THREE PIECES
OF GLASS

THREE PIECES
OF **GLASS**

WHY WE FEEL LONELY IN A
WORLD MEDIATED BY SCREENS

ERIC O. JACOBSEN

BrazosPress

a division of Baker Publishing Group
Grand Rapids, Michigan

© 2020 by Eric O. Jacobsen

Published by Brazos Press
a division of Baker Publishing Group
PO Box 6287, Grand Rapids, MI 49516-6287
www.brazospress.com

Printed in the United States of America

Library of Congress Cataloging-in-Publication Data
Names: Jacobsen, Eric O., author.
Title: Three pieces of glass : why we feel lonely in a world mediated by screens / Eric O. Jacobsen.
Description: Grand Rapids, Michigan : Brazos Press, a division of Baker Publishing Group, 2020. | Includes bibliographical references and index.
Identifiers: LCCN 2019041773 | ISBN 9781587434228 (paperback)
Subjects: LCSH: Loneliness—Religious aspects—Christianity. | Belonging (Social psychology) | Digital media—Religious aspects—Christianity. | Fluorescent screens—Miscellanea.
Classification: LCC BV4911 .J33 2020 | DDC 261.5/2—dc23
LC record available at https://lccn.loc.gov/2019041773

ISBN 978-1-58743-492-1 (casebound)

20   21   22   23   24   25   26   7   6   5   4   3   2   1

CONTENTS

ACKNOWLEDGMENTS

I would like to acknowledge some of the conversation partners, colaborators, and encouragers who helped me with this project along the way. Hazel Borys, Mark Childs, Andy Crouch, Lee Hardy, Wendy Hoashi-Erhardt, Lance Kagey, Richard Mouw, Joseph Myers, Ron Rienstra, Laura Smit, and James K. A. Smith provided fresh insight and needed feedback as the ideas for this project began to bubble to the surface. After I took a long hiatus to focus on pastoral work, my spiritual director, Sara Singleton, helped me navigate the path back into writing again. Bob Hosack at Baker was patient and gracious in giving me time and space to let this book become what it needed to be. Lisa Williams, as always, helped me sound smarter than I actually am and helped me get the manuscript ready for the first, second, and third pitch. And project editor James Korsmo quickly caught the spirit of what I was trying to say, and his suggestions, like the rug in *The Big Lebowski*, "really tied the room together."

This project went through many iterations, and it took a long time to figure out if any of it was helpful. So I am particularly grateful to those groups who gave their time and attention so I could field test the ideas. Friends at First Pres Tacoma; Colorado Springs Presbyterian Church; Providendia Church in West Palm Beach; Third Church, Richmond, VA; and the Members Christian Caucus of the Congress for the New

Urbanism all listened well, asked great questions, and helped me distinguish the wheat from the chaff.

My Friday-morning guys group kept me grounded week by week and offered prayer and encouragement on those days when this project felt like a chore. My children—Kate, Peter, Emma, and Abe—were understanding when I had to skip some family time to work on this project and provided a steady supply of good excuses to set the writing aside and reengage the world. They unwittingly served as an important focus group as I watched them figure out how to find places to belong among their friends, in the church, and in our walkable neighborhood. And my wife, Liz, not only has been my faithful companion on this journey but is also the one who inspires me every day with her ability to create communities of belonging out of the most unlikely ingredients.

This book is dedicated to Judi Jacobsen, for whom every trip to the store has been a master class in civic belonging.

INTRODUCTION

Where Everybody Knows Your Name

The door opens, flooding the bar with natural light. An ordinary-looking, heavyset man appears and is greeted by a chorus of voices: "Norm!"

Thus begins the first episode of *Cheers*, the TV sitcom that dominated the airwaves during the 1980s. *Cheers* made the top-ten list of the Nielson ratings in eight of its eleven seasons. The "Norm" greeting became a standard trope for the show. It fit perfectly with the theme song's chorus, "You want to be where everybody knows your name."

There were many reasons for *Cheers*' popularity, but perhaps the most compelling was this theme's resonance with audiences. Viewers remained loyal because they longed for a place where they were known well enough to be greeted on arrival by name. This was true in the '80s and is even more so today. This longing, while ubiquitous, is not well understood.

What specifically do we long for when we want a place where everybody knows our name? Why do we seem to be moving further away from it each passing year? And how might we encourage the development of these kinds of real places so we don't have to settle for watching people enjoy fictional ones? The answer, surprisingly enough, has to do with three pieces of glass—the car windshield, the TV, and the smartphone.

These three pieces of glass represent key choices we've made at the societal and individual levels to devalue face-to-face contact with other people for the sake of efficiency, autonomy, and entertainment. But saying this only helps us to understand the problem. The more difficult part is to figure out how to solve the problem. This book is an attempt to do just that. But before we get into that project, let's begin by digging a little deeper into that desire to be greeted by name.

When I arrive home, I'm greeted by people who know my name and greet me with names that betray an even more intimate connection, such as "Dad" or "Honey." Yet I, too, long for that "Norm" experience. What Cheers (the bar) offers that my home does not is a particular kind of connection that I describe as "civic." Additionally, the Cheers setting is quasi-public, making it a kind of forum for developing relationships with people who are different culturally and/or socioeconomically. As society becomes increasingly polarized and fragmented, settings where one can comfortably interact with people different from oneself are increasingly important.

Cheers is also a real brick-and-mortar place (or at least the Bull and Finch Pub in Boston that it's based on is) where people have to be bodily present for the proper greeting to take place. This real place is a neighborhood bar, meaning that many of its patrons live in relative proximity to one another and are likely to bump into one another outside of the bar. Cheers is in Boston, which influences the topics that are discussed (Red Sox) as well as some of the tensions that exist between patrons (class, nationality, education level, etc.).

The term that best captures the object of that longing we have for a place where everybody knows our name is "belonging." This book focuses on the kind of belonging that involves real people gathering in real places in the civic realm. This is the kind of belonging that seems to have diminished in the past few decades. And it is this kind that many desire to experience today.

Three distinct but interconnected forces are largely responsible for the demise of this kind of belonging. They are significant, but the first seems to have the dubious distinction of being the driving force in this crisis of belonging. This is a kind of centrifugal force that pulls us inward toward isolated or private environments and away from public engagement. These are the notorious three pieces of glass that were mentioned earlier. The car, the television, and the smartphone have made our lives easier and more entertaining, but together they have vastly reduced the frequency, duration, and quality of our public interactions.

The second force has to do with the public realm itself. Let's say you decide to forgo your car, TV, and smartphone for one day to experience face-to-face connection with neighbors. You leave your private realm, and, after a walk that is longer and less satisfying than you imagined, you can't find any place to stop, enjoy some leisure, and interact with neighbors. You might find a fast-food restaurant or a coffee shop, but they don't seem like places where anybody is greeted by name.

Over the past fifty years, we have seen a marked decline in the physical settings that constitute the public realm. Some neighborhoods have bars that successfully function as a connecting hub for local residents, but the vast majority of American neighborhoods have no such amenity. And bars like Cheers, even when they are present, constitute only one subsection of the civic realm.

Other kinds of civic-realm settings have been more normative: plazas, squares, parks, and even sidewalks and corners. But in the last half century, these settings either have not been built or have been built so poorly that they fail to gather anyone other than those unfortunate souls who have no other options.

The third force pushing against our desire to belong is the frenetic pace that has taken over our lives. We are too hurried to invest in or maintain deep relational connections. And since, through the internet and phone, we are able to connect with people and places across an incredibly wide geographical stretch, we seem to have a hard time connecting with the places where we actually live.

So we find ourselves in a difficult situation. With the option of binge-watching our favorite show and ordering groceries online, we have fewer compelling reasons to leave our homes. If we were to leave to hang out in the neighborhood, there is likely no central gathering spot for us.

And frankly we are so tired and have such little discretionary time, we aren't in the mood to risk going out and connecting spontaneously.

Our lives are enviable by almost any standard. We enjoy good food and entertainment in comfortable homes with those we love. Yet we can't help but envy Norm's belonging a little.

Before we jump into attempting a solution to this problem of belonging, we must first ask if this problem needs fixing. This book is written from a Christian perspective, so it's important to frame this issue theologically before proceeding.

To a Christian who looks to the Bible as the ultimate source of truth, a longing for a place where we are known by name does not necessarily merit investing time and energy into seeking a solution. I must ask whether God really cares that my neighbors and I don't have a good setting to cultivate our relationships with one another and with the place we call home.

We can begin by asserting that the kind of belonging that is truly satisfying to humans who are made in God's image is belonging within God's realm: "I would rather be a doorkeeper in the house of my God than dwell in the tents of the wicked" (Ps. 84:10).

For this passage, it's tempting to identify the church as "the house of my God" and the neighborhood bar as the "tents of the wicked." Our goal then would be to get Norm out of the bar and into a church, and then maybe to see the neighborhood bar close its doors for good.

But this approach to the issue ignores one important truth: the presence of God is not limited to the building of the local church. God can be present and at work in any location—including a neighborhood bar. In Colossians, Paul reminds us that Jesus is at work in every setting: "For in him all things were created: things in heaven and on earth, visible and invisible, whether thrones or powers or rulers or authorities; all things have been created through him and for him. He is before all things, and in him all things hold together" (Col. 1:16–17). Jesus is not only the creator of all things; he is the one who allows them to carry out their functions properly. A place like Cheers has an organic logic, and insofar as that system works to bless and enrich human life, Jesus is the one working behind it.

It is important to clarify here that I am not suggesting that the local church is not more significant to God's intent for humanity than the local bar is. The writer of Hebrews notes the importance of the common life of the church, "not giving up meeting together, as some are in the habit of doing, but encouraging one another—and all the more as you see the Day approaching" (Heb. 10:25). Clearly, Christians are called to gather together for the purpose of fellowship, mutual encouragement, and worship. I would argue that the specific location for these gatherings is not all that important but that it is essential that Christians gather regularly.

In the book of Acts, we get a picture of the rhythms of the early church that may help us see more clearly the distinct roles of different settings for gathering: "Every day they continued to meet together in the temple courts. They broke bread in their homes and ate together with glad and sincere hearts, praising God and enjoying the favor of all the people. And the Lord added to their number daily those who were being saved" (Acts 2:46–47). Luke is primarily telling us about the activities that the emerging disciples of Jesus did as a Christian community (meeting together, breaking bread, praising God). But he also tells us that they were "enjoying the favor of *all* the people." The "all" here suggests that this includes the people in Jerusalem who were not part of the Christian community.

For the Christian community to "enjoy the favor of all the people" within their local community, there would have needed to be settings for them to interact with non-Christians. The kinds of settings that allow Christians to naturally interact with their non-Christian neighbors vary from culture to culture, but certainly a neighborhood bar can provide one type of setting for this kind of interaction.

We know that God has called us to belong to and participate in the local church. We know that the local church is called to invite people to experience belonging in God's kingdom through a life-transforming encounter with Jesus Christ. While ultimately we do want all our neighbors to experience kingdom belonging, I don't believe that this is the only reason that God cares about the kind of belonging that all people experience in the places they live. I also believe that God can use the kind of belonging that people experience in a place like Cheers as a foretaste of what it is like to belong to God's kingdom.

And if God can use a place like Cheers to accomplish his will in the lives of people, then God's people can support the work of a place like Cheers. In the book of Jeremiah, we pick up the story of God's people exiled in Babylon. During this difficult time, the temptation must have been great to circle the wagons, try to strengthen what bonds they could within the community of faith, and wait until this exile came to an end and they are returned to Jerusalem.

But through Jeremiah, the people are given the clear mandate: "Seek the welfare [*shalom*] of the city where I have called you into exile" (29:7 ESV). The Hebrew word *shalom* is often translated as "welfare" or "peace," but it means much more than just the absence of conflict. It means human flourishing in all of its dimensions (physically, relationally, and aesthetically). The people were to seek flourishing not just for the enclave of the faith community but for the people of the city as a whole.

I believe that belonging in place is an essential (but often overlooked) element of shalom. In fact, belonging might be not so much an *element* of shalom so much as shalom itself considered from a particular perspective. Belonging can be thought of as the subjective experience of shalom. When we experience shalom, we feel like we belong.

The experience of shalom feels like belonging, but the converse is not necessarily true. Some forms of belonging that are not grounded in shalom are high-school cliques and street gangs. These forms tend to be malformative to our personhood and destructive to the social and natural environment. Belonging that is anchored in shalom can be described as kingdom belonging; belonging that is not based in shalom can be described as worldly belonging.

After establishing that place-based belonging is desirable for us as well as important to God, the only question that remains is, How do we get from here to there? How do we cultivate settings in which everyone knows our name (as well as the names of the others who show up)? The answer (spoiler alert) is that we don't (only) read a book about it. In order to solve this problem, we're going to need to pay close attention to those three pieces of glass. This is because the problem of our lack of belonging has emerged not so much from erroneous thinking as from building certain kinds of settings for daily life and adopting certain societal practices that have altered the way we bodily interact with one another and with the places we live. To successfully remedy the problem of belonging, we need to address it in the realm of the built environment, of institutions, and of individual and communal practices.

Therefore, the solution to the problem of belonging involves first being aware enough that we begin to recognize the cost we incur when we choose to invest our limited time and energy in some of the common practices that alienate and isolate us from the people and places proximate to us. The time and resources we spend on our phones, watching TV, and driving our cars not only shape us in ways that work against our sense of belonging; they also prevent us from investing time and resources in other practices that cultivate belonging.

But awareness and restraint won't alone solve the problem of belonging. We need to rethink the kinds of buildings and public spaces we're building and consider how to construct a built environment that encourages belonging. We also need to look to alternative practices that are more affirming of body, place, and story; we need to recover and cultivate practices and conceptual categories that strengthen a sense of belonging with and among our neighbors.

To put this point a bit more directly, sitting on our couch watching a television show where fictional characters enthusiastically greet one another is a step in the wrong direction. Whatever solutions we ultimately find will most likely involve switching off the TV, putting down the smartphone, and getting out of the car and venturing into the local setting of whatever place God has called us to live, where we face the risk of being greeted or ignored. This is a risk I believe we are called to take. It's not just we who want to be "where everybody knows your name." Our neighbors want this as well. More importantly, God wants this for us and for our neighbors. Seeking the shalom of the cities and neighborhoods to which we've been called will involve addressing this crisis of belonging in our own lives and in the lives of our neighbors.

DEFINITIONS

What does it mean to belong? Is it simply to have my name included on the rolls of my church? Does it have to do with where my home is? Is it a legal question regarding to whom I'm married and which children claim me as their father? Why do I sometimes feel as if I don't belong when I'm in a group of acquaintances? Are there different kinds of belonging for different settings? And if so, do I need to experience every kind of belonging to feel at peace? And last, how does the belonging we can experience in the here and now connect to the belonging that we will experience when Christ returns and establishes his kingdom on earth? In this section we attempt to come up with a definition of belonging simple enough to be useful but complex enough to account for the various nuances of this vital concept.

ONE

WHAT IS BELONGING?

A Season Abroad

In the winter of my junior year of college, I traveled to Scotland to study at the University of Aberdeen. I arrived on campus just after the beginning of the new year. Growing up in Seattle, I thought I was impervious to winter gloom, but I was not prepared for this. The sun went down at three in the afternoon, and the old stone buildings made everything feel damp and chilly. The whole town had a lackluster feel, due in no small part to the economic slump of the North Sea oil industry.

I didn't know anyone and felt very much alone. The food was unfamiliar, I had a hard time understanding the thick Scottish brogue, and the educational system was hard to navigate. My first Sunday there, I showed up to the beautiful old stone chapel on campus only to find its massive doors locked. The next week, I asked a theology professor about local churches, and he suggested a few.

The following Sunday, I walked in a misty rain through an industrial neighborhood to a church located in an ugly warehouse. The interior was unremarkable: a simple stage and rows of metal folding chairs on a concrete floor. After the welcome, the worship team led us in a praise chorus that I recognized immediately. Soon tears were streaming down my face. For the first time in weeks, I felt a powerful sense of belonging. After worship I stayed for fellowship and enjoyed getting to know some of the members of the church.

That experience of belonging was a turning point in that lonely season of my life. Belonging on Sunday permeated the rest of the week and helped me feel less lonely when I wandered the unfamiliar campus or spent an evening reading alone in my room. I traveled a lot on weekends, so I never got much involved in the life of that church, but I looked forward to returning there on weekends when I happened to be in town. Each time I felt a significant sense of belonging.

Belonging as Organized Complexity

During that season abroad, if someone had asked me how I was doing, I'd have said I was struggling with loneliness. My friends were back in school getting ready to begin a new term, and I was waking up each day in a single room thousands of miles away. This was before cell phones and Skype, so my primary form of communication with home was the aerogram letter. I longed for even an hour of face-to-face time with a friend.

This is a common way of understanding loneliness: as a lack of relational connection with another person. In chapter 9 I explore in detail why this approach is inadequate, but for now, I want to use this common pattern of thinking as a way of teasing out a more robust understanding of belonging. To do this, we need to draw a lesson from the field of urban planning.

Jane Jacobs's seminal book *The Death and Life of Great American Cities* has a perceptive chapter titled "The Kind of Problem a City Is."[1] There she tries to account for why so many attempts at solving urban problems by so-called experts have failed. Jacobs contends that it has to do with a basic misunderstanding of what kind of problem a city presents. Jacobs describes three basic kinds of problems that call for different kinds of solutions.

Problems of simplicity look at two variables, and the solution involves adjusting one variable to positively influence another variable. City planners often treat parking as a problem of simplicity. We can estimate how many users a building will have and then require a certain number of parking spots to ensure that they will all have access to the building.

Problems of disorganized complexity involve too many variables to measure, so solutions are often based on statistics and complex modeling. Traffic engineers often deal with problems of complexity when recommending how many and what types of roads will be required in a particular area. Jacobs believes that dealing with the city as a problem of simplicity and as a problem of disorganized complexity both are too simplistic and fail to understand the internal logic of a city and neighborhood.

Jacobs advocates seeing the city as a problem of organized complexity. She sees the city as a kind of living organism that tends to function effectively even when we don't understand how. Jacobs takes an inductive approach to dealing with cities and neighborhoods. She advocates paying attention to particulars and building general theories from there rather than beginning with general theories. Jacobs is aware of how one particular element in a city or neighborhood (like a park) exists as part of any number of complex systems that work together to shape the success or failure of the particular element.

I contend that belonging is a concept best studied as a case of organized complexity. It is tempting to deal with the crisis of belonging as a problem of simplicity: a loneliness problem whose proposed solutions tend to involve setting up friendships for people who lack them. Belonging can also be studied as a problem of disorganized complexity. We can look at the changing demographics of single-person households and try to account for them in terms of aging and mortality statistics. But belonging is much more nuanced and too complex to be fully comprehended using these kinds of methods. To understand the crisis of belonging and to work toward effective solutions, we first need to understand belonging as a complex but ultimately coherent phenomenon essential to human thriving.

Belonging as Relationship, Place, and Story

What does it mean to belong? While it seems like a straightforward concept, it can be tricky to pin down a precise definition. If we restrict ourselves to the variety of belonging we experience as humans, as opposed to, say, the way that my shirt belongs to me, it simplifies things.

Human belonging can include institutional, geographical, social, and/or cultural dimensions. We belong if we are on the official rolls of an organization. However, it is not unusual for a member of my church to report feeling they just don't belong. The social dimension of belonging is often what people mean when they say they belong (or don't belong). I feel I belong if I sense acceptance among a group of people. This can be formal, like belonging to a family, or informal and fluid, like belonging to a group of friends.

Belonging is often connected to geography. I have a sense of belonging if I have lived in a particular locale a long time, especially if I'm a third-generation resident. It's possible to speed up the geographic sense of belonging by deliberately engaging with the natural and built environment of a place.

Last, there's a cultural aspect to belonging. I feel like I belong if I don't have to think too much before I speak or engage in an activity. Cultural belonging has to do with an internalization of the norms, patterns, and lexicon of a particular group or place.

The following is a working definition of "belonging" for the purposes of this book: "a sense of fitting in with a particular place, a particular group of people, and/or with the ethos or narrative of a place." You belong when you don't have to work too hard for a sense of acceptance.

Levels of Belonging

The belonging I felt in the social hall of the church in Scotland, I learned later, represented one of four experiential levels of belonging. The congregation knew that I was an American college student on a short-term stay in Scotland. I didn't know any particular people in that church very

6

well—where they lived, who they were related to, or what they did for a living. The powerful belonging I felt at that church was the kind of belonging appropriate to a church social hall.

Joseph Myers, in his book *The Search to Belong*, asserts that belonging is not a simple unidimensional concept.[2] We do not simply belong or not belong to particular persons or groups. If we belong, we belong in different ways. Drawing on the insights of sociologist Edward T. Hall, Myers articulates four distinct levels within which we may or may not belong to persons or groups. These spaces not only provide the context for our belonging but also are governed by a set of rules and spatial relations that communicate and reinforce the kind of belonging that pertains in that setting. The four levels of belonging are *intimate, personal, social,* and *public.*

Intimate belonging is the kind of belonging we experience with our spouse or maybe a best friend. Myers describes this kind of belonging as "naked and unashamed."[3] We don't keep any secrets from those with whom we experience intimate belonging. *Personal belonging* is the kind of belonging we experience with our families and close friends. We tend to know very well those with whom we experience personal belonging. We have mutually disclosed information that is personal and assumes a high level of trust.

Social belonging is the kind of belonging we experience with people whom we recognize but may not yet know very well. We experience social belonging at church coffee hour, the neighborhood dog park, or a PTA meeting. Social belonging is important but often overlooked. It is important for our identity formation. In settings geared for social belonging, we are often asked to explain who we are to another person, and it is often in formulating and articulating an answer to that question that we figure out who we are. Social belonging is also important to personal and intimate belonging. In settings for social belonging, we often self-select those with whom we want to experience personal or even intimate belonging.

Public belonging is the kind of belonging we experience with those whom we may not know personally but with whom we are connected through some external commonality. We experience public belonging as fans of the same sports team, as worshipers in the same sanctuary, or as denizens of the same town.

In considering these distinct levels of belonging, it's important to avoid some common misunderstandings of how they work. First, we should understand that we all have a need to belong at all four levels. These levels of belonging are distinct but not sequential. We don't move from public belonging to social belonging to personal belonging to intimate belonging. Rather, each of us needs to experience belonging at all four levels throughout our lives.

Furthermore, many of our relationships can exist at more than one level of belonging. More precisely, those with whom we experience one level of belonging should "scale up" to the larger realms of belonging. We experience intimate belonging with our spouse but also interact with our spouse at personal, social, and even public levels. It is important that we know how to navigate our spousal relations at all four of these levels if we want to have a healthy marriage.

With lots of programing targeted at marriages and small groups, the Christian community has focused perhaps too much attention on intimate and personal belonging. This is not a bad thing, since intimate and personal belonging are very important. However, at the same time, the Christian community has often neglected to recognize the importance of the civic level of belonging and in doing so has missed an opportunity to mitigate some critical aspects of loneliness within the congregation and the larger community. In the next chapter, we will explore the particular importance of the civic level of belonging.

TWO

THE SPECIAL NEED
FOR CIVIC BELONGING

Checker Friends

I remember returning home to Seattle after my freshman year of college. I'd run down to the local grocery, and the checkout clerk started asking me about my first year away. This took me by surprise, since I hadn't mentioned anything about being home for the summer. I wondered how this random checker at Safeway knew *anything* about me, let alone something so current as the fact that I'd just gotten home from college.

Then I realized that this must be one of the checkers my mom chats with. I put two and two together: this man had been receiving weekly updates on my status, sometimes accompanied by pictures. My mom has been talking with checkers and other folks in lines forever. She used to embarrass me by pulling out family pictures and giving the guy at the register a quick update while he bagged our groceries. These conversations weren't particularly deep or important, but they are one way my mom (and her family, by extension) is known by and knows some of the people in our neighborhood.

My mom and this checker were friends, but not close friends. He had never been to our house, and they didn't normally discuss sensitive matters. Their friendship is one example of what is known as "civic friendship." This term can be used to capture a wide range of people we connect with on a casual basis. Civic friendships can include those people with whom we chat or even just greet often enough to maintain some kind of mutual recognition. Civic friendships range from those we greet by name (and are greeted back by name) and know a bit about their context, those to whom we say hello with just enough inflection to acknowledge recognition, and those we acknowledge when we discover that our experiences of belonging overlap in some way.

Civic friendships might seem random and inconsequential, but I believe they play a critical role in our experience of belonging to a particular location. In this chapter I will clarify the meaning of civic friendship and explore its particular role in belonging.

Private and Civic Spheres for Belonging

The four levels of belonging we surveyed in chapter 1 help bring some specificity to the kinds of belonging that we experience. To connect these levels of belonging to other conversations, it can be helpful to group the levels of belonging into two distinct spheres.

It is common practice in the social sciences to distinguish between the private and public aspects of our lives. I use "civic" in place of "public" when engaging in these kinds of conversations, because I believe that important gradations exist between the people we know in our neighborhood and those we know in a wider context, such as our city or town. So, for our purposes, the private sphere involves our associations with family and close friends. The civic sphere involves all of our associations with people who are not family and close friends.

We can see how the levels of belonging line up with the spheres below.

Sphere	Belonging Level
Private	Intimate
	Personal
Civic	Social
	Public

The private sphere includes both intimate and personal belonging. The most common setting for these levels of belonging is the home. The home is a container for the intimate belonging that we share with our spouse. It is also the container for the personal belonging we enjoy with our immediate and extended family. And it is often where we spend time with our close friends and perhaps a small group.

The civic sphere includes both social and public belonging. The settings for these levels of belonging are varied, but usually outside of the home. Social belonging includes civic friendships where there is some kind of personal connection, even if it seems very minor. This would include the checker or banker who knows your name but also the dog walker that passes by while you retrieve your morning paper. You may not know each other's name, but your greeting indicates that you're more than complete strangers.

Public belonging in the civic sphere is less personal than social belonging. Public belonging usually involves an external factor you have in common with another person. When thinking about the civic sphere, we can consider public belonging the kind of belonging that you share with another person who is a resident of your city or town. You may not know each other personally, but you share some common connections to the stories, natural environment, built environment, and characters of your common locale. If you were to run into someone from your town in another country, you would likely feel a welcome sense of connection and mutual belonging. Belonging publicly isn't necessarily geographic; fans of the same sports team or owners of BMW motorcycles can share a kind of public belonging. For the purposes of this book, we focus on the kind of public belonging that we experience with people who live in our area.

Belonging and Shalom in Private and Civic Life

Over the past few decades, the religious aspect of our lives has migrated more and more into the private sphere. That has been the result of both external and internal forces. Externally, how our society has dealt with the messiness of an increasingly religiously pluralistic culture has been demanding that everyone leave their religious convictions at home when entering the public square. Internally, Christians have largely written off the civic realm as too complicated and have focused their attention on relationships within the community of faith or among friends and family. This privatization of religion is specific to our culture at this time and is by no means a universal phenomenon.

A good case can be made that the Bible encourages the community of faith to be involved in civic friendships in their community. When the people of God had been exiled to Babylon, the prophet Jeremiah was given a word from God that was to frame their thinking about this challenging period.

> This is what the LORD Almighty, the God of Israel, says to all those I carried into exile from Jerusalem to Babylon: "Build houses and settle down; plant gardens and eat what they produce. Marry and have sons and daughters; find wives for your sons and give your daughters in marriage, so that they too may have sons and daughters. Increase in number there; do not decrease. Also, seek the peace and prosperity of the city to which I have carried you into exile. Pray to the LORD for it, because if it prospers, you too will prosper." (Jer. 29:4–7)

They had hoped that he would bring a message of deliverance—that they would soon return to the promised land. Instead, Jeremiah brought the sobering news that they would be in exile another seventy years. This meant that most of them would spend the remainder of their earthly lives in exile.

Rather than promising deliverance, Jeremiah provides a strategy for living in exile, one focused on seeking shalom. To experience shalom is to experience the fullness of God's intent for human existence. And as we noted in chapter 1, belonging can be thought of as the subjective experience of shalom. So Jeremiah is commanding the people of God to work on belonging in this place of exile.

When we can say that we are making progress toward shalom, we are concurrently experiencing a greater sense of belonging. It can be helpful to conceptualize shalom as a set of external objective characteristics and belonging as an internal subjective experience, but in actuality it is impossible to maintain a clean distinction between these two concepts. As we'll soon see, one of the delightful surprises for God's people is that we can experience shalom belonging even in very difficult circumstances.

In fact, this particular aspect of the shalom-belonging connection is one of the important lessons from this key teaching on shalom. We have been working with a definition of belonging that involves relationships, place, and story. And at the time of Jeremiah's message, the people of God are in the midst of a crisis in two of these three elements.

They have been exiled as a community so they can fairly easily maintain a sense of relational belonging. But they have been physically removed from the promised land, so with regard to place they seem destined for a season of alienation rather than belonging. Also, they have been transplanted into the cultural milieu of Babylon, which involves not only a completely different set of practices and patterns but also a very different story from the one that shaped their life in the promised land.

The context of their exile does not seem very shalom-like, and yet they've been instructed to pursue shalom in this setting. There are clearly some significant limits as to how they can go about this task. They can't fix the place issue by moving back to the promised land, and they most likely can't fix the cultural issue by overturning the dominant culture of the Babylonians. So seeking shalom, or pursuing belonging, is going to involve small, incremental shifts within the external realm of their new life as well as internal shifts in their mental framework.

The other instructive part of this story is the way this command to seek shalom is to be pursued in both the private and the civic realm. The first part of Jeremiah's message addresses the private realm: "Build houses and settle down; plant gardens and eat what they produce. Marry and have sons and daughters; find wives for your sons and give your daughters in marriage." In pursuing shalom via these specific things, they will experience a greater sense of belonging in the private sphere.

The second part of Jeremiah's message addresses the civic sphere: "Seek the peace and prosperity of the city to which I have carried you into exile. Pray to the LORD for it, because if it prospers, you too will prosper." Here, Jeremiah invites the people of God to turn their imagination to the realm outside their front doors and outside of the places that they gather as a community. Jeremiah doesn't provide as much specific direction for shalom-seeking in the civic sphere as he does for the private sphere. Perhaps this is because shalom-seeking in the civic realm is going to look different in different contexts.

Jeremiah's lack of specificity should not, however, be taken to mean that it's not important. He instructs the people to take direct action on behalf of their city of exile—to "seek"—as well as to ask for God to work for the good of the city—to "pray." Whereas his admonition about investment in the private sphere is given without any rationale, he provides a clear rationale for investing in the civic realm: "for if it prospers, you too will prosper" (literally, "if it achieves shalom, you will achieve shalom"). As the people of God find ways to get involved with the civic life of this alien culture and to work and pray for its good, they will experience a greater sense of belonging even in the midst of exile.

I believe there is a particular need for Christians today to pay attention to the second half of Jeremiah's message. Like others in our culture, many Christians feel an acute need to belong. The good news is that shalom belonging is a fundamental promise of the gospel. However, due to a variety of factors, the overriding tendency within the US Christian community has been to pursue belonging in the private sphere while largely ignoring the possibility of belonging in the civic sphere.

Civic Friendship

In contemporary attempts to measure loneliness, researchers have asked people how many persons they have in their life with whom they can discuss important matters. They calculate how many people live alone (or "alone" with children). What such studies measure as a barometer of loneliness are relationships within the private sphere. The studies that look at household size are basically measuring intimate relationships, because a second adult in the household is likely to be a spouse, romantic partner, or close friend. The studies measuring how many others people have with whom they can discuss important matters is tracking personal relationships.

Intimate and personal relationships are important to an overall sense of well-being, but they aren't the only kinds of relationships we need in order to have a sense of belonging. And people who lack sufficient intimate and personal relationships can still achieve a sense of belonging and avoid acute loneliness through a robust network of relationships in the civic sphere. Chapter 9 examines how relationships in the civic sphere can lead to the formation of private and intimate friendships, but in this chapter we focus on the value of civic relationships in and of themselves.

Peggy Thotis is a sociologist who has done extensive research on the impact that different social roles have on people's sense of well-being,[1] what we've been calling civic friendships. Thotis calls these friendships "lighter relationships" to distinguish them from the more demanding relationships we have with spouses, children, and coworkers. Thotis tracks how lighter relationships can "boost feelings of self-esteem, mastery, and physical health."[2] While the more weighty relationships with spouses and children add a lot to our lives, they also can wear us out. Charles Montgomery, drawing from Thotis's research, notes, "Women's 'obligatory' roles as spouses, parents, or employees tended to demand lots of time and energy and were more likely to translate into what she called 'role strain.' That wasn't the case with light, voluntary roles in life, which were unambiguously associated with well-being. The more social roles people have in life, the stronger they become in both mind and body."[3]

Relationships in the civic sphere not only give us a greater sense of well-being, they also help us feel a stronger sense of belonging. John Helliwell, a social scientist who has done extensive research on happiness, claims there is a strong correlation between social belonging, trust, casual relationships, and happiness.[4] Charles Montgomery cites Helliwell's "perfect triangle" of happiness:

- people who feel that they "belong" to their community are happier than those who do not;

- people who trust their neighbors feel a greater sense of that belonging; and
- that sense of belonging is influenced by social contact.

In Helliwell's research, then, social contact with neighbors can be just as important for happiness as contact with close family and friends.

One difficulty with the problem of loneliness may be in how we think about loneliness. When people consider intimate friendship as the only significant form of human relationship, they can miss some of the other ways we connect with one another. This can lead to people perceiving themselves to be more lonely than they actually are, because in their focus on intimate friendship, they miss out on the other kinds of friends they have. It can also lead to missed opportunities to invest in civic friendships.

Walking Home

I have to admit, I admire my mother's ability to cultivate civic friendships with grocery checkers, but sadly I did not inherit her gift. Perhaps I'm a bit more of an introvert, but when I'm running to the store to pick up some milk, I don't feel like talking about my kids. However, I do like knowing the checker's name, and it makes me feel good when they know mine.

My office is a little over a half mile from my home, and if I choose to walk home along the commercial center of our neighborhood (as opposed to riding my bike along the bike corridor), I have a pretty good chance of being greeted by a dozen or so business owners who know me by name. I have a civic friendship with at least one person at the dentist's office, the pub, the tailor's store, the financial planner's office, the grocery store, the coffee shop, the dry cleaners, the nail salon, the bank, the pharmacy, the art school, the auto shop, and the printer. That's not counting the residents and people from our church that I might greet as well.

Being recognized by people in your neighborhood might seem inconsequential if you haven't experienced it, but it feels good and contributes significantly to my sense of belonging here. Of course, I believe that we do need intimate and social relationships in the private sphere in order to avoid loneliness and feel a secure belonging. But our desire for belonging in the private sphere shouldn't eclipse our significant need for belonging in the civic sphere. Unfortunately, many of the decisions we've made individually and as a society have had a negative effect on civic belonging. I am convinced that learning to value this sphere and invest in it is key to overcoming the crisis of belonging in our culture. Before we jump into that conversation, we need to do a little more work to sharpen our understanding of how belonging in the here and now connects to belonging in the kingdom of God.

THREE

SIGNS, INSTRUMENTS, AND FORETASTES OF BELONGING

Church as Sign, Instrument, and Foretaste of the Gospel

After spending forty years in India, missionary Lesslie Newbigin returned to his native England and found it to be alarmingly secular. As he considered strategies for reintroducing the gospel to post-Christian England, Newbigin realized that the local church would need to serve as a "hermeneutic of the gospel" for society. No longer could the church exert a gospel influence on society by proclaiming the good news within the walls of the church and waiting for the people who needed this message to come and hear it.

Newbigin was convinced that the only way that the church could influence society was by serving as "sign, instrument, and foretaste of the gospel":

> If the gospel is to challenge the public life of our society, . . . it will only be by movements that begin with the local congregation in which the reality of the new creation is present, known, and experienced, and

from which men and women will go into every sector of public life to claim it for Christ, to unmask the illusions which have remained hidden and to expose all areas of public life to the illumination of the gospel. But that will only happen as and when local congregations renounce an introverted concern for their own life, and recognize that they exist for the sake of those who are not members, as sign, instrument, and foretaste of God's redeeming grace for the whole life of society.[1]

There are a couple of aspects of Newbigin's insight here that I really appreciate. I like how he is focusing his attention on how the gospel can have an impact on the public life of society. Newbigin is rightly rejecting the privatizing impulse found within so many Christian communities that we noted in chapter 2. Like Jeremiah with the Israelites, Newbigin is directing the Christian community to take an interest in shalom in the civic realm of society. Newbigin's focus on what is going on outside of the walls of the church ultimately led to the missional movement within the church.

The other thing that I like is how Newbigin breaks down the impetus for gospel progress into three distinct aspects. He calls for the church to be a sign, instrument, and foretaste of the kingdom within the civic (he calls it "public") realm. These distinct terms are extremely useful, so it is important that we take a moment to specify what they mean.

A *sign* points to the thing signified. A church acts as a sign of the gospel when it demonstrates gospel-transformed lives in a way that is visible to the outside world. An *instrument* is a catalyst that allows someone to access and appropriate the good under consideration. A church acts as an instrument of the gospel through its ministry of evangelism. Evangelism allows and encourages those outside of the community of faith to experience a life-transforming encounter with the gospel. A *foretaste* is a partial experience, but not the full experience itself. The church acts as a foretaste of the gospel when it allows those outside of the Christian community to experience some of the benefits of Christian community. Churches can serve as a foretaste of the gospel by including those outside of the community of faith in

19

celebrations, service projects, and other activities vital to the life of the community.

In this book, we will be utilizing Newbigin's rubric, but with a couple of changes. In the first place, instead of advocating for the *gospel* in the civic realm, we will be focusing on belonging as one aspect of a holistic witness of the gospel. As we noted in chapter 2, belonging and the gospel are interrelated. Our acceptance of the gospel leads us toward shalom and should result in a greater experience of belonging in God's kingdom. On the other hand, a positive experience of belonging especially within a Christian setting can point someone toward the gospel.

The other change that we will make to Newbigin's rubric is to allow that institutions and settings outside of the church can effectively function as foretastes of belonging. In our use of Newbigin, we will look at ways that the church can act as a sign and instrument of belonging for society. We will note how the church can serve as a foretaste of belonging as well, but we will be especially attentive to how certain foretastes of belonging are generated outside of the church.

This is where Norm's experience of Cheers can fit in. I am making the claim here that a neighborhood pub in which a person like Norm can experience acceptance and belonging in a way that enriches his life is a foretaste of the kind of belonging that God wants for all of us. Of course God wants Norm to experience belonging in ways that are far richer and more comprehensive than Cheers can offer him, but Norm's experience in Cheers offers the possibility of whetting his appetite for the kind of belonging that God wants for him.

Church as an Instrument of Belonging

At the end of Jesus's public ministry, just before his ascension into heaven, he gave his disciples instructions for carrying out his mission without his physical presence: "All authority in heaven and on earth has been given to me. Therefore go and make disciples of all nations, baptizing them in the name of the Father and of the Son and of the Holy Spirit, and teaching them to obey everything I have commanded you. And surely I am with you always, to the very end of the age" (Matt. 28:18–20). The Great Commission is perhaps the clearest expression of the fundamental calling of the church.

Jesus's final instructions to his disciples can be understood as a mandate for the church to serve as an instrument of belonging. The church is called to be a catalyst of belonging through evangelism, baptism, and discipleship. These three basic tasks are fundamentally about helping people fully experience the belonging for which they were created. Through evangelism, the church invites those who don't yet belong to the community of faith to be included. Baptism celebrates those who have recently experienced belonging. And discipleship is a process of enculturation whereby the experience of belonging is extended into all areas of life and becomes embedded in various individual and community practices.

Of course both evangelism and discipleship can happen outside of the purview of the institutional church. Individual Christians and participants in parachurch ministries share their faith with others all the time. And individuals and participants in parachurch ministries help others learn to live as disciples of Christ. This reality may have a lot to do with the high degree of individualism in the contemporary West. A careful reading of Scripture portrays the church as God's primary agent for evangelism and discipleship. No one in Scripture embodies faithfulness to the Great Commission more than Paul, and Paul pursued evangelism and discipleship often through the planting and nurturing of local churches.

The church, then, has a key role to play in helping alleviate the crisis of belonging in our culture. Through evangelism and discipleship, the church can help individuals who feel displaced and lonely to find a place in God's family and God's kingdom.

As instruments of belonging, the church and its members must always be ready to invite someone from the outside into an experience of belonging: "Always be prepared to give an answer to everyone who asks you to give the reason for the hope that you have" (1 Pet. 3:15).

21

However, in many contexts, people aren't typically asking about the "hope that [we] have," so the church needs to be prepared to be a sign of belonging in a society that is indifferent to the gospel.

Church as a Sign of Belonging

What might it mean, then, for the church to serve as a sign of belonging? We can best answer this question by utilizing the four levels of belonging discussed in chapter 1. When I use the term "church" in this context, I am referring to the members of the congregation, not to the building or the formal programs run by them.

Public belonging is the kind of belonging that we experience when we share some kind of external influence in common. The kind of belonging we experience with one another in Sunday worship is an example of public belonging. The church can be a sign of kingdom belonging at the public level by ensuring that the focus of the service remains on Jesus Christ. Churches can easily become tools for nationalistic or political campaigns, and those that resist being used in those ways demonstrate the reality of what it means to declare Christ as the only Lord.

The church can be an effective sign of public belonging by handling the various elements of the service in a way that allows everyone to feel included. We live in a highly mobile culture, and among those who gather for worship on a Sunday, some have been coming for decades while many have been coming for only a few weeks. Many have previously been involved at other churches. Most people attach their sense of belonging in worship to a certain style of music, the order of worship, level of formality, and so on. Helping everyone feel as if they belong involves being very careful when making changes and giving ample explanations for why things are the way that they are.

Social belonging is the kind of belonging that we experience among people who are familiar to but not necessarily well known by us. The church can be a sign of kingdom belonging at the social level by exhibiting exceptional diversity in its fellowship activities. Our culture has a tendency to cluster at the social level according to race, age, income, or political affiliation. A church coffee hour that allows some diversity in one or more of these delimiting characteristics can be a countercultural sign.

Personal belonging is the kind of belonging we experience when we know and are accepted by a small group of people who know us well. Members of a church might experience personal belonging in the context of their own families or through a small group. A church small group can be a sign of kingdom belonging when neighbors or coworkers witness a network of nonfamilial relationships that encourage openness and honesty and provide a support network to help its members navigate the challenges of everyday life.

Intimate belonging is the kind of belonging in which we share everything and have no secrets. Although spouses, best friends, or mentors can all experience intimate kingdom belonging in a Christian context, I will mention briefly the kind of intimate belonging we find in a marriage relationship. A Christian marriage can be a sign of kingdom belonging insofar as the couple demonstrates unconditional love, durable faithfulness, mutual respect, intimacy without insularity, simple delight in each other, and a willingness to serve others. For someone who has only experienced intimacy in a transactional way (I will stay with you only so long as you meet my needs), this kind of intimate belonging can be a powerful sign of the kind of belonging that God intends for us.

Foretastes of Belonging

There is a group of glassblowers in Tacoma, Washington, called the Hilltop Artists. They have a number of programs under their umbrella, but their mission is "using glass arts to connect young people from diverse cultural and economic backgrounds to better futures."[2] Kids who enroll in this program learn to blow glass at temperatures up to three thousand degrees, which is very exciting for most adolescents.

But the larger benefit is that the kids get connected to a wider community of peers and adults who care about them and who can connect them to wider opportunities and to social services if that is necessary. Kids who participate on the production team of the Hilltop Artists have a 100 percent high school graduation rate, and many of them go on to postsecondary education.

The opportunity to blow glass draws lots of kids to this program, but what keeps them there is a strong sense of belonging. Walking into the hotshop on a Tuesday night, one is likely to find music blaring, some donated snacks lying about, and a few clusters of young people working intently together to create amazing works of art. There will be a few adults scattered around as well, talking casually with some of the kids taking a break between projects.

Often when I encounter settings like the Hilltop Artists' hotshop, I have two thoughts in quick succession. The first thought is that this feels like shalom. Everyone in the room is experiencing a strong sense of belonging, and from that secure place they are challenging themselves and growing in their relationships with one another. And my second thought is that, when the people of God gather, it should feel more like this. There are Christians involved in the Hilltop Artists' program, but it is a secular program. What does it mean when a secular program does a better job of establishing shalom for a group of people than the church is able to do?

Don't get me wrong, the church can and does provide a profound sense of belonging for its members in certain contexts. There are many ways that the Christian community can also provide a foretaste of belonging for those outside of the faith. As I mentioned above, when a church community allows those who are not yet members and/or not yet Christians to participate in community celebrations or to participate in a service project, they are offering a significant foretaste of belonging for those who are included in these things.

However, I want to focus our attention here on these kinds of foretaste experiences that take place outside of the Christian community, because I believe that they are not uncommon and I believe that the Christian community can partner with these kinds of places, groups, and institutions for gospel impact if we can learn to see and understand them a bit better.

As we explore this topic, it will be helpful to employ the concept of common grace, which provides a framework for making sense of the really good things that emerge outside of the community of faith. "Common grace" refers to nonsalvific blessings that God provides regardless of one's status in the community of faith. The fact that these blessings are nonsalvific distinguishes them from the blessing of regeneration, which comes only from confessing one's sins and accepting the forgiveness available through Christ's atoning death on the cross.

The blessings of common grace are usually broken down into three categories. The first is natural blessings. God sends rain for crops to grow, and both Christians and non-Christians benefit from it. The second is restraint from evil. Even though all are sinners, people choose not to engage in evil activities even when it would be to their advantage to do so. Sometimes this restraint is attributed to the role of human conscience, which also is a gift from God. And the final category of common grace is civic virtue, which has to do with the good things people do for others even when there is no direct benefit for doing so.

When places, groups, and institutions with no explicit connection to the community of faith cultivate a strong sense of belonging for people, we can attribute this to common grace. This particular form of common grace can be best understood as civic virtue. This kind of belonging can evoke a feeling of shalom among those who experience it. However, as delightful as this kind of belonging is, it can never achieve the level of belonging or the experience of shalom that will be experienced when God's kingdom is fully established. This kind of belonging can be a foretaste of God's kingdom, but it is not the kingdom itself.

Families, even non-Christian families, often exhibit traits characteristic of belonging. What holds a family together is a commitment to the relationship rather than goods or services exchanged. The kind of belonging that soldiers who have been in active combat together possess strikes me as another example of a foretaste of kingdom belonging. Soldiers are encouraged to be faithful to one another, to be reliable, and to serve one another self-sacrificially.

Grief support groups can also fall into this category. People are generally accepted into these groups unconditionally, and members are encouraged to be empathetic and compassionate with one another. Groups that form around helping members achieve personal goals (like losing weight or running a marathon) can exhibit the belonging characteristic of transformation; however, they can also turn in the direction of interpersonal shaming and toxic competitiveness. And of course a neighborhood pub where regulars enjoy the experience of "everyone knowing their name" can offer a significant foretaste of belonging.

Incremental Belonging

This notion of secular groups offering a foretaste of kingdom belonging leads to the idea of incremental belonging. Incremental belonging builds off of the notion that ultimately we all need to belong to God by receiving forgiveness from our sins and being adopted into his family. Any other experience of belonging can be understood as a step toward that ultimate belonging, a step away from it, or perhaps a distraction from it. Obviously, it will be difficult to tell for sure how each particular instance of belonging functions with regard to our ultimate belonging, but we can use a couple of case studies to help identify some potential markers of either progress or regress in this regard.

The first case study has to do with the role a family, especially a loving father, can play in a person's journey to salvation. Salvation in the Bible involves being adopted into God's family and experiencing God as a loving Father. At the same time, we all have earthly fathers, and some of us have been blessed to have a good relationship with our earthly fathers.

It has generally been understood that having a good relationship with one's earthly father makes it easier to accept the generous offer that God makes to be our heavenly Father. One reason for this is that having a good experience with our earthly father allows us to more vividly imagine what is being offered when God extends his offer to be our Father. Now, not having a good relationship with one's earthly

26

father does not prevent one from accepting God's offer to be our Father; it just means that there may be a few more barriers to overcome.

For this reason we can say that there is every reason to hope that every person has a good relationship with their earthly father, both for the immediate blessing that it represents and for the potential future blessing of establishing a relationship with the heavenly Father.

There are other experiences of belonging that function in this way. My wife is a theater teacher and directs a spring musical at our local public high school every year. Her vision is to make the spring musical an event not just for the "drama kids" but for the whole school. Consequently, she usually has a very diverse cast, including kids that don't fit in with any other groups at school. For many kids, being in the cast of the spring musical is their first really meaningful experience of belonging with their peers.

For some kids, this experience can function as an on-ramp to an experience of belonging in the Christian community. There was a high school kid who visited the youth group at our church a few times when he was a junior. He was very shy and kept the earbuds from his phone in his ears throughout youth group. It was extremely difficult to draw him out and engage him in conversation. The following year, he auditioned for the spring musical and got a part in the cast. This was a really positive experience for him. He made lots of new friends and really came out of his shell when he was with the cast. There were a few other members of the cast who were involved in our youth group. So, in the late spring of his senior year, he came back to youth group, and it was like he was a different person. He didn't wear his earbuds, was easy to engage in conversation, and even took the initiative to connect with others.

Empty-Calorie Belonging

An important counterpoint to incremental belonging that we need to keep in mind is idolatrous belonging. An idol is a human-made object that for the idolater takes the place of the real God. For some, an idol is preferred to the real God because it initially seems to offer us more control over our devotional practices and more permission to do what we want while promising similar benefits offered from the real God.

In reality, however, the idol offers no real benefits to the idolater and makes increasing demands on its devotee. The classic idol was the golden calf made by God's people after their deliverance from Egypt. They claimed that it, rather than God, was their deliverer from slavery, and they convinced themselves that proper devotion to this god could best be shown through licentious carousing.

By fixing their attention on this idol, the Israelites took their eyes off of the real God who had just delivered them, and they missed a crucial opportunity to encounter and be blessed by the God who had rescued them from Egypt. Fortunately, this instance of idolatry was short-lived and the Israelites were given another chance to engage with this God.

The pursuit of belonging can, in like manner, be a kind of idolatrous quest that can work against the ultimate belonging that God offers to us. I call idolatrous belonging "empty-calorie" belonging because it is analogous to the way junk food affects our experience of healthy food. If we are ravenously hungry, we might choose to eat something like a bag of potato chips and a cookie. This will probably taste good and alleviate our hunger. But it will also accomplish two other things that are less beneficial for us. It will likely take away our appetite for any healthy food that is later presented to us. It will cultivate our desire toward junk food. And second, if this choice becomes a pattern, it will lead to significant health problems.

The idolatrous pursuit of belonging usually leads to a form of belonging that works against the values of God's kingdom. Many fraternal organizations (in both collegiate and noncollegiate settings) offer a kind of belonging that mimics the belonging available in the local church. These groups often have quasi-religious ceremonies and expectations of involvement among their members that act to dissuade many of their members from getting involved in a local church.

Of course not every member of a fraternal organization is going to get sucked into idolatry through these quasi-religious ceremonies. Those who have experienced genuine worship through their belonging to a local church are likely to see through the folly of these ceremonies.

They might even participate with their mouths and their bodies, but in doing so their hearts are not engaging in idolatry.

Because of the rituals, fraternal organizations are an easy example of idolatrous belonging, but there are lots of other ways one can pursue belonging in an idolatrous way that don't involve such rituals. Belonging to a highly competitive sports team, a boating club, or even a neighborhood pub can prevent someone from experiencing belonging at church and ultimately belonging to God.

This gets us back to the question we posed in the introduction. Is Norm's experience of belonging in Cheers a step toward real belonging, or is it an idolatrous substitute for the kind of belonging he most deeply needs? The answer is that it could be either. It can depend on the values and intentions of those who own and manage the place and the collection of people who gather there. Or in many cases, it has to do not with the management or the community but rather with the state and intentions of the person who patronizes the place.

Catalysts of Belonging

As disciples of Jesus, we are called to partner with him in announcing the good news that the kingdom of God has come and in inviting others to be included in God's kingdom. There are many ways that we can be obedient to that call directly, and there are ways that we can pray for and cheer for others who are engaged in this work even if they are not part of the community of faith.

As members of Christian churches, Christian families, and other types of Christian communities, we can make every effort to ensure that our community truly reflects characteristics of God's kingdom and functions effectively as a sign of the kind of belonging that God wants for all of us. As individuals and as groups of Christians, we can be prayerful and intentional about our role as instruments of belonging for those who are outside the Christian community, by being ready to share the gospel with others when it is appropriate. And finally, we can take note of the places, groups, and institutions within our community

29

that are functioning well as positive foretastes of belonging. I don't believe that we need to try to take over these entities and "baptize" them as Christian ministries, nor do we even have to get involved with them ourselves. But we can cheer for them and pray that they would continue to thrive and that those who experience a foretaste of belonging in these settings would have their appetite for belonging piqued and would have an opportunity to experience the more satisfying experience of belonging to God's kingdom.

KINGDOM BELONGING

So far we've been talking about belonging as mostly a good thing. Nobody likes to feel lonely or alienated, and belonging seems to be the desired solution to these pressing problems. As we noted in the introduction, we all long to be somewhere "where everybody knows your name." In the previous chapter, we discovered that this longing to belong is a multifaceted concept. We long to belong at numerous levels that work within the private and the civic spheres of life. The discovery of these different aspects of belonging has served to highlight just how important belonging is to numerous aspects of human flourishing. This seems to be one of those concepts that can easily cross over from the Christian community to the secular

realm and back again. If there was a button that could be pushed that would increase a sense of belonging across the board, who would hesitate to press it?

But the reality is that some kinds of belonging are not altogether good and can be quite hurtful and even destructive. Street gangs offer a kind of belonging that encourages violence and illicit activity. Cliques of popular kids in high school can destroy the self-image of those who are excluded and can elicit anxiety and body-image issues in those who feel that they need to continually earn the right to be included. And then, of course, there are experiences of belonging that could go either way. Youth sports teams can provide an extremely positive or negative experience of belonging depending on the culture that is cultivated by the coaches and encouraged by the parents.

Clearly, not all experiences of belonging are equally valuable. And as we evaluate various manifestations of belonging, we might find differing opinions about which ones fall into the good category and which ones don't. For this reason, we will need to develop an evaluative framework for assessing the value of various kinds of belonging. In this section, we will be developing a biblical theology of belonging.

FOUR

THE **CHARACTER**
OF **KINGDOM BELONGING**

Koinonia

After a decade in full-time ministry, I was called to return to academia to pursue a PhD. This turned out to be an exciting adventure for my family and me. The last time I'd been in graduate school was much simpler. My wife and I had just gotten married, didn't have any children yet, and were setting up our life together. But this second foray into graduate school involved me leaving a full-time job, a house, and a network of support, and also moving a family of five into an eight-hundred-square-foot apartment in a place none of us had ever lived. On top of all that, when we moved, neither my wife nor I had a job, so we were going to be without a steady income for the foreseeable future.

This might very well have been a disaster but for the fact that our apartment was located in a residential community owned by the seminary, with the very fitting name of Koinonia, a Greek word that is often translated "fellowship" or "community." For us, this apartment complex lived up to its name. Koinonia consisted of ninety apartments arranged in three three-story buildings that framed a common grassy area, a small playground, a basketball court, and a community building. We served as the community coordinators for the first floor and had a corner apartment directly adjacent to the walking path leading to the common area.

What made Koinonia a distinct living arrangement was that all of the residents had three things in common. We were graduate students at a seminary, we were all disciples of Christ, and we were all poor. Beyond those three things, there was quite a bit of variety among us. There were twenty-somethings, retirees, newly married couples, and established families with kids. There was a mix of single and married households. And there was a lot of cultural and ethnic diversity; among the ninety apartments were probably forty different nationalities.

The trust level among newcomers was established pretty quickly, and strong bonds were often formed by helping one another and sharing resources. As a family of five in a small apartment with one bathroom and a tiny kitchen, we benefited greatly from this arrangement. If our bathroom was being used, no one thought twice about using a neighbor's. We didn't have a microwave in our kitchen, but that wasn't a problem, because our neighbor did. We had just one car, and I remember my wife calling from the grocery that was five miles away and asking if I could pick up our son from baseball practice in ten minutes. I said yes without any hesitation, even though I knew she had the family car. I walked out our front door and called out, "Car?" to the first person I saw. She reached into her pocket and threw me a set of keys without saying a word. Five minutes later I was watching the last few minutes of my son's practice, ready to drive him home when it was over.

Not only did we share resources, we spent a lot of time enjoying one another's company as well. None of us could afford much travel, so people were around on weekends and holidays and usually up for doing something fun and cheap. We didn't arrange many play dates, because the kids just ran around in a loose clump collectively supervised by the adults in the community. On Friday afternoons, we parked ourselves on the concrete slab outside our front door and served drinks to people as they came home for the day.

From a financial perspective, those three years at Koinonia represent the poorest years of our married life. And yet they hold some of our happiest memories. We think of that time as deeply formative for us individually and as a family unit. We experienced a profound sense of belonging at Koinonia, a little taste of shalom.

Characteristics of Kingdom Belonging

When I think of belonging from a kingdom perspective, my thoughts often turn to Koinonia. Of course, not everything was perfect in this community. We had plenty of challenges, and I'm sure not every resident felt as enthusiastic about it as we did. But for us, it certainly felt kingdom-ish. While these kinds of experiences can be helpful in getting a feel for what God's kingdom is like, it is better to turn to Scripture to help us get a clearer picture of kingdom belonging. In this chapter we look at eight identifying characteristics of kingdom belonging.

Unconditional

In the first place, kingdom belonging finds its basis in God's unconditional love. God chose Israel to be the recipients of his blessing not because of any characteristics or merit on their part but simply because he chose to love them. With the incarnation of Jesus in the New Testament, non-Jews are extended an offer to belong to God's kingdom that is based on that same unconditional love.

Because of its basis in God's unconditional love, belonging in God's kingdom is never earned or deserved. Therefore, humility and gratitude are appropriate characteristics of those who belong to God's kingdom. If humility and gratitude are not present within someone who belongs to God's kingdom, it is an indicator of a basic misunderstanding at play. Most people are susceptible to a strong tendency for feelings of entitlement to develop over time. And it is common for humility and gratitude to fade over time. Therefore, it is necessary for those who belong to God's kingdom to be reminded of the gospel on a regular basis.

Covenantal

Second, kingdom belonging is covenantal. A covenant is an agreement between two parties that establishes a relationship. There may be certain expectations associated with the covenant, but it is the relationship that is paramount. In contrast to covenants, contracts are agreements that involve relationships, but in contracts the expectations are paramount, the relationships secondary.

Our relationships with our children tend to be covenantal. We have expectations for our children (obedience, chores, meals together), but we don't fire them from the family when those expectations aren't met. Our relationship with the person we hire to mow our lawn is contractual. As soon as the relationship ceases to be beneficial to either party, the contract is voided, and we hire someone else or start mowing our own lawn.

Covenants and contracts are not always as easy to clearly distinguish. Your relationship with the grocery store checker is contractual—you pay three dollars and she gives you milk. But as you go to the store every week, you develop a friendship. One week you forget your wallet but still would like some milk. Because of the relational trust that has built up, she lets you take the milk and pay for it the next time you come in, or she pays for it out of her own pocket. This is because your contractual relationship has started to take on some covenantal characteristics.

An example on the other end of the continuum is marriage. A marriage is (or is supposed to be) a covenantal relationship. There are expectations in a marriage such as sexual union, maintaining a household, raising children, and so on. But the relationship is more important than any of these expectations. When a couple gets divorced, a lawyer is brought in to help transform a covenantal relationship into a contractual relationship. Expectations regarding finances, property, and child-rearing all become clearly spelled out in a legally binding contract.

Kingdom belonging is clearly covenantal. God reached out to Abram with a covenant promise to bless him and to bless the world through his offspring. Through Christ, non-Jews have been included in this promise, grafted into the covenant. Because God's kingdom is covenantal in nature, belonging to the kingdom is secure and peaceful. Those who belong to God's kingdom are not anxious about their status in the kingdom. The story of the prodigal son beautifully depicts the covenantal character of the kingdom. The father doesn't welcome the disobedient son home grudgingly but joyously runs to welcome his son home and instigates a celebration.

Invitational

There are clear distinctions between those who do and those who do not belong to God's kingdom. However, it is important to remember that kingdom belonging is always inclusive, porous, and invitational.

This becomes abundantly clear in the New Testament, but we see hints of this quality in the Old Testament as well. When God set into motion his plan to redeem sinful humanity by calling Abram to be the recipient of his blessing, he promised that Abram would be a conduit for blessing for the whole earth (Gen. 12:3). We see this inclusive tendency in passages such as Leviticus 19:33–34: "When a foreigner resides among you in your land, do not mistreat them. The foreigner residing among you must be treated as your native-born. Love them as yourself, for you were foreigners in Egypt. I am the LORD your God." At this time, God was focusing his blessing on Israel, but he wanted the Israelites to maintain a compassionate heart toward those on the outside.

This invitational quality becomes more prominent in the New Testament. Jesus included gentiles (non-Jews) in his ministry and often praised their faith. When describing his ministry focus, he made this invitational aspect abundantly clear: "For the Son of Man came to seek and to save the lost" (Luke 19:10). In Jesus's final instruction to his disciples, he tells them to take the message of salvation "to the ends of the earth" (Acts 1:8).

In the early church, God communicated this inclusive plan clearly with Peter, who set the pattern for the rest of the church: "So then, even to Gentiles God has granted repentance that leads to life" (Acts

11:18). Finally, the second half of Acts is dominated by Paul, who leads numerous missionary journeys and models a missionary impulse that has characterized the Christian church ever since.

Since the kingdom of God is invitational, those who belong to the kingdom should resist the natural tendency toward insularity that characterizes most human groups. Churches should not think in terms of meeting the expectations of the members but rather should always be attentive to those who are not yet part of their fellowship.

Compassionate

The kingdom of God reflects God's special concern for the marginalized, hurting, and vulnerable. In the Old Testament, God reveals himself as a God who cares for the poor and vulnerable: "For the LORD your God is God of gods and Lord of lords, the great God, mighty and awesome, who shows no partiality and accepts no bribes. He defends the cause of the fatherless and the widow, and loves the foreigner residing among you, giving them food and clothing" (Deut. 10:17–18).

God commands his people to reflect his character by showing compassion for the poor in their midst: "Do not take advantage of a hired worker who is poor and needy, whether that worker is a fellow Israelite or a foreigner residing in one of your towns" (Deut. 24:14).

God requires not only that his people not take advantage of the poor but also that they make deliberate efforts to ensure that their needs will be met. The gleaning laws are one of many examples of this type of command: "When you are harvesting in your field and you overlook a sheaf, do not go back to get it. Leave it for the foreigner, the fatherless and the widow, so that the LORD your God may bless you in all the work of your hands" (Deut. 24:19).

In the New Testament, we witness Jesus taking this obligation to care for the poor and vulnerable and making it a central focus of his ministry. Challenging expectations for a Jewish rabbi, Jesus showed special concern not only for the poor but for every kind of marginalized person. Jesus scandalized Jewish leaders and his followers by reaching out to women, the unclean, and sinners.

The story of the hemorrhaging woman in Luke 8 is a typical example. Jesus has been summoned by the leader of the local synagogue to come and heal his daughter, but on the way Jesus encounters a woman who is suffering from a bleeding disorder and who desires his help. Jesus interrupts his journey not only to heal this woman but also to talk with her and generally bolster her dignity in front of the crowds. By attending to this woman, who many would have considered unimportant, before attending to Jairus, Jesus demonstrates the value of caring for the poor and marginalized.

This care for the poor was carried on in the early church. In his first epistle, John instructs his readers to care for the poor as a way of emulating Jesus's self-sacrificial love: "If anyone has material possessions and sees a brother or sister in need but has no pity on them, how can the love of God be in that person?" (1 John 3:17). And James warns his readers not to show favoritism toward the rich: "Suppose a man comes into your meeting wearing a gold ring and fine clothes, and a poor man in filthy old clothes also comes in. If you show special attention to the man wearing fine clothes and say, 'Here's a good seat for you,' but say to the poor man, 'You stand there' or 'Sit on the floor by my feet,' have you not discriminated among yourselves and become judges with evil thoughts?" (James 2:2–4).

Because concern for the poor, hurting, and vulnerable is a high value in the kingdom of God, those who belong to the kingdom should be people of compassion. It is common when people see someone who is poor or hurting to assume that this is because they are under God's judgment or are somehow less deserving of God's favor than others, but the Bible teaches God's people not to think like this. God's people are to be tenderhearted toward the poor, to accompany them in their suffering, and to offer practical help.

Diverse

We note above that the kingdom of God is invitational and compassionate. One natural outcome of this value that we can give special consideration is the fact that diversity is highly valued in God's kingdom.

This value can be seen in God's activity long before he instigates his plan of salvation. We see evidence of God's love for diversity in the way he created the world: "So God created the great creatures of the sea and every living thing with which the water teems and that moves about in it, according to their kinds, and every winged bird according to its kind. And God saw that it was good" (Gen. 1:21). God could have created a simpler world with one or two kinds of bird and one or two kinds of fish, but instead he created a world with such abundant variety that even today we are discovering new species.

This valuing of diversity takes on a new importance with the coming of Jesus and his offer of free forgiveness to all people. Because belonging to the kingdom is anchored in God's unconditional love, external characteristics don't play a role in one's belonging status. In fact, diversity is encouraged because it provides a clearer witness to the source of one's belonging: "There is neither Jew nor Gentile, neither slave nor free, nor is there male and female, for you are all one in Christ Jesus" (Gal. 3:28). This is made abundantly clear in explicit descriptions of the kingdom: "People will come from east and west and north and south, and will take their places at the feast in the kingdom of God" (Luke 13:29).

Diversity in belonging goes beyond ethnic, socioeconomic, or gender distinction, however. Kingdom belonging values diversity in gifts, natural aptitudes, and experience. Paul's notion of the church as an interdependent body illustrates this aspect: "The eye cannot say to the hand, 'I don't need you!' And the head cannot say to the feet, 'I don't need you!'" (1 Cor. 12:21).

That diversity is an important value in God's kingdom has two implications for those who belong to it. The first is that belonging to the kingdom challenges us to truly value those things that make others different from us. It's easier to identify with and value those attributes in others that are similar to ours, but God challenges us to take the more difficult approach of valuing difference. The other implication is that there is freedom and encouragement for those who belong to God's kingdom to discover and develop those attributes that make us distinct. Since our unity is in Christ, we can avoid the temptation to seek uniformity to strengthen group identity within the kingdom of God.

Transformative

Kingdom belonging is transformative. Through belonging, we are shaped in ways that are healing and beneficial. Sin not only severs our relationship with God and strains our relationships with others but also distorts and pollutes the goodness conferred on us in our created existence. To recover that goodness, we need to experience victory over not only the punishment of sin (justification) but also the power of sin (sanctification). For this reason, kingdom belonging is meant to be transformative.

This aspect begins in the Old Testament with the covenant expectations that God communicated to the Israelites. "When you enter the land the LORD your God is giving you, do not learn to imitate the detestable ways of the nations there" (Deut. 18:9). The law showed what a transformed life was supposed to look like and provided a framework of right and wrong that could guide individuals and the community. Unfortunately, the law was not able to help the Israelites actually achieve transformation: "Therefore no one will be declared righteous in God's sight by the works of the law; rather, through the law we become conscious of our sin" (Rom. 3:20). In the New Testament, Jesus fulfilled the law through his obedience. He also died on the cross to achieve forgiveness for us and to break the power of sin that kept us from being able to keep the law.

A major theme of the New Testament, then, is the transformation for the disciple of Jesus. This is picked up in at least two different ways. The first is ontological, having to do with the change within the essence of our being when we belong to God through Christ: "Therefore, if anyone is in Christ, the new creation has come: The old has gone, the new is here" (2 Cor. 5:17). The second aspect of this truth is ethical/vocational: "I urge you to live a life worthy of the calling you have received" (Eph. 4:1). The call to belong in God's kingdom comes with a promise that one can and will be formed into the kind of person who fits into God's holy kingdom.

Delightful

When the first humans were placed in the garden, God provided everything that they needed for belonging there: "The LORD God made all kinds of trees grow out of the ground—trees that were pleasing to the eye and good for food" (Gen. 2:9). These trees were created not only to meet the humans' need for physical food but also to meet their need for beauty.

From this, we can discern that for God, beauty is not peripheral but essential to human thriving. God created us with bodies designed to apprehend and delight in his creation's beauty: "The heavens declare the glory of God; the skies proclaim the work of his hands" (Ps. 19:1). He invites us to experience the goodness of his provision with our senses: "Taste and see that the LORD is good" (Ps. 34:8). Because of this intent of God's, our delighting in the particular locale where God has placed us is an important aspect of what it means to belong somewhere. Whenever I'm on an extended trip or when I move to a new location, an important watershed of belonging in that place for me is when I find something that brings me delight. This might be a pastry at a local coffee shop, a bench with a view, or a fragrant walking path.

This aspect of God's intent for humanity has been difficult for many people to accept. They have tended to imagine a more austere picture of God and his will for us. Time and time again, humans have reasoned that what God must want is that we deny ourselves sensory delight.

When Paul encountered this erroneous way of thinking among the Christians in Colossae, he identified it as a belonging issue. As ones who had been reconciled to the God who created the world and declared it all good, how could they believe that denial of bodily delight would be pleasing to God? "Since you died with Christ to the elemental spiritual forces of this world, why, as though you still belonged to the world, do you submit to its rules: 'Do not handle! Do not taste! Do not touch!'?" (Col. 2:20–21). Now of course there are good reasons for certain kinds of abstention for those who belong to God. But these reasons are for the purpose of moving toward the right use of God's creation rather than denying the goodness of that creation.

Productive

The ethical/vocational aspect of calling involves more than just personal transformation for the sake of becoming holy. When we belong to God's kingdom, we are conscripted into God's activity in the world. I call this characteristic of the kingdom "productive" to underscore the work that we have been given to do. This aspect of kingdom belonging is described in more detail in the next chapter, so I only mention it here.

It's easy to think of belonging to the kingdom in terms of the benefits bestowed on its members. Kingdom membership involves forgiveness of sin, the promise of eternal life, and transformation. But membership in the kingdom is also about active participation in what God is doing in the world.

The Effect of Kingdom Belonging

When my wife and I were contemplating the possibility of my returning to school to pursue a PhD, we mostly considered how a structured academic program would shape me and help me develop tools that would help me better live out my vocation. We knew that this experience would also have an impact on our family, but we mostly thought of this aspect in terms of what we would have to sacrifice as a family in order to achieve these other gains.

We were not expecting the powerful impact that the sense of belonging we experienced at Koinonia would have on each member of our family and on the family as a whole. Not only did the community help us manage the challenges we faced with very limited resources, they also helped us quickly establish deep connections to the place and the people proximate to our home. This relatively short period was a time of tremendous growth for each one of us, and during this time we each experienced deepening love of and trust in Christ. We look back on that time now as a treasure that we wouldn't want to trade for anything. Our experience of kingdom belonging left an indelible imprint on us.

The cumulative effect of kingdom belonging on the individual and on communities is that kingdom belonging brings shalom, freedom, purpose, and hope. Shalom comes from the peace one has in the security that one's status in the kingdom is secure. Freedom comes from being encouraged to be the person one was created to be. Purpose comes from knowing one's life is neither meaningless nor self-referential but instead is an important part of God's plan for all of creation. And hope comes from the fact that one's belonging is tethered to an already-accomplished future that is drawing the present toward itself.

FIVE

THE **CHARACTER** OF **WORLDLY BELONGING**

Trying Hard to Be Liked

I was going to a large public university, and I wanted to find a smaller community where I could feel like I belonged. The Greek system seemed like a good option, since some of my siblings had enjoyed a good experience with a fraternity or sorority. At my school, you didn't join a house until after your first semester.

The process of joining a house was a weeklong period called "rush." You begin that week by visiting all of the houses for a brief introduction. Each evening, the members of the houses go through the list of visitors and invite some of them to return. When you receive your list of houses that have invited you to return, you choose those that you find interesting. Each day the lists get shorter, and the time at the houses gets longer, until the last day, when you are invited to join one house.

As with most Greek systems, different levels of prestige were associated with each house. It was a large system, with over forty total houses, but everyone knew there were five fraternities clustered on one prominent street that were the "good houses." Even people not in the system knew that. At the time I attended, one house included a Dutch prince on its active membership rolls.

My good friend and roommate had already been offered a spot at one of the good houses in the winter of our freshman year. Because my friend and I had been on the same level of social prestige in high school, we both took this as a positive sign of my being invited to one of the good houses. It also meant I had a slight advantage (or so I thought) over other students going through rush. Each evening of rush week, my friend could give me insider information from the selection meeting he'd attended at one of the prestige houses. He wasn't established enough to persuade the members to choose me, but he could give me updates on how I was doing.

Unfortunately, I wasn't doing very well. I'm slightly introverted, and large social gatherings, especially ones that require a lot of small talk, make me nervous. One involuntary way I express my nervousness is to yawn. So at my first meet and greet at my friend's house, I must have yawned a few times while talking to members. Later that night, my friend gave me the postgame analysis, and it wasn't good. "Dude, I really think a lot of these guys could really like you, but a few guys really shot you down and said that you looked really bored to be there," he reported.

Even after I had offended some members by yawning in their faces, my friend had convinced them to invite me back for a second day. The stakes were higher now, so I was going to make every effort not to yawn and to be likable. I have since discovered that my trying to be liked generally has the opposite effect. There exists a personality type that instinctively knows what will make people like them, and that type can easily become that desired person. Unfortunately, I don't have that trait.

The next day at my friend's house, I think I did manage to suppress any yawns. However, I was even more nervous. Between trying to remember not to yawn and trying to figure out what I could say that would make me more likable to these guys, there wasn't much bandwidth left to carry on an interesting conversation. That night my friend delivered the disappointing news that I wasn't going to be invited back. Neither of us was surprised.

The good news is that I did continue to visit other houses and managed to find one where I did feel comfortable. It wasn't one of the prestige houses, but it was a good group of guys, and with them I felt more comfortable being myself. I ended up joining this group.

I am not anti-Greek-system. I think fraternities and sororities provide a good option for students to experience belonging, especially at large schools. And I believe that many make a sincere effort for rush to be more about helping individuals and groups to find a good fit than about arranging students according to some kind of ranking system. However, at some level, human nature being what it is, we tend to bring our insecurities into systems like this and use them to ascertain our own worth. When we do that, the kind of belonging that we experience can feel very different from what we have seen as kingdom belonging. The term that we can use to describe this other kind of belonging is "worldly belonging."

Worldly Belonging

Worldly belonging is the polar opposite of kingdom belonging. Like kingdom belonging, it is sought after by those who feel alienated and lonely. But unlike kingdom belonging, worldly belonging ultimately fails to satisfy those who pursue it. And the effect of worldly belonging on the individual, the community, and the environment is negative.

A scriptural example of worldly belonging is in the story of the tower of Babel: "As people moved eastward, they found a plain in Shinar and settled there. They said to each other, 'Come, let's make bricks and bake them thoroughly.' They used brick instead of stone, and tar for mortar. Then they said, 'Come, let us build ourselves a city, with a tower that reaches to the heavens, so that we may make a name for ourselves; otherwise we will be scattered over the face of the whole earth'" (Gen. 11:2–4). These people are feeling anxious and unsettled, so they devise a plan to bolster their sense of belonging.

The key here is that they desire to establish a sense of belonging by "making a name for themselves" rather than relying on God to establish their identity. This points to a fundamental distinction between kingdom belonging and worldly belonging. Worldly belonging is something

47

that humans attempt to develop on their own initiative, and kingdom belonging is received as a gift from God.

Characteristics of Worldly Belonging

In this story we don't see the full negative implications of worldly belonging, because the Lord steps in to frustrate their plans. But as we trace worldly belonging throughout the rest of the Scriptures, we can identify some common characteristics: it is exclusive, contractual, enemy focused, and malformative.

Exclusive

Worldly belonging is based on some common characteristic or attribute the group finds valuable; thus worldly belonging tends to be exclusive. Group identity is strengthened not only by making clear distinctions between who's in and who's out but also by keeping people out.

One unfortunate development we see in the biblical story of salvation is how the people of God under the old covenant drifted from kingdom belonging to worldly belonging. The old covenant exemplified a type of belonging that made clear distinctions between who was in and who was out. But it was also invitational in its posture toward outsiders.

Over time, this invitational aspect was largely forgotten. The religious leaders we meet in the New Testament equated belonging with a rigid understanding of holiness and maintained group identity by cutting people off who didn't fit their standard of holiness. These leaders were scandalized by Jesus's willingness to reach out to outsiders.

Contractual

Worldly belonging tends to be contractual rather than covenantal. What sense of belonging exists is based on the mutually beneficial nature of the relationship between the individual and the group. This can lead to instability, because the individual can be removed from the group at any time. Likewise the individual might remove herself from the group if she no longer derives benefit from belonging to it.

A key attribute of kingdom belonging is its covenantal character. In many contexts, however, there's a strong pull toward contractual relationships, which can lead to a challenging dynamic for a new or immature Christian. If our experience of kingdom belonging is weak, it's easy to fall back into some of the contractual worldly-belonging relationships. Paul warns the Colossians about this dynamic: "Since you died with Christ to the elemental spiritual forces of this world, why, as though you still belonged to the world, do you submit to its rules . . . ?" (Col. 2:20). The Christians in Colossae have been included in the kingdom of God and can enjoy the benefits of God's covenantal love. However, they are not experiencing this covenantal love as fully as they should, and they therefore derive their sense of belonging from the world. Since the world tends to encourage contractual belonging, these Christians feel pressured to submit to a set of rules to maintain their sense of belonging.

Enemy Focused

Worldly belonging not only excludes outsiders, it also readily and commonly identifies enemies as a way of building cohesion and commitment among the belonging group. We need to acknowledge that this has also been an attribute of kingdom belonging at a particular point in salvation history. This focus on the enemy was present in the Old Testament as God was first establishing his special relationship with the Israelites and forming their identity as a distinct people. God warned his people to "not be like the other nations."

> The LORD your God will cut off before you the nations you are about to invade and dispossess. But when you have driven them out and settled in their land, and after they have been destroyed before you, be careful not to be ensnared by inquiring about their gods, saying, "How do these nations serve their gods? We will do the same." You must not

49

worship the LORD your God in their way, because in worshiping their gods, they do all kinds of detestable things the LORD hates. They even burn their sons and daughters in the fire as sacrifices to their gods. (Deut. 12:29–31)

The other nations followed practices detestable to God and harmful to the people. As God taught his people a way of goodness, beauty, and justice, the other nations served as a counterexample of life away from a relationship with God. This enemy focus in the Old Testament was behind both God's instruction to remove the other nations from the promised land and his warning not to follow their practices.

The long-term lesson here is to not divide the world between "us" and "them" but rather to show the ugliness of sin and its corrosive impact on individuals and communities. In the New Testament, Jesus makes clear that the real enemy is sin, not any particular group of people. Since we all sin, we all deserve the punishment the "other nations" received. Outside of Christ, we are under the curse of sin and, as such, are enemies of God. Of course, Jesus teaches this not to condemn us with it but rather to offer us forgiveness and a restored relationship with God: "For if, while we were God's enemies, we were reconciled to him through the death of his Son, how much more, having been reconciled, shall we be saved through his life!" (Rom. 5:10).

This development in salvation history fundamentally changes our perspective on the concept of enemy. Sin is the enemy, and we all need Christ to overcome its power over us. Others who don't yet know Christ are to be thought of no longer as our enemies but rather as people like us in need of liberation from sin.

This is a radical shift in the common understanding of enemies. It took a while for its implications to sink in for the disciples and other would-be followers of Jesus. Some were looking to him to conquer the oppressive force of the Roman army, others expected him to publicly condemn overt sinners, and still others hoped he would give them an edge over the despised Samaritans: "And he sent messengers on ahead, who went into a Samaritan village to get things ready for him; but the people there did not welcome him, because he was heading for

Jerusalem. When the disciples James and John saw this, they asked, 'Lord, do you want us to call fire down from heaven to destroy them?' But Jesus turned and rebuked them" (Luke 9:52–55). Jesus refused to treat any person as his enemy. He extended the possibility of forgiveness and restoration to all. Nonetheless, the tendency to identify other people as enemies exerts a strong pull on people, including Christians, so we see enemy focus as a common aspect of belonging both within and outside of the Christian community.

Malformative

Worldly belonging tends to be malformative to character. One mechanism by which worldly belonging can be malformative is to create a split between our presenting self and our authentic self. If the group we want to belong to is highly restrictive or intolerant of weakness or flaws, we often try to construct a presenting self that is acceptable to the group.

As the divide between our presenting and authentic selves becomes more entrenched, we begin to believe that the presenting self is who we are. More significantly, we start to believe that the presenting self is what God sees. This is problematic in two ways. The first is that, since the presenting self requires work to maintain, it makes our relationship with God dependent on our effort.

The second problem is that it moves our authentic self away from our conscious awareness. And this makes it easy for the Enemy to twist and distort our authentic self without our noticing. This dynamic is what the Bible describes as captivity to sin.

When we are captive to sin, we find what God requires of us distasteful instead of life-giving. We ignore God and his instructions and pursue things that promise much more than they deliver. As our deep need for peace, joy, and belonging continues to go unmet, we ramp up our pursuit of the wrong things. When belonging is the need we're trying to meet in this way, we gravitate toward the worldly kind of belonging described above.

Because God desires us to thrive and his instructions to us are meant for our flourishing, when we ignore God and his instructions the result harms the individual and the wider community. Paul describes what becomes of human life when we turn from God:

> Furthermore, just as they did not think it worthwhile to retain the knowledge of God, so God gave them over to a depraved mind, so that they do what ought not to be done. They have become filled with every kind of wickedness, evil, greed and depravity. They are full of envy, murder, strife, deceit and malice. They are gossips, slanderers, God-haters, insolent, arrogant and boastful; they invent ways of doing evil; they disobey their parents; they have no understanding, no fidelity, no love, no mercy. Although they know God's righteous decree that those who do such things deserve death, they not only continue to do these very things but also approve of those who practice them. (Rom. 1:28–32)

Because God is the source of life, worldly belonging ultimately leads to death. John provides evidence for this truth in Cain's decision to murder his brother: "Do not be like Cain, who *belonged* to the evil one and murdered his brother" (1 John 3:12, emphasis added). When Moses was preparing God's people to enter the promised land, he made clear the connection between the kind of belonging God wanted for them and life, versus the alternate kind of belonging and death: "See, I set before you today life and prosperity, death and destruction. For I command you today to love the LORD your God, to walk in obedience to him, and to keep his commands, decrees and laws; then you will live and increase, and the LORD your God will bless you in the land you are entering to possess" (Deut. 30:15–16). And when Jesus's disciples contemplated how to replace Judas, they described his fate in terms of belonging. They prayed for God to provide another "to take over this apostolic ministry, which Judas left to go where he belongs" (Acts 1:25).

Making Distinctions

Generating a list of kingdom-belonging characteristics helps us recognize the kind of belonging manifested in any given circumstance or context. One might be tempted to think that exercising this kind of discernment is unnecessary, since an individual or group that self-identifies as Christian should be exhibiting kingdom-belonging characteristics.

Unfortunately, this is not always the case. Because worldly belonging is so prevalent, it's not uncommon for Christians to exhibit worldly-belonging characteristics. This is partly why we are encouraged not to take everything at face value, but rather to "test the spirits" (1 John 4:1). Similarly, Jesus tells a miniparable to explain how the foundation of our lives will be revealed by the things our lives produce: "By their fruit you will recognize them" (Matt. 7:16).

The good news is that Christian groups or individuals are not doomed to remain in worldly-belonging mode indefinitely. Christ has the power to overcome any of the worldly-belonging characteristics if we recognize the error of our ways and ask Christ's help in recalibrating around kingdom belonging. One reason for articulating the characteristics of worldly belonging is to assist individuals and groups in seeing where they may have strayed from the parameters of kingdom belonging.

Groups that offer their members an experience of worldly belonging tend to be exclusive, contractual, enemy focused, and malformative. However, it is important to know that worldly belonging is not necessarily "hell on earth." The experience of this kind of belonging can have perceived value and feel pretty good at times. However, the benefits of worldly belonging tend to be short lived and become less satisfying over time.

Also, I'm not claiming that every instance of belonging that isn't explicitly Christian automatically qualifies as "worldly." Chapter 3 introduced the notion of common grace to account for non-Christian groups that exhibit kingdom-belonging characteristics. Unfortunately, we are also going to consider some explicitly Christian examples of worldly-belonging characteristics. It's important to keep in mind that the purpose of articulating these distinct ways of belonging is to establish an evaluative framework for making sense of any instance of belonging.

Unsatisfied

Having a friend who belonged to a "prestigious" fraternity in college afforded me an insider's perspective on this kind of elite group. As my friend transitioned from pledge to active member, he got to know the individual members better and to experience what that kind of belonging felt like. From the outside, it looked like an enviable society of the few who lived a charmed existence.

The guys presented themselves as good-looking and confident. They were successful in school and sports. They didn't all come from wealthy families, but they seemed to be the kind of people who would secure good jobs upon graduation and comfortably take their place among the privileged class. Not only did these guys seem to possess every manner of positive qualities, they didn't seem to struggle like the rest of us, and for them big transitions (like going to college) didn't involve awkwardness and angst.

But as my friend got to know the young men in this fraternity in their daily lives, a slightly different picture began to emerge. He started to see that the confident exterior was in many cases an act that had been adopted to satisfy the expectations of high-achieving parents and to be accepted among their peer group. Some of the guys built coping mechanisms that helped them avoid dealing with some of the complex feelings going on under the surface. Others admitted to their struggles privately in unguarded moments but worked hard to keep those struggles hidden from the outside world. As my friend put it, "people who act like they have their [stuff] together either don't have a lot of [stuff] to get together or they are really good actors."

I'm not suggesting that my friend's fraternity was a pure example of worldly belonging and that there were no elements of kingdom belonging to be found there. I am quite certain that more than a few guys were fairly well grounded (like my friend) and didn't get caught up in the elite status of that particular house. I'm also sure there were traditions and aspects of their culture that were healthy and good. It's likely also that this fraternity tapped into some of my insecurities, so my experience there would have had a high likelihood of being malformative.

In any case, for me that particular group at that time in my life represented worldly belonging. I was in the midst of a major life transition and feeling uncertain about a number of things. Getting a bid at that elite house would have provided a rush of affirmation and an immediate sense of belonging that would have outweighed the tumultuous stew of emotions I was feeling. But I am convinced that the long-term effect of this kind of belonging would not have been life-giving for me and would not have contributed to the shalom of the world. It doesn't really matter, because I could not surmount the barriers to belonging to that house.

The kind of belonging I really needed also can present significant barriers to overcome. Those barriers are not insurmountable, but they can be counterintuitive, so it's important to understand some of the dynamics that are at play between belonging and not belonging and also how a sense of belonging can ebb and flow under certain conditions. To better understand these dynamics we will now turn to exploring the shape of kingdom belonging.

SIX

THE **SHAPE** OF **KINGDOM BELONGING**

A Recovery of Belonging

The movie *Babette's Feast* tells the story of a remote Danish Protestant Christian community that has lost its way.[1] The founder died years ago, leaving his two daughters to lead the aging community. They haven't had any converts for years and have settled into a joyless existence where petty feuds and lingering tensions conspire with a philosophical commitment to austerity to make daily life exceptionally miserable.

This grim situation is interrupted by the arrival of Babette Hersant, who's seeking refuge from persecution in France. Babette is brought in as a volunteer cook, and over the next fourteen years she gains the trust of the community by bringing small improvements to their simple meals. One year, Babette wins the lottery and is awarded enough money to return to France and resume her former life. She decides instead to spend it all on one lavish feast for the community.

This beautiful act of selfless sacrifice causes the members of the community to remember the joy they once had in their faith, and many of them reconciled with one another. When the sisters realize that Babette has spent her entire windfall on one meal, they are aghast and become concerned that Babette will be poor for the rest of her life. To this, Babette replies, "An artist is never poor." The sisters realize what a gift they have received from Babette, and as they consider how God will continue to utilize this beautiful soul in heaven, one sister declares, in one of my favorite movie lines of all time, "Oh, how you will enchant the angels."

Babette's Feast illustrates some of the complex elements of belonging. When the community was first founded, it may well have been an inviting community where people experienced both love from one another and a stable setting to experience belonging. Even their austerity may have been counterbalanced by the camaraderie of brothers and sisters who share a deep commitment to a common mission. Over time, the community seemed to have lost some of that vitality, and what held them together was the familiarity of a particular location and a pattern of existence that depleted their joy and passion as it continued to meet their physical needs.

Babette, an outsider who had the least legitimate claim to belonging among the community, nevertheless helped them experience renewal by relocating their sense of belonging around a shared experience of delight. The story reminds us that belonging isn't a static concept, nor are its boundaries easy to demarcate. In this chapter, we look at some of the conceptual nuances that need to be kept in mind when thinking about belonging.

Centered-Set Belonging

Belonging is a universal human experience. In the previous two chapters, we contrasted kingdom and worldly belonging in terms of some of the elements that characterize them. But part of what makes kingdom belonging distinct can't be captured in terms of particular attributes. One dynamic of kingdom belonging is its structural and dynamic characteristics.

In the book of Philippians, Paul encourages the members of the Christian community to live in a way distinct from the rest of the world.

> Join together in following my example, brothers and sisters, and just as you have us as a model, keep your eyes on those who live as we do.

For, as I have often told you before and now tell you again even with tears, many live as enemies of the cross of Christ. Their destiny is destruction, their god is their stomach, and their glory is in their shame. Their mind is set on earthly things. But our citizenship is in heaven. And we eagerly await a Savior from there, the Lord Jesus Christ, who, by the power that enables him to bring everything under his control, will transform our lowly bodies so that they will be like his glorious body. (Phil. 3:17–21)

Paul doesn't specifically mention belonging here, but belonging is implied in his reference to citizenship. He describes the members of the church in Philippi as citizens of heaven, which is his way of saying that they belong to God. To understand what Paul is saying here, we need to know a bit about his audience.

Philippi was an important Roman colony, and many of its residents were Roman citizens. This was somewhat unusual, because only a fraction of the people who lived in the Roman Empire but outside of Italy were Roman citizens. Roman citizenship was automatic to free men born in Italy and to their male descendants who lived elsewhere. Others had to be granted citizenship or buy it. Philippi contained an unusual number of Roman citizens because a lot of retired Roman soldiers lived there. Roman citizenship for those living in Philippi was not geographical; citizenship had nothing to do with living within the city of Philippi and everything to do with one's relationship to Rome.

This is similar to how Paul understands being a citizen of heaven. It is not about living within the bounds of a place called heaven (or the kingdom of God); rather, it is about one's relation to Jesus, who reigns over the kingdom of God. Paul's understanding of belonging to God's kingdom, then, can be considered a centered rather than a bounded set.

A bounded set is a group defined by boundaries (see fig. 1). It's easy to visualize a bounded set if we take all the striped balls on a pool table and gather them in one area. Inclusion in the group is determined by whether one is inside or outside a set of boundary characteristics. Inclusion in a centered set, by way of contrast, is determined by one's

Figure 1

Bounded Set

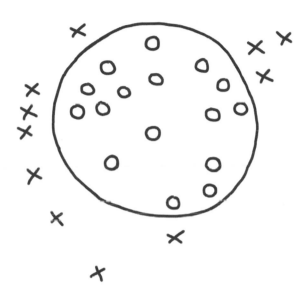

relationship to the center. One is included in the set if one is oriented toward the center, and not included if one is oriented away from the center. The Camino de Santiago is a historic pilgrimage terminating in the city of Santiago, Spain. There are multiple starting places and multiple routes to travel, but all of them lead to Santiago. Pilgrims in this context can be thought of as a centered set because the defining characteristic of them is that they are all heading toward Santiago.

Membership in God's kingdom is not fundamentally about living within any particular boundaries (geographical or otherwise); rather, it is about one's relation to Jesus, who is at the center of God's kingdom. This was not always the case.

When God first established Israel to be a holy nation and a demonstration of his goodness and righteousness to the world, the kingdom he established through them was a bounded set. The conditions for belonging to this group were keeping the law and being a descendant (sort of) of Abraham. Belonging to God's kingdom also involved living within the promised land and communing with God through temple worship in the holy city of Jerusalem. Violating the covenant requirements and expectations resulted in being removed from the temple and the city either temporarily or permanently.

Things took a dramatic turn with the incarnation of Jesus and his announcement of the kingdom. These changes were part of God's plan from the beginning, but they seemed very radical when announced by Jesus. Jesus extended the invitation to belong to the kingdom broadly. He invited men and women, Jews and gentiles, healthy and sick, rich and poor. People responded to his invitation of belonging to the kingdom by either accepting his offer and becoming a disciple or rejecting it. Through this method, Jesus collected an eclectic group of disciples who had little in common with one another but who all had a vital relationship with Jesus.

Figure 2
Centered Set

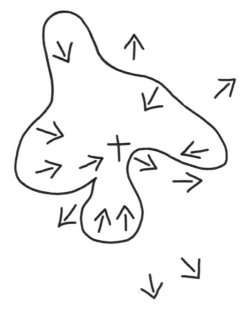

It is helpful to visualize the centered set as a random bunch of arrows with a cross in the center (see fig. 2). The cross represents Jesus, and the arrows represent the people who encountered Jesus. Some of the arrows point directly toward the cross, which represents those who respond positively to Jesus by confessing their sins and accepting his offer of forgiveness. Some arrows point away from the cross; they represent those who reject Jesus's offer of forgiveness either because they are confident in their own righteousness or because they don't care about being part of God's kingdom. The arrows pointing toward the cross are members of the group; the arrows pointing away from the cross are not. It's a little tricky to draw a boundary around this centered set, but it can be done. The boundary of the centered set ends up being messy and uneven, because the centered set tends to deemphasize the boundary.

The Progression of Belonging in God's Kingdom

Getting back to Paul's message to the church in Philippi, we need to acknowledge that the Christian life is about more than one's orientation to Jesus at the center. It is also about how we live our lives. That's why Paul encourages the Philippians to model their lives on faithful disciples and not live like those who are enemies of the cross. One's belonging to the kingdom of God involves a turning toward Jesus. That is the critical initial step but by no means the end of the story. As we noted when listing attributes, kingdom belonging is meant to be transformative. Paul encourages the Philippians to begin living differently, and he also promises a complete transformation of their bodies when Christ returns and brings everything under his control.

Being a disciple of Jesus means living one's life more like his; that is, there are some bounded-set aspects of discipleship. Paul warns the Philippian Christians about falling back into pagan practices: "Their god is their stomach and their glory is their shame." He wants them to live within the boundaries of a faithful Christian lifestyle, but he doesn't want them to make the mistake of thinking that living this way is the basis for their belonging to the kingdom.

In other letters, he warns Christians about trying to earn membership in God's kingdom by their behavior. To the Ephesians, he proclaims: "For it is by grace you have been saved, through faith—and this is not from yourselves, it is the gift of God—not by works, so that no one can boast" (Eph. 2:8–9). Those in Philippi were in danger of rejecting God's righteousness in favor of pagan practices, but those in Ephesus were in danger of trying to maintain righteousness by their own efforts.

Figure 3

Centered Set
with Transformation

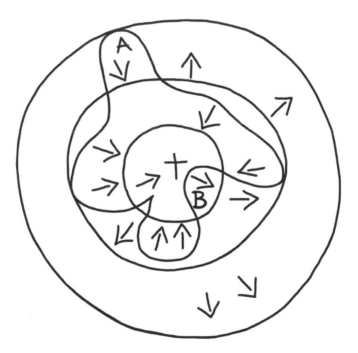

We can capture this more nuanced understanding of belonging to the kingdom of God by adding another layer to our diagram (see fig. 3). We can add concentric circles to represent one's behavior, attitude, and posture toward others. The closer one is to the center (Jesus), the more one's behavior, attitude, and posture toward others are like Jesus's. This layer allows us to note a couple of important case studies involving belonging to God's kingdom. First, we can look at person A, a former pagan who has been living his life diametrically opposed to Jesus's model. However, this person has just repented of this lifestyle and accepted forgiveness from Jesus. His behaviors and attitudes are deeply embedded in his context; it will take some time for those things to change. Because he has turned toward Jesus, he fully belongs in God's kingdom. He now begins a long, slow journey of transformation that will bring him closer to the center.

Now look at person B, a Pharisee who is offended by Jesus and has rejected his offer of forgiveness. He believes he is able to maintain perfect righteousness by keeping his community's interpretation of God's law. From a lifestyle perspective (we'll set attitude and posture aside for the moment), his life looks more like Jesus's than does the former pagan's. Like Jesus, he worships God, he prays, and he avoids participation in the pagan lifestyle. But he does not belong to God's kingdom, because he has rejected Jesus's offer of forgiveness.

This case reveals a significant inaccuracy of our chart, because while his external behavior may look more similar to Jesus's, his heart is very different. Whereas Jesus is humble and compassionate toward others, this Pharisee is proud and judgmental toward others.

While this chart isn't perfect, it does show the somewhat quirky and counterintuitive aspects of belonging to God's kingdom when seen as a progression. The theological terms that can be used to track this progression are "justification," "sanctification," and "glorification." Justification involves forgiveness of sin and a restored relationship with God. This is complete and instantaneous when we confess our sin for the first time and accept Jesus as our Lord and Savior. Justification establishes us as belonging to God's kingdom.

Sanctification is the long, arduous process of being transformed in our behaviors, attitudes, and postures toward others to be more like Jesus. Sanctification begins when we first confess our sins and accept Jesus as our Lord and Savior, but this process involves times of progress and times of apparent regress. Our belonging to God's kingdom is in no way based on our sanctification, but sanctification is the normal and expected process that those who belong to God's kingdom should experience in their earthly lives.

Glorification is what we will experience when Christ returns and takes up his rightful role as king in the kingdom of God. Glorification marks the final step to belonging to God's kingdom. When we experience glorification, we will no longer struggle with sin in our attitudes or our actions. In this aspect, glorification represents the final step of sanctification. But glorification also involves something new: our bodies will be transformed, no longer serving as settings for pain, sickness, or death. After making the claim that our citizenship is in heaven, Paul goes on to describe this glorification by claiming that Christ "will transform our lowly bodies so that they will be like his glorious body" (Phil. 3:21).

The Kingdom as Place

The promise of glorification reminds us that our current struggle with sin will come to an end, and, redeemed, our bodies will be transformed as glorious resurrection bodies. Another important aspect of glorification, however, is the setting in which we will experience it. In the present time, the kingdom of God is a relational, not a geographical, kingdom. As we've seen, this has significant implications for how we belong to God's kingdom. But when Christ returns to reign over his rightful kingdom, the kingdom will be both geographic and relational. This means that belonging in God's kingdom will change in terms of how we experience place-based belonging.

Scripture teaches us that when Christ returns to reign in glory, it will be in the context of a "new heaven and earth" (Rev. 21:1). This is an evocative image, and we don't know a lot about what that setting will be like. However, a few other passages of Scripture provide a bit more detail about the physical and sociological attributes of God's kingdom as a geographic place.

The most well known of these passages comes from the Revelation of John where he describes the new Jerusalem:

Then the angel showed me the river of the water of life, as clear as crystal, flowing from the throne of God and of the Lamb down the middle of the great street of the city. On each side of the river stood the tree of life, bearing twelve crops of fruit, yielding its fruit every month. And the leaves of the tree are for the healing of the nations. No longer will there be any curse. The throne of God and of the Lamb will be in the city, and his servants will serve him. They will see his face, and his name will be on their foreheads. There will be no more night. They will not need the light of a lamp or the light of the sun, for the Lord God will give them light. And they will reign for ever and ever. (Rev. 22:1–5)

We see here a redeemed city filled with the radiance of God's glory.

Particularly interesting is how it recasts the garden of Eden in an urban milieu. Because of humanity's disobedience, people were removed from the garden and cut off from the tree of life. Now we see this same tree accessible once again to humanity, but this time it is in the middle of a great city rather than in an intimate garden.

The prophet Zechariah gives us a slightly different perspective: "This is what the LORD Almighty says: 'Once again men and women of ripe old age will sit in the streets of Jerusalem, each of them with cane in hand because of their age. The city streets will be filled with boys and girls playing there'" (Zech. 8:4–5). To be clear, this is initially an image of what Jerusalem should be like after the exile, but I believe that this can also be used to fuel our imaginations for what the new Jerusalem will be like when Christ returns. What I love about Zechariah's picture of shalom in Jerusalem is its ordinariness. Here shalom is depicted not in terms of the splendor of the setting or the presence of the king but rather in the simple everyday interaction of the inhabitants of the kingdom. Zechariah illustrates my notion of belonging as the subjective experience of shalom.

In contrast to the urban images from Revelation and Zechariah, the prophet Micah's picture of the kingdom draws from wilderness and agrarian motifs:

In the last days

> the mountain of the LORD's temple will be established
> as the highest of the mountains;

> it will be exalted above the hills,
>   and peoples will stream to it.
> Many nations will come and say,
>   "Come, let us go up to the mountain of the LORD,
>   to the temple of the God of Jacob.
> He will teach us his ways,
>   so that we may walk in his paths."
> The law will go out from Zion,
>   the word of the LORD from Jerusalem.
> He will judge between many peoples
>   and will settle disputes for strong nations far and wide.
> They will beat their swords into plowshares
>   and their spears into pruning hooks.
> Nation will not take up sword against nation,
>   nor will they train for war anymore.
> Everyone will sit under their own vine
>   and under their own fig tree,
> and no one will make them afraid,
>   for the LORD Almighty has spoken. (Mic. 4:1–4)

For some reason, these rural images of the kingdom of God have been more prevalent in our imagination. One famous instance of this is the Peaceable Kingdom series by Edward Hicks (see fig. 4). Hicks highlights the peacefulness of the kingdom in terms of a cessation from strife. In the animal kingdom, predators and prey dwell together without fear. In the human realm, Native Americans and colonists enjoy fellowship without warfare. And where humans engage the natural world, children fearlessly play near wild animals and steep cliffs.

As noted, the geographic elements of the kingdom of God are a future rather than a present reality. However, the picture we hold in our minds of what that geographic kingdom will look like can impact how we think about the kingdom and what it means to belong to it today. I believe for reasons that will become clear later that it is important for us not to neglect the aspects of the future kingdom that involve the cities, towns, and built environment.

Christians have leaned toward the rural aspects of the physical setting of God's coming kingdom in part because of a particular view of

FIGURE 4. *Peaceable Kingdom* by Edward Hicks

restoration. The first picture of shalom we see in Scripture is of God and a nuclear family in the garden of Eden. It is a beautiful picture, and it is understandable that some would assume that God's future kingdom will involve some kind of return to that idyllic state.

But that reading ignores the fact that the other major picture of God's coming kingdom is an urban image: the new Jerusalem coming down from heaven to earth. In this picture, the network of human relationships has grown beyond the natural family to be more of a full-blown society. Here we witness shalom not only in the natural setting but also in a built environment that involves at least walls, gates, and streets.

A reasonable conclusion to draw from these two images of shalom that bookend the narrative of salvation is that Eden does not represent the final state for creation, especially as the ultimate setting of belonging for humanity. This suggests that God's intent was for his creation to be developed. In Genesis 2:15 we read that God placed the first humans in the garden to "work it and take care of it." This involves both preserving creation from destruction and developing its potential in ways that will bless humanity. Developing the potential of creation can involve both metal pipes for indoor plumbing and oil paints for Rembrandt's masterpieces.

This idea of humanity developing the potential of creation adds a dynamic and progressive element to salvation history. A static understanding would be that God's will for creation and for humanity's role in it was fixed at some early point and that faithfulness to God involves preserving this pristine moment in history. Redemption would involve some kind of return to the garden of Eden. A dynamic approach incorporates both the beginning and the end of the history of salvation. The garden is what shalom looks like for humanity at the beginning of the story, and the new Jerusalem is what shalom looks like for humanity at the story's end (see fig. 5).

Between these two poles we can insert the rest of human history as the progression of time along the vertical axis. As generations come and go, humans continue to develop creation in ways that honor God and bless humanity (medicine) and in ways that dishonor God and harm humanity (pornography). We can depict the God-honoring development of creation through the progression of time as a vector of shalom. If humanity collectively were perfectly obedient to God throughout history, then they would experience shalom, blessing, and favor with God as they made their way from the garden to the new Jerusalem.

But the story is much more ambivalent. Some of what humans do in developing creation honors God, but much of it is prideful, oppressive, and exploitative. Such sinful expressions of humanity's vocation can be depicted as a vector line straying away from the shalom line.

This diagram provides a helpful illustration of the kind of situation that disciples of Jesus face continually. We find ourselves part of a particular society at a particular point in history, and there is much that we see around us that is clearly not honoring God. One common response that seems congruent with the narrative of Scripture is to disengage with society and focus on the private realm of our family and friends and the unsullied realm of nature. In chapter 13 we will look at a prominent

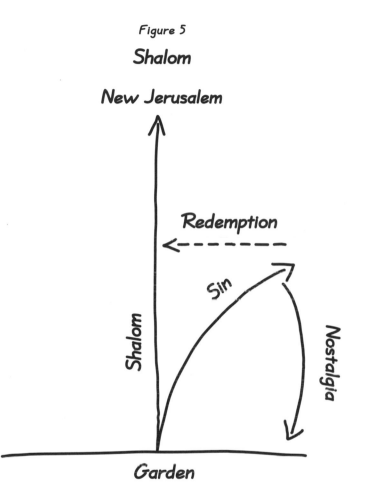

Figure 5

Shalom

Christian community that exemplified this approach. This response sees redemption in terms of returning to the garden before things got complicated. I characterize this approach as nostalgic, because it is fueled by a desire to return to an idealized place that no longer exists.

A response that is better in line with the full witness of Scripture is to see redemption as an attempt to influence society to move away from sin and toward shalom while properly accounting for the development of culture through the progression of time. In his book *Creation Regained*, Al Wolters explains this with a metaphor of the healing of a human being.

Imagine a child who is struck with a debilitating disease as an infant. As the child grows, much of her development is normal and good, but some of it is afflicted with the disease. When the child is twelve, a cure is developed, and she undergoes the necessary treatments. When the doctors declare her cured, our expectation is not that she will now be a completely healthy infant but rather that she will be a healthy twelve-year-old. The nostalgic approach sees redemption in society like hoping a twelve-year-old will become a baby. The approach I advocate sees redemption as a twelve-year-old free of disease while remaining a twelve-year-old.

I believe a nostalgic desire to return to the garden is behind a common preference for the images of God's future kingdom that focus on the rural and on the private realm. This approach is often accompanied by a general distrust of society and culture. It can lead to thinking of escapism and even austerity as Christian faithfulness. These strategies limit the ways that Christians can seek the shalom of the cities to which they have been called (Jer. 29:7). And they seem to have a corrosive effect on the experience of belonging.

The Kingdom as a Feast

The future kingdom of God is described not only as a place but as an event—specifically, a celebration meal for the wedding of the Lamb of God (Christ) and his bride (the church): "'Let us rejoice and be glad and give him glory! For the wedding of the Lamb has come, and his bride has made herself ready. Fine linen, bright and clean, was given her to wear.' (Fine linen stands for the righteous acts of God's holy people.) Then the angel said to me, 'Write this: Blessed are those who are invited to the wedding supper of the Lamb!' And he added, 'These are the true words of God'" (Rev. 19:7–9).

This evocative text gives us a picture of belonging to God's kingdom as a joyous time of worship spilling over into a shared experience of sensory delight. Supper implies raw ingredients from creation that are prepared and presented according to a culture of the table that has been developing along the progression of human history. People have carried out their task of developing God's creation by figuring out new ways to bring out the potentials inherent in the materials of creation by employing methods of baking, boiling, roasting, frying, and other methods to create sumptuous meals.

Redemption at the Table

Babette Hersant is depicted as an agent of redemption by leveraging her God-given talent as an artist, her training in the long-developed tradition of French cooking, and some choice specimens of God's creation to create a once-in-a-lifetime meal:

- "Potage à la Tortue" (turtle soup) served with Amontillado sherry
- "Blinis Demidoff" (buckwheat pancakes with caviar and sour cream) served with Veuve Cliquot Champagne
- "Cailles en Sarcophage" (quail in puff pastry shell with foie gras and truffle sauce) served with Clos de Vougeot Pinot Noir
- endive salad
- "Savarin au Rhum avec des Figues et Fruit Glacée" (rum sponge cake with figs and candied cherries) served with Champagne
- assorted cheeses and fruits served with Sauternes
- coffee with vieux marc Grande Champagne cognac[2]

This beautiful and self-sacrificial act helped remind the members of the austere Christian community of the goodness of creation and perhaps even the redeemability of human culture. Through this meal, the members of the community opened themselves again both to being recipients of God's gifts and to the goodness of one another.

This was a community meal and not a celebration of the Lord's Supper, but it is not too much of a stretch to see it as a kind of foretaste of the marriage supper of the Lamb and the kingdom of God. This redemptive meal gave its participants a renewed experience of belonging to God, to his good world, and to each other.

SEVEN

STRANGERS AND KINGDOM BELONGING

Gander

The musical hit *Come from Away* tells the story of how the citizens of Gander, Newfoundland, became the unexpected hosts for seven thousand strangers when thirty-eight planes were forced to land there following the events of 9/11. Gander is portrayed in the musical as a tight-knit community where everybody knows everybody else. And at first it seems likely that the people of Gander will function like a bounded set. It's a setting in which one might expect to see a stranger shunned because they lack the familiarity and connection everyone else has. And these seven thousand strangers are not just relationally unfamiliar but differ from the local residents in every conceivable way. They represent a diverse mix of ethnicities, nationalities, religions, sexualities, and languages.

But the residents of Gander don't shun these seven thousand strangers. Rather, they do just the opposite: they welcome them with open arms. They offer them shelter in the local school and put them up in their homes. Many of the stores offer provisions free of charge. They organize teams to cook meals and take care of other needs. They even offer quiet space in the library for Christians, Muslims, and Jews to pray. The hospitality of the Ganderites goes beyond these necessities; they invite the strangers to share in their lives. They throw parties for them and even extend an offer to make any of them honorary Newfoundlanders by participating in a lighthearted ritual.

This unexpected welcome has a profound effect on the people stranded on this remote island. These former strangers are pleasantly surprised to have their needs met so graciously by this community thrown into a role they didn't ask for because of events in another country. The stranded passengers find Gander a safe place where they can let down their guard and even begin to process some of their fears about the unimaginable events that have just taken place. The experience on Gander was so impactful that some passengers returned to Gander to celebrate the ten-year anniversary of their time there.

The story told in *Come from Away* is an important reminder that a stranger doesn't have to be an object of fear or a category of person to exclude. Rather, a stranger can be a reminder of the common humanity we share with every single person. And it can be a litmus test of our ability to see the image of God in people we haven't yet met.

Strangers and Hospitality

In chapter 4 we included "invitational" as a key element of kingdom belonging. This element radically impacts the role that strangers play in the kingdom of God and has significant implications for how we understand the concept of belonging. The term "stranger" can imply someone who doesn't belong. But because of the invitational nature of the kingdom of God, a stranger should be treated with the same consideration given to someone who does belong. Ultimately, strangers should be given the opportunity to themselves belong: "When a foreigner resides among you in your land, do not mistreat them. The foreigner residing among you must be treated as your native-born. Love them as yourself, for you were foreigners in Egypt. I am the LORD your God" (Lev. 19:33–34).

Because regard for strangers is so fundamental for kingdom belonging, hospitality is upheld throughout Scripture as an important virtue for kingdom people: "Do not forget to show hospitality to strangers" (Heb. 13:2). Christine Pohl insists that hospitality must include "making a physical place in our lives, families, churches, and communities for people who might appear to have little to offer."[1]

God wants his people to be hospitable because God is hospitable. This is important to keep in mind because it is easy to read the flip side of God's hospitable provision of Canaan to the Israelites as an act of racist aggression against the Canaanites already living in the land. It would take a separate chapter to fully resolve this apparent contradiction; but in short, the Canaanites were under God's judgment for truly horrendous practices (e.g., child sacrifice), they were given time to repent of their ways, and every Canaanite who helped the Israelites was welcomed into the community (e.g., Rahab, the Kenites).[2] God ultimately placed the Israelites in the promised land not to create a permeant dwelling for that people group which would exclude all other people groups but rather to establish a foundation for a kingdom that would eventually include people from "every nation, tribe, people and language" (Rev. 7:9). This ultimate purpose for the land is confirmed in how God instructed the Israelites to conduct themselves with regard to others once they were settled in the land.

In the Old Testament, we see hospitality made manifest primarily in the fair and gracious treatment of foreigners. In the New Testament, hospitality becomes a key element of the mission strategy of the early church. The Jewish church makes room for the gentiles. And the geographic footprint for the church expands to make room so that all nations can be included in God's kingdom.

This hospitality theme continues as the early church expands and develops. Because the mandate of evangelism requires so much traveling for the community, and because traveling can be dangerous and challenging, a strong informal tradition of hospitality grows among the churches. But hospitality is not restricted to fellow believers. It is for those who are not part of the Christian community and particularly for the marginalized who find themselves on the outside of most communities.

Within the ancient world, hospitality was encouraged. But for the most part, that hospitality was of the instrumental type. One was encouraged to be hospitable to people from whom one could derive some benefit; having one's boss over for dinner was considered a good idea. Christian hospitality was distinct in that Christians offered hospitality to those from whom one would not expect to benefit and to those who could not return the favor. "Then Jesus said to his host, 'When you give a luncheon or dinner, do not invite your friends, your brothers or sisters, your relatives, or your rich neighbors; if you do, they may invite you back and so you will be repaid. But when you give a banquet, invite the poor, the crippled, the lame, the blind, and you will be blessed. Although they cannot repay you, you will be repaid at the resurrection of the righteous'" (Luke 14:12–14).

Selfless hospitality made the Christian community stand out among their secular neighbors. Their willingness to expose themselves to risk caring for the sick during the plague was exceptional. This tradition eventually led to the creation of hospitals, which were initially Christian institutions.

Banishing Strangers

Since strangers play such a distinct and critical role in kingdom belonging, it is worth taking a brief look at how strangers have had an impact on recent development patterns that in turn influence the general posture toward strangers in the United States. Basically, we have dealt with the issue of strangers by excluding them from many residential neighborhoods (at least middle- and upper-class ones). This approach has had the unintended consequence of increasing the number of people who are strangers to us and making us more fearful of them.

One way we banish strangers from residential neighborhoods is through a planning tool known as zoning. Chapter 16 looks at this in detail, but for now we'll highlight only one feature of it having to do with strangers.

Zoning basically classifies buildings into different zones according to their use. Houses go in one zone; commercial buildings go in another zone. While this seems normal to us now, when zoning was introduced, some thought it was an unfair limitation on property owners' rights.

Eventually, the US Supreme Court had to determine whether prohibiting all commercial buildings from a residential neighborhood was constitutional. It's important to keep in mind that prior to the adoption of zoning codes, most cities had some kind of nuisance regulation on the books. For example, cities could deny a permit for a slaughterhouse or cement factory in a mostly residential neighborhood. Zoning made this separation much more comprehensive. There could be no commercial development of any kind in a residential neighborhood. A standard zoning code would prohibit not only industrial buildings but also retail, services, and restaurants.

So the question is, Why can't you have a corner grocery or coffee shop in a residential neighborhood? It turns out that the answer is "Because of strangers." The majority opinion for the case explains: "A place of business in a residence neighborhood furnishes an excuse for any criminal to go into the neighborhood, where, otherwise, a stranger would be under the ban of suspicion."[3]

Note how the words "stranger" and "criminal" are used almost interchangeably here. Whether or not Justice Sutherland actually believed that strangers tend to be criminals is not important. What is worth noting here is that zoning set into motion a powerful tool to ban strangers from residential neighborhoods. Zoning has also been used to separate people according to socioeconomic levels (see chap. 16).

Another policy tool that has contributed to the banishment of strangers from residential neighborhoods is the cul-de-sac. This strategy can be seen in what would become the street plan for the neighborhoods built between 1950 and 2000. Traditionally, residential neighborhoods were built on a simple grid. A parcel of land was apportioned into a series of blocks divided by a regular pattern of streets and sidewalks. The new approach, however, involved developing major arterials that led to feeder roads that ultimately led into cul-de-sacs, where the houses were.

This approach purportedly was taken to increase safety. Cars wouldn't speed as they approached the end of a cul-de-sac, so kids could play there in relative safety. After a few initial studies seemed to indicate a decrease in accidents, the Institute of Transportation Engineers recommended cul-de-sacs over the grid pattern.[4] From this recommendation, cul-de-sacs made it into engineering standards. This approach actually isn't a lot safer, since cars can move very fast on arterials and feeder roads, making it unsafe for anyone (young or old) who leaves the confines of the cul-de-sac.

In any case, dampening the speed of cars through neighborhoods wasn't the only impact cul-de-sacs had on these new residential neighborhoods. They also were particularly effective in banishing strangers. A typical cul-de-sac is a dead end that serves anywhere from four to eight houses. A person walking into a cul-de-sac would have to live in one of those several houses or be visiting a resident in order to not arouse suspicion. On a block grid, one can justify walking on a sidewalk on any street on the basis of being on the way to somewhere else. But on a cul-de-sac there is no possibility of passing through on the way to somewhere else. Strangers are effectively banished from the neighborhood.

Most of the residential construction of this period was built according to strict zoning regulations that separated residential buildings from commercial. Most residential housing units were placed on an arterial, feeder road, cul-de-sac street plan. These two practices were effective in protecting residents from contact with strangers. In some respects this decreased contact with strangers near our homes made us feel safer, but in other ways it may have increased our overall fearfulness of strangers and contributed to the condition of unease in the public realm we're experiencing today.

Strangers—Fixed or Fluid

This notion of creating neighborhoods that banish strangers might sound a little harsh when stated like that, but is banishing them really such a bad idea? Strangers sometimes are criminals, and even when they're not, they can make us feel uncomfortable. The problem with the logic behind practices that seek to minimize our exposure to strangers isn't that they're enacted for the purpose of increasing our perception of safety. The problem is that they use a notion of strangers that is too static.

When we think of the word "stranger," we might picture a person who looks a little odd or menacing to us. We often forget that the concept of stranger is not fixed but is relationally fluid and context specific. Few people are strangers to everyone. Most people have at least a few friends or acquaintances. Our status as stranger in a particular situation depends on the nature of the relationship we have with the person who encounters us. There are situations where we ourselves are the strangers.

In or around our own home, those we don't recognize are strangers. However, when we are somewhere unfamiliar to us, we are the strangers. If we happen to find ourselves lost in an unfamiliar setting—one set up to discourage strangers—it can be very uncomfortable. If I'm lost in a place that includes a coffee shop or a hair salon, I can easily pop in and ask where I am or how to find an address. If I'm lost in a residential subdivision built on the cul-de-sac model in the middle of a weekday, I'll be hard-pressed to find another person out in the public realm.

We can think of every relationship as existing on a continuum of familiarity. On one end of the spectrum are the people we consider close friends. On the other end of the spectrum are people who are complete strangers to us. There are lots of people who fall between these two points. Not only does this way of viewing the issue reveal that "stranger" and "friend" are not black-and-white categories; it also shows they are not stable.

People who initially are strangers to us can become acquaintances and even friends over time if the conditions are favorable. On the other hand, people who are acquaintances can become strangers to us over time if the conditions of our environment don't encourage or even allow spontaneous interaction. A neighborhood in which homes are designed for access through the garage and where there are no local coffee shops provides very little opportunity for neighbors to chat informally on a regular basis, so relationships among neighbors can atrophy.

City Gates

It is important to think about neighborhood design that generally encourages people to move along a continuum from stranger, to familiar face, to acquaintance, and possibly to friend. However, I think it's perhaps a little naive to completely discount the real danger that certain strangers might bring to the private sphere of our homes. Thus, it's important to consider some of the cultural differences between our context and the context of the Old Testament, out of which so many of the hospitality texts emerged. A key difference to note is the role of city gatekeepers.

The people of God in the Old Testament were a fairly cohesive community. In a town or even a city, everyone who lived there knew everybody else. An arriving stranger would pass through the city gates, where he or she would be met by the elders who gathered there. From this encounter, the elders could screen the newcomer to determine whether this stranger presented any danger or concern to the community. They were literally gatekeepers for the town.

Another difference has to do with sharing information. If someone from the town were to offer hospitality to a passing stranger, the whole town would know. If anything concerning were to happen with the stranger in that particular household, the neighbors would be available to help maintain peace and order.

In our culture, communities tend to be much more fragmented and isolated than in the ancient world. If one household were to welcome a stranger into their home, they could often do so without the knowledge of or any sense of support from the wider community. Neither do they have the benefit of elders at the gate to screen for any red flags. It can thus be challenging (and possibly unwise) to simply invite a stranger into one's home in response to the hospitality mandates in Scripture.

Christine Pohl suggests that we consider alternative strategies to cover the gatekeeping and communal-knowledge functions when thinking about how to offer hospitality to strangers. She refers to these kinds of settings as "threshold places."[5] One effective way to cover both of these roles is to look to institutions to act as mediating entities between individuals and strangers. Food banks, homeless shelters, drop-in centers, free medical clinics, and so on can provide opportunities for us to connect with strangers and extend hospitality to them without exposing ourselves or our households to undue risk. In some cases, institutional mediation can lead to bringing a stranger into one's home. A clear example of this kind of hospitality is a good foster-care program, especially one that helps families offer emergency foster care for crisis situations.

It is especially appropriate for a local church to function as a mediating entity and catalyst for individuals to extend hospitality to strangers. Churches can partner with and provide host sites for any of the institutions mentioned above. Because Christian churches are institutions built on the authority of the Bible, they can play a unique role of advocating for hospitality to strangers and encouraging their members to consider ways to extend hospitality to those in need. For those who claim to follow Jesus, it is difficult to ignore the importance of hospitality: "Then the righteous will answer him, 'Lord, when did we see you hungry and feed you, or thirsty and give you something to drink? When did we see you a stranger and invite you in, or needing clothes and clothe you? When did we see you sick or in prison and go to visit you?' The King will reply, 'Truly I tell you, whatever you did for one of the least of these brothers and sisters of mine, you did for me'" (Matt. 25:37–40).

The View from Below

When thinking about how to deal with strangers in our housing choices and in the way we design neighborhoods, our first instinct is often to exclude them or to minimize our chances of encountering them. However, this instinct does not align with scriptural teaching. Scripture not only consistently mandates hospitality but also admonishes God's people to remember that they were once strangers. This is, I believe, a key to adopting a gracious posture toward strangers.

The seven thousand passengers who were stranded in a foreign country on the day after 9/11 weren't expecting to be strangers in a strange land, but for the next week that's what they were. It's important to remember that "strangers" aren't some category of people we'd rather ignore; strangers are any of us under certain conditions. We would do well to think of ourselves as the stranger before deciding how we want to deal with strangers.

Treating strangers with decency and consideration can be powerful testimony to our common humanity. The seven thousand passengers were not customers from whom the residents of Gander could hope to profit, nor were they fellow citizens who shared some external characteristic with the local residents. They were treated well because they were people in need who showed up at the right doorstep. This basic act of hospitality testified to the inherent worth and dignity of humans created in the image of God. A community treating those who don't belong as if they do is a story that strikes a chord with a broad audience. At one point in history, this kind of self-sacrificial love was a distinctive characteristic of the people of God. May it be so again.

EIGHT

KINGDOM AND COVENANT BELONGING

Finding My Job

On the introvert/extrovert spectrum, I find myself slightly on the introvert side. I like people and enjoy being in the company of others, but I prefer being with individuals or small- to medium-sized groups. I tend to get a little overwhelmed at large gatherings.

In the latter, I have learned, it helps me to have a job. Sometimes I offer to take coats as people arrive; my favorite is serving drinks. A job helps me find my place, to feel like I belong without the pressure of having to engage in multiple short conversations around the room. It's funny, but when I no longer feel the pressure to engage in conversation, I tend to relax and actually enjoy talking with people.

I realize that this is not how everybody functions. Lots of people love going to parties and easily navigate social situations. But the fact that finding a job helps me overcome my particular challenge with parties suggests that work may play some kind of a role in our experience of belonging.

This is an important point because of the numerous negative connotations of work. It is often seen as a grim necessity we must participate in so that we can get the things we need and want. Food, clothing, shelter, and movie tickets cost money, so we must work. Lots of people are counting the days to retirement, when they can enjoy life without work.

But it has been my observation that life without work is not as delightful as people make it out to be. It's fairly common to experience some kind of an identity crisis once the novelty of retirement wears off. And people who don't have to work because of inheritances can have a hard time finding themselves and their place in the world. Our work doesn't have to be born of necessity, nor does it need to be paid work. But work in whatever form we engage with it seems to play a vital role in our identity formation as well as our sense of belonging. We were, after all, created to work. The God in whose image we have been made works, and he has called us to participate in his kingdom through our work.

Kingdom and Covenant

In chapter 4 we identified "productive" and "covenantal" as two characteristics of kingdom belonging. In this chapter we give these characteristics special consideration, because they bring to light more-nuanced aspects of kingdom belonging.

Productivity, in particular, is an aspect of kingdom belonging that can lose its meritorious status when it becomes too dominant. Thus, to understand the role of productivity in kingdom belonging, we need to see it in light of covenantal belonging and to better understand the collective vocation of the human race.

Mike Breen believes that the entire Bible can be best understood through the dual lens of covenant and kingdom.[1] Covenant has to do with the relational aspect of God's plan to redeem creation. Covenant has to do with our restored relationship with God as our Father and with our experience of being adopted into his household. Kingdom, on the other hand, has to do with our vocation as representatives of the King to the rest of creation. Kingdom has to do with the responsibility that comes with our status as members of God's kingdom. Breen shows not only how these fundamental themes shoot through the entire Bible but also how they help to balance each other out. Too much emphasis on covenant makes for lazy Christians who can easily develop a self-referential faith. Too much emphasis on kingdom makes for burned-out or shrill Christians who are tempted to believe that God cannot accomplish his purposes without their help.

If kingdom and covenant are fundamental themes in the Bible, then it should come as no surprise that they play a key role in our experience of belonging as well. We can see these themes play out on a regular basis in the life of the church. When someone wants to make the leap from a visitor who attends a church regularly to a member who belongs, they often attend a new members' class. Thus, they are presented with the gospel and are informed (or reminded) that they have been invited into God's family through the grace made possible by Christ's death on the cross. On this basis they are qualified to become a member of the local church, a status also granted to them on the basis of grace. Belonging to the local church when it follows this pattern is particularly focused on the covenant aspect of belonging.

However, it has been my experience, as a pastor who oversees a membership process that looks like this, that for most people this step will not suffice for them to establish a strong sense of belonging. Joining a small group of some kind does help, but even that is usually not going to be the thing that makes them feel like they are really a part of the community. What is usually needed is for them to find a place to serve the church. They need to experience the feeling that their contribution is necessary to the ministry and mission of the organization.

Finding a place to serve the mission and ministry of the church connects them more to the kingdom theme than the covenant theme. While this is certainly true, I would never want someone to just serve in the church and never experience that unconditional love and acceptance that is connected more with the covenant theme. What this suggests, therefore, is that a strong sense of belonging to God's kingdom involves both kingdom belonging and covenant belonging.

Work and the Kingdom

We must not ignore the "more than just covenant" aspect of kingdom belonging, because it is critical to our sense of belonging. But we also need to be aware of this aspect because our work is an important aspect of God's strategy for the world. Our vocation (or calling) as Christians is both to be a beloved child of God (covenant) and to be agents and representatives of God's work in the world (kingdom). This is because God carries out his activity in the world either by direct action in the world or indirectly through his agents. Our work can be seen as God's indirect work in the world.

In taking this aspect of our vocation seriously, we need to be careful to avoid some common misunderstandings about our work in the kingdom. In the first place, it must always be clear that working for God's kingdom is not the way we earn our place in the kingdom. As noted earlier, our belonging to the kingdom is a gift, and any work we do doesn't make us any more deserving of a place in the kingdom. When we fail to fully understand God's grace, we tend to see our work as a way to earn God's favor.

However, another reason for this misunderstanding is that our culture encourages a narrow view of work as necessary chore. From this standpoint, if we win the lottery, the first thing we would do is quit our job. But the Bible teaches a very different view of work. The work that we are given to do as humans is an honor related to the fact that we are made in God's image. We were given work to do in the garden before the first sin and its consequent punishment: our ancestors worked in paradise. Therefore, work is not fundamentally a punishment in the Bible, but this fact gets distorted after the fall.

Work, when understood properly, is more blessing than curse. But work must be kept in balance with rest, because our productivity is never meant to represent the entirety of our identity and purpose. One reason for the institution of the Sabbath was to build in a regular time to enjoy the goodness of our created existence without being productive.

This productive aspect of the kingdom goes back to the beginning. In the first creation account, we witness God giving the creatures that he made in his image a special set of instructions for their work: "God blessed them and said to them, 'Be fruitful and increase in number; fill the earth and subdue it. Rule over the fish in the sea and the birds in the sky and over every living creature that moves on the ground'" (Gen. 1:28).

These instructions, known as the "creation mandate," provide the basic vocation for all humanity. The creation mandate can be broken down into three sub-mandates:

- procreation mandate—be fruitful and multiply
- stewardship mandate—subdue the earth and rule over the creatures
- cultural mandate—fill the earth

Most of the work that we do as humans can be placed under one of these three creation mandates. And since these mandates come not just before the call of Abram but also before the fall, we can claim them as valid and good for all humanity, not just for the people of God.

Work, Toil, and Reconciliation

The fall, however, did have a significant impact on human vocation. One consequence of humanity disobeying God's command and turning from his sovereign authority was that they were removed from the garden and their work became toil. Work continued to be good and productive, but now elements of frustration, fruitlessness, and pain entered into it.[2] Most work now is a combination of good and toilsome elements.

The other major consequence of the fall is that humans now live under the dual curse of alienation from God and deep suffering in the world. God's plan to solve both of those problems was spearheaded in the ministry and mission of Jesus, who proclaimed the good news of the kingdom and then died and rose again to make a way for humans to be reconciled to God and to experience relief from suffering by being included in the kingdom. A key vocation for disciples of Jesus, then, is to be agents of this reconciling work: "All this is from God, who reconciled us to himself through Christ and gave us the ministry of reconciliation: that God was reconciling the world to himself in Christ, not counting people's sins against them. And he has committed to us the message of reconciliation" (2 Cor. 5:18–19).

We can see two kinds of expressions for this "ministry of reconciliation" in two of Jesus's teachings to his disciples in the Gospel of Matthew. The first focuses on evangelism and is expressed in the Great Commission: "Therefore go and make disciples of all nations, baptizing them in the name of the Father and of the Son and of the Holy Spirit" (Matt. 28:19). The second focuses on acts of compassion and is expressed in the parable of the sheep and the goats: "'When did we see you a stranger and invite you in, or needing clothes and clothe you? When did we see you sick or in prison and go to visit you?' The King will reply, 'Truly I tell you, whatever you did for one of the least of these brothers and sisters of mine, you did for me'" (Matt. 25:38–40).

Kingdom and Worldly Work

Being participants in God's mission to and for the world involves more than just evangelism and mercy, however. These vocations that are appropriate for disciples of Jesus do not cancel out the vocations that are part of the creation mandates. Almost any kind of vocation or activity we might involve ourselves in could be done in such a way that it brings glory to God or in a way that detracts from God's glory.

In a similar way that we have been thinking about belonging, we can divide up our work as kingdom oriented or worldly oriented. Some Christian traditions have tended to make this distinction according to the kind of activity that our work is connected to (see fig. 6). For this way of thinking, going to church, engaging in Bible study, doing evangelism, and participating in church programs of whatever kind is kingdom work. Teaching, farming, plumbing,

Figure 6
Model of Two Kingdoms

Kingdom	Worldly
Worship	Farming
Bible Study	Teaching
Evangelism	Art
Church Program	Plumbing
Fellowship	Business
	Politics

lawyering, and creating art would be considered worldly work. I believe that this way of thinking fails to recognize the scope of God's work in the world.

A better way of understanding our work comes from the Dutch Calvinist tradition. According to this tradition everything we do is done *coram Deo* (before the face of God) (see fig. 7). Therefore, it doesn't matter whether our work falls within the parameters of the work of the church. Paul provides a helpful framework for making distinctions in our work: "Whatever you do, work at it with all your heart, as working for the Lord, not for human masters" (Col. 3:23). What matters is whether we do our work as if for the Lord—as Dutch Calvinist tradition puts it, whether our work is "God honoring" or "God dishonoring."

From this perspective, a plumber does kingdom work if her work increases shalom and if she is working as to the Lord. On the other hand, the work of a pastor who ignores the Bible and spouts racist propaganda during worship is dishonoring to God and is therefore worldly work.

Figure 7

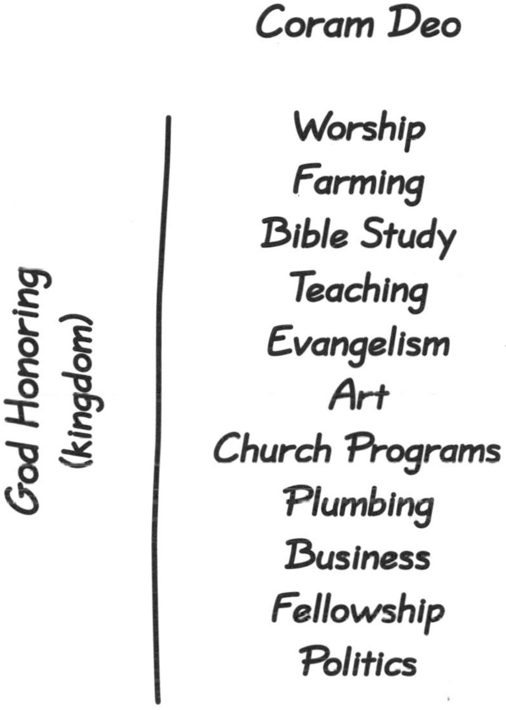

Coram Deo

| God Honoring (kingdom) | Worship
Farming
Bible Study
Teaching
Evangelism
Art
Church Programs
Plumbing
Business
Fellowship
Politics | God Dishonoring (worldly) |

Communitas

The concept of belonging is closely related to the concept of community. And true community is always rooted in both the covenant and kingdom aspects of God's kingdom. As people strive to experience a deeper sense of belonging, they frame this pursuit as a desire to be part of a community. This isn't a bad desire, but it's one for which it is relatively easy to miss the target. Community is one of those elusive goals that cannot be pursued directly but must come as a by-product of another type of goal.

As noted above, belonging in the kingdom involves both a covenant (relational) dimension and a kingdom (responsibility) dimension. As also noted above, we need to engage with both the covenant and the kingdom aspects of God's kingdom to fully experience belonging.

This reality has significant implications for how we pursue and experience community within the local church. The local church potentially offers both community (covenant) and mission (kingdom) to disciples of Jesus. However, the order in which we pursue these things can make a difference. Jeff Vanderstelt, who founded the Soma Community, explained it to me this way: When the church starts with fellowship and then plans to add mission later, they often don't achieve mission or fellowship in the long run. But if they pursue mission first, they are likely to achieve both mission and fellowship.[3]

This resonates with my experience. When a church doesn't have a clear sense of mission, it's very easy for its people to treat community selfishly, as a consumer product. During fellowship times, they ignore newcomers and hang out with their friends and complain about the coffee. On the other hand, when the church puts together a challenging mission trip, those who participate often gain a profound experience of community.

The reason for this counterintuitive dynamic involves a concept known as "communitas." Alan Hirsch describes it as a strong communal bond that is formed through challenge and/or strife.[4] Hirsch, leaning on Victor Turner's research on liminality and community among various African tribes, cites the example of one tribe that incorporates a critical experience of communitas as a rite of passage into adulthood. In this particular tribe, the men live separately from the women and children. When a group of boys reach adolescence, they are taken from the women to live on their own, far from their settlement, for an extended period. At the end of this time, the boys are welcomed back to the community as men and are allowed to live with the rest of the men.

This time of living away is extremely challenging, even dangerous. The boys learn important life skills and grow in confidence. However, the most important thing is that these boys experience communitas. They form connections to one another that are strong and long-lasting.

Communitas is often experienced by soldiers deployed together, members of sports teams who overcome challenges to become champions, and neighbors who survive some kind of acute crisis together.

Communitas is why such strong bonds of community are formed among participants in a mission trip. A church that maintains a strong mission focus and continually mobilizes the people to engage together in mission will usually experience a strong sense of internal communitas.

Belonging and Believing

One final reason for including both covenant and kingdom elements in our understanding of belonging to God's kingdom is that it expands our imagination to consider alternative routes to belonging. For instance, we tend to think of evangelism as the requisite first step for someone seeking an experience of belonging in the kingdom. First a person hears the gospel and responds by confessing his sins and accepting the forgiveness offered through Christ. Then he finds a local church to join, learns the patterns and practices of a disciple, and begins to experience a sense of belonging to the kingdom through belonging to the church. We can describe this path as "believing to belonging," and it is a fairly common pattern for how someone experiences belonging in the kingdom.

However, another route to belonging is becoming increasingly common. It can be described as "belonging to believing." In this case, a person begins his journey to the kingdom by experiencing a sense of belonging through a local church community. For instance, a person who is not a disciple of Jesus signs up with a local church to go on a mission trip to build houses in Mexico because a friend who is going on that trip has told her about it. She goes on the trip and is deeply impacted by the experience of community and the opportunity to serve people in a challenging context. By the end of the trip, she feels a strong sense of belonging to the group. Then she begins to ask about the belief system that grounds this group and motivates them to serve others in this way. Over time, she is introduced not just to a belief system but to the person of Jesus and ends up confessing her sins and accepting Jesus's forgiveness. In this case, the belonging came first and the believing came after.

The Price of Belonging

> Community is not something you have, like pizza. Nor is it something you can buy. It's a living organism based on a web of interdependencies—which is to say, a local economy.
>
> James Howard Kunstler, *The Geography of Nowhere*

Belonging, like community, is one of those goals that can't be pursued directly. If we desire the experience of belonging and try to go after it as a stand-alone goal, we will almost never reach it. However, if we focus instead on discovering our job (or vocation), we are likely to find ourselves connecting with others who are drawn to a similar purpose. If we resist the temptation to bolt at the first bump in the road and are willing to take some relational risks, over time we are likely to feel that we belong.

This doesn't mean there won't be people who will attempt to sell us the experience of belonging. As we will discover in chapter 11, belonging can be an effective marketing tool. Corporations have discovered that if they can tap into our deep desire to belong, they can sell us anything. But those who belong to God and understand the covenantal and kingdom elements of his kingdom should be among the first to see right through this strategy.

The belonging we experience through Christ is not easy. It's not a golden ticket to a place called heaven. It's an invitation to become a participant in a community called to be family together on mission. Many will balk at what's involved with this kind of belonging. Those who can push through the fear and inertia and lean in to the kind of belonging that God wants to give will find the belonging for which they have been created.

PART THREE

THE **GOSPEL** AND **BELONGING**

Tim Keller asserts that the gospel is a relatively simple message told in three different ways in Scripture. One way is that of a covenant that was established, broken, and then repaired. Another way is of exile and homecoming. And finally, the gospel is a story of a King who returns to liberate his people from slavery.[1]

Each of these three ways of proclaiming the good news of the gospel relates to the three aspects of belonging introduced in chapter 1. We often feel alienated in our relationships because our alienation from God through the broken covenant affects all our other relationships, and we so long for full reconciliation. We each have a deep longing for home because we carry within us a fundamental desire to return

93

to the garden from which we have been exiled. And hovering around our experience of enslavement to fear is our need to be anchored in the liberating power of the good story of the kingdom of God. This way of framing the gospel of the liberating King is a bit different from how Keller describes it; so don't hold him responsible if you're not convinced. But I think that it's a compelling idea.

In this section, we'll explore how the gospel is made manifest in each of these aspects of belonging.

NINE

THE PROMISE
OF COMMUNITY

Loneliness

Sue was in her midnineties and had been a member of our church for sixty-eight years.[1] She was opinionated and stubborn and proud of her independence. Unlike the majority of her peers, who had moved into some kind of assisted-living facility, Sue had been able to stay in her own home and manage most of her own affairs. Her husband had died almost twenty years ago, and all of her kids had moved out of state, but Sue was doing just fine. Or so we thought.

It turns out this self-reliance, while impressive, was a mixed blessing for Sue. Days would go by without her having any meaningful interaction with another person. She would often get invited to join another family from church for Thanksgiving or Christmas meals, but other holidays would come and go without anyone to share them.

Her kids were pretty good about calling on her birthday and on Mother's Day, but sometimes they forgot. It's not that they didn't care for her, it's just that Sue seemed so content that they assumed she had other friends checking in with her. The truth is that Sue was lonely and too proud to mention it. One October day, Sue was found dead in her basement; it was determined that she had fallen on some stairs three days prior. This experience was extrememly upsetting to our community, not only because of the loss of a friend, but also because it brought to our attention the problem of loneliness in our midst.

Loneliness is painfully difficult. Most of us have experienced at least temporary bouts of it. All of us know people who deal with chronic loneliness.

To some degree loneliness is an unavoidable by-product of our modern industrialized society, but we've witnessed a sharp increase in this malady in the past couple of decades. According to the General Social Survey, in 1985 the number of people with whom the average American discussed important matters was three. In 2004, that number had dropped to two. And what is even more concerning is that in 2004, 25 percent of the respondants reported that they didn't have a single person with whom they could discuss important matters. That number had tripled since 1985.[2]

We tend to think of loneliness as mostly a problem for the elderly, but it's becoming clear that it is not only an issue for that demographic. A gnawing sense of loneliness is growing for other population groups as well.[3] Twentysomethings recently out of college and working their first jobs can have a hard time putting together a social network to replace the close-knit community they experienced in college. Young moms spending large swaths of their day in the company of toddlers are surprised to discover how much they miss adult conversation. Many single fortysomethings are anxious about never finding a life partner and spending the latter half of their lives alone. Divorced dads in their fifties lose touch with their children and find their carefree autonomy a poor replacement for their former paternal role. Sixtysomethings who can't afford to retire feel trapped in dead-end jobs that sap the energy and drive that might be applied to social pursuits.

The Epidemic of Loneliness

Loneliness has long been studied as a psychological or sociological phenomenon, and more recently as a medical and even public health issue that can have more significant negative effects than obesity. Prolonged loneliness can lead to increased levels of a stress hormone (cortisol) in the bloodstream. Loneliness can cause vascular resistance, which can raise blood pressure and decrease blood flow. And loneliness can set off a danger signal in the brain that affects the production of white blood cells and compromises the immune system's ability to fight off infections.[4]

A 2012 study of 1,604 people over age sixty showed that 43 percent reported chronic loneliness. Those who were lonely lost mobility more quickly and had more difficulty performing routine tasks. In follow-up studies six years later, the subjects who struggled with loneliness had died at a much higher rate than those who didn't.[5]

The difference in mortality rates between those who are lonely and those who are not suggests that loneliness poses more of a health risk than either smoking or obesity. Let that sink in for a moment. Think of the resources and efforts we've expended to encourage people to avoid behaviors that put them at risk for taking up smoking or becoming obese. Can we even imagine those kinds of resources being allocated to alleviate loneliness?

It isn't just being by ourselves that is hard to take; it is the feeling of being excluded by others. We may remember times from childhood when a group formed and we weren't a part of it. Or we walked through the cafeteria looking for a place to sit and eat but did not see one friendly face. Adults don't like to feel left out any more than kids; they can just do a better job of hiding those painful feelings.

Jacqueline Olds and Richard Schwartz, professors of clinical psychiatry at Harvard, have extensively researched the experience of loneliness and claim that humans as a species are hardwired to experience significant distress when feeling left out. They cite the emerging science of attachment theory, which has demonstrated that human health and resilience come from the quality of our formative and current attachments—more so than our independence. When children fail to experience attachment early in life, they have a hard time not only forming and maintaining relationships but also navigating all sorts of aspects of adult life.

Created for Relationship

Clearly loneliness is not good for us relationally, emotionally, or physically. This is because we were not intended to be alone. We were, in fact, created for relationship. In the Bible the first clue we have to this truth can be found in the first creation account in the opening chapter of Genesis. After six days (five and a half, really) creating everything else, God turns his attention to creating humans: "Then God said, 'Let us make mankind in our image, in our likeness'" (Gen. 1:26).

The first thing to notice here is the plural pronoun God uses to refer to himself. This is one of the early hints of biblical support for what will become a fully developed doctrine of the trinitarian nature of God.

God is three persons and yet is also one God. God the Father, God the Son, and God the Holy Spirit are each distinct persons of the Trinity who exist in a mutual relationship of love and cooperation. A word that describes the trinitarian nature of God is "perichoresis." This literally means "to dance around," and it suggests that the relationship among the persons of the Trinity is not formal and static but dynamic and even beautiful.

It's interesting that this trinitarian hint is dropped at the same time we're told that humans are created in God's image. Insofar as this language presents God as the model of perfection for humans, it communicates that however else we might think about perfection, it does not include isolation or autonomy. This idea challenges contemporary Western notions of maturity involving self-reliance and independence. God, who is perfect, does not present himself to us as an isolated individual but rather reveals himself to us as a community of love and cooperation.

As we move into the next verse, this idea that we were intended to be in community is reinforced: "So God created mankind in his own image, in the image of God he created them; male and female he created them" (Gen. 1:27). This passage seems to suggest that it is only when we are in community (male and female) that we represent the image of God. To take this passage to mean that we must be married (male and female) to be fully human is an overreach. Jesus was not married and

98

is still definitely considered to be "fully man." However, Jesus did live his life in loving community.

The relational nature of human life is also affirmed in the second creation account. In this account, God creates man and places him in the midst of a garden. After descriptive material about the context of the garden and the man's role in it, God identifies something vital that is missing. Up until this point, God has spoken only positive affirmations of his creation: it is "good." But here he offers his first negative assessment, and it has to do with the man's lack of relationship: "The LORD God said, 'It is not good for the man to be alone. I will make a helper suitable for him.'"

In a bit of a strange twist in the story, God presents the animals to the man with the express purpose of "see[ing] what he would name them" (Gen. 2:19). It is later revealed that this was also a kind of bizarre speed dating situation: "So the man gave names to all the livestock, the birds in the sky and all the wild animals. But for Adam no suitable helper was found" (Gen. 2:20).

This passage, then, affirms that humans are meant to be in community, and while humans are blessed by animals in many ways, what we really need is human relationships to experience the "good" that God intends for us.

This idea is reinforced in the scene depicting the meeting of the first two humans. God brings the newly created woman to the man, who responds with a poem of celebration: "This is now bone of my bones and flesh of my flesh; she shall be called 'woman,' for she was taken out of man" (Gen. 2:23).

Besides the simple joy the man expresses because his "not good" condition of loneliness has been remedied, there is interesting wordplay going on. So far the narrator has referred to the man as "*Adam*," which is related to the Hebrew word for earth (*adama*). This name highlights the importance of humans being made from the earth. But when the woman is presented to the man, he responds by giving his new partner and himself matching names. He says, "She shall be called 'woman' [*isha*], for she was taken out of man [*ish*]." Where the narrator names the man in relation to the earth, the man names the woman in relation to himself.

At the beginning of the Bible, then, relationality is established as key to human thriving. Of course, as the narrative continues to the crisis, it is not surprising that it is the relationships that suffer. After Adam and Eve make the fateful decision to violate God's command by eating of the fruit from the tree of the knowledge of good and evil, it immediately causes a rift in their relationship: "And [God] said, 'Who told you that you were naked? Have you eaten from the tree that I commanded you not to eat from?' The man said, 'The woman you put here with me—she gave me some fruit from the tree, and I ate it'" (Gen. 3:11–12).

This fracturing of human relationships continues with their children as Cain murders Abel. From that point on, strife among humans becomes a persistent element of the human condition. Throughout history, humans do find ways to make it work and live in community with one another. However, the specter of alienation continues to plague humans to this day.

Attempts at a Solution

As consciousness of the loneliness epidemic rises among academics and social-service providers, we see some attempts to address the problem coming to the fore. One example of this approach is the Silver Line Helpline, a loneliness prevention program out of England. This program involves setting up a call center that clients (mostly seniors) can use to get answers to common questions about daily living.[6] The real reason for the service, however, is to help alleviate loneliness.

Most callers have some kind of practical question, about cooking for instance. It usually becomes pretty clear as the conversation develops that the deeper purpose of the call is human connection. Some clients call once per day. One client calls every hour to ask the time. The staff is able to field most of the initial calls but can also try to link the client with a volunteer who can call more regularly and even write letters.

I would call this kind of approach to the problem of loneliness a relational approach, in that it frames the problem of loneliness mostly in terms of a lack of meaningful relationships. The relational approach gravitates toward solutions that attempt to increase instances of relational connection that the lonely person will have each day or week. To utilize Jane Jacobs's idea of three basic ways to understand a problem, which we discussed in chapter 1, I would say that the relational approach treats loneliness like a problem of simplicity. Like many other attempts to solve societal problems as problems of simplicity, these kinds of approaches are destined for failure.

Instigating Friendship

If the clearest metric of loneliness is the fact that people don't have other people to talk to about important matters, then solutions such as a call center make a lot of sense. People who have one or two people who call to check in with them regularly are less lonely than people who don't. The most direct way to address this particular problem is to identify those who don't have people checking in with them and then recruit and deploy people to do that.

For some people struggling with loneliness, such programs offer some relief. However, even in these programs' early stages, we can see some significant limitations in their ability to alleviate the growing problem of loneliness. The first problem has to do with scale. The sheer number of lonely people who could use a friend is overwhelming. It would be difficult to figure out who all the lonely people are. Many people are hesitant to self-identify as lonely, so call-center programs usually downplay the real reason for their existence and publicize other reasons to call in. Another difficulty in managing programs like these is finding suitable "friends" who can call and check in, and then pairing up clients and callers.

This organizational issue suggests a second problem. When a caller is successfully assigned to a client, there's a good chance that it won't feel like a good match. Between interests, personality, and values, there are numerous factors that make a friendship either work or not. If there's not a good match between client and caller, the calls may continue, but the relationship will feel forced or even a little chilly. Regardless of other factors, one unavoidable limitation of these kinds of programs

101

is that the client understands himself or herself as a client and knows that the person who calls has been assigned to do so.

A final limitation with a call-center program is that the majority of the interactions are not going to be face-to-face but rather mediated by a telephone or screen. While phone conversations can be meaningful, most people prefer face-to-face interactions.

Fundamentally, the problem with the call-center approach to the issue of loneliness is that it is a programmatic solution to a relational problem. Human relationships are notoriously difficult to program. And this includes the church. For this reason, Joseph Myers and others advise churches to be wary of relying too much on church programs to build community and rather recommend that churches focus on developing environments where relationships can develop and grow organically.[7]

So what kind of environment would encourage friendships to grow organically? There are three conditions that are most helpful to the formation of friendships:

1. Proximity
2. Repeated unplanned interactions
3. A setting that encourages people to let down their guard and confide in people

Of course, the existence of these three conditions doesn't guarantee that friendships will form, and they won't cause two incompatible people to become friends, but they increase the likeliness of friendships forming.

Now, a strategy of creating friendship environments for all the lonely people out there may have as many if not more logistical hurdles than the programmatic approaches. For now, we can flag these conditions as desirable and deal with their feasibility later.

Loneliness as a Belonging Issue

When we let go of the relational/programmatic approach to solving the problem of loneliness and start to think about the kinds of environments that encourage friendships to form spontaneously and organically, we are beginning to understand loneliness as a problem of organized complexity. To frame loneliness as a problem of organized complexity, we can begin with our need to experience belonging.

We were created for shalom, which means that we were created to experience belonging—a sense of fitting in with a particular place, a particular group of people, and/or the ethos or narrative of a place. Belonging is complex because it involves aspects of relationships, place, and story. Belonging is complex, but it is not disorganized or random, since it is part of God's good purposes for human existence as part of the created order.

We can think of loneliness not simply as a lack of relational interaction in an individual's life but rather as a deficit of belonging that is experienced at the individual level but is usually connected to wider societal issues. To address these issues, we need to look not only at the web of relationships a person has (or doesn't have) but also at how the place they live encourages (or discourages) connection and how stories are generated and shared in that environment.

Seeing loneliness as a problem of organized complexity through the lens of belonging is more involved than the relational/programmatic approach that is getting a lot of attention right now. And there's probably good reason for focusing on that kind of approach. It's a lot easier to set up a call center or recruit "friends" to visit elderly clients than to address the issue of a physical environment that isolates people from their neighbors. But if we really want to see a decrease in the epidemic of loneliness, I believe that we need to frame the issue as a deficit of belonging.

The Opposite of Loneliness

On May 27, 2012, Marina Keegan published an article in the *Yale Daily News* titled "The Opposite of Loneliness."[8] In it she notes that we don't have an adequate word for the one thing that she most wants in life: "We don't have a word for the opposite of loneliness, but if we did, I could say that's what I want in life.'"[9] I believe that Keegan is not alone in this conviction. We know that loneliness is a serious problem, but we don't have a clear sense of what its opposite is. From a societal perspective, we know what we're against (loneliness), but since we don't have an adequate word for its opposite, we don't really know what we're for.

Keegan takes a stab at describing what the opposite of loneliness is like in her experience: "It's not quite love and it's not quite community; it's just this feeling that there are people, an abundance of people, who are in this together. Who are on your team. When the check is paid and you stay at the table. When it's four a.m. and no one goes to bed. That night with the guitar. That night we can't remember. That time we did, we went, we saw, we laughed, we felt. The hats."[10]

In her casual, rambling style, Keegan picks up the three aspects of belonging we've been exploring. There is a relational element to the opposite of belonging (love, community, people), but it's more. There is also the element of experiences in place (you stay at the table, no one goes to bed). And there is the element of story ("We did, we went, we saw. . . . The hats.").

Keegan was killed in an automobile accident soon after this essay was published, a few days after graduation. The only bright spot in this tragic story is that Keegan had experienced a sense of belonging in her community before her life was cut short.

Unlike Sue's death, which went unnoticed for days, Keegan's death snatched her from a community of friends who were deeply embedded in their common place and in one another's stories. The shock waves of Keegan's passing spread immediately and left a deep hole among her community at Yale. What's concerning for a Christian looking at these contrasting stories is that Sue was an active member of her church when she died alone and unnoticed. If Keegan had a faith community, she never mentioned it, and yet she died as someone who had at least tasted a sense of belonging and knew that she wanted more.

Maybe this is as it should be. The first shall be last and the last shall be first and all that. Maybe we're not supposed to experience too much belonging during our earthly sojourn, and maybe those who do aren't interested in the kind of belonging that God is offering. Maybe, but I don't really think so. I think that Sue could have and should have experienced a much greater sense of belonging in her own neighborhood without taking away her taste for the promise of ultimate belonging in the kingdom. And I think that Keegan understood her taste of belonging among her friends at Yale was just that—a foretaste. Concerning that "opposite of loneliness," Keegan said "that's what I want" rather than "that's what I have." I believe that if the church did a better job of being a sign and instrument of belonging in the world, Keegan might have been drawn to something like that.

EXCURSUS

Social Capital

When we work with the relational/communal aspects of belonging, social capital can be a helpful conceptual tool. "Social capital" is a term coined by sociologist Robert Putnam to describe the quality of relationships in a community as an economic asset.[1] Putnam makes the point that social capital is a significant asset not unlike human or resource capital. Human capital has to do with the skills and abilities of a potential workforce, and resource capital has to do with the availability of natural and human-made resources. It's easy to see how the wealth a particular community is able to generate is correlated with human and resource capital. Putnam makes the point that this is also the case with social capital.

When we say that a community has a high degree of social capital, we mean there is a rich saturation of interconnected relationships between people and a high degree of trust. This can have an impact on wealth generation in a couple of ways. I refer to them as "opportunity benefits" and "security benefits." On the opportunity side, there tends to be a good degree of networking and sharing of information, allowing some people to connect to opportunities and others to collaborate. On the security side, when trust levels are high, there's less need to allocate expense and energy to protect one's interests. We don't need as many lawyers when deals can be reliably sealed with a handshake, and we don't need security guards when neighbors look out for each other.

Social capital can be broken down into two distinct kinds: bonding and bridging. "Bonding social capital" is the social capital that exists among people who know one another well. Extended families, tight-knit ethnic enclaves, religious communities, and some neighbors can enjoy a high degree of bonding social capital. People who enjoy a similar socioeconomic or educational level can too. Bonding social capital often involves deep, close relationships. It tends to be the kind of social capital that comes to mind when we first start paying attention to this concept.

"Bridging social capital" is the kind that can exist among people who differ from one another in some significant ways. Bridging social capital is a measure of relationships that cross lines of similarity—friendships and associations formed among people of different racial groups, religious communities, or neighborhoods.

The kinds of relationships that constitute bridging social capital are not normally as deep or close as those we find in bonding social capital. But the relationships of bridging social capital can be highly valuable in their own way. They can mitigate some of the negative effects of prejudice and hostility. They can also help expand imagination and expose people to other ways of life. Such exposure can help pull people out of a negative cycle of poverty or inspire some highly creative collaborations.

It has been said that bonding social capital helps people get by, while bridging social capital helps people get ahead. Young mothers in a poor neighborhood can rely on bonding social capital to get help with childcare, financial support, relational encouragement, and information about social services. But they likely need bridging social capital to get connected to educational, training, and job opportunities that might help them improve their socioeconomic situation.

As we explore the crisis of belonging in contemporary society, it is important to keep social capital in mind. As already noted, relationships play a key role in our sense of belonging. Putnam tracked social capital in terms of the economic value of relationships. Because we are tracking belonging, our use of the term will be a little different, but valuable nonetheless.

TEN

THE PROMISE OF HOMECOMING

Homesick

Every three years my family goes on an extended trip. Usually this means spending four to six weeks in another country. We love these trips. Through them, we've been exposed to people and cultures we have come to deeply appreciate and who have shaped our family. Our relationships with one another have grown through these trips. By far, our best family stories come from these intentional times spent together.

Yet occasionally on these trips I feel blue because I'm missing home. They say home is where the heart is, but this experience challenges that notion for me. I'm with the five most significant people in my life, whom I happen to love and enjoy very much, yet I still manage to feel homesick.

So what, exactly, am I homesick for? I think I miss my home itself: my bed, my favorite chair, my coffee maker. I'm also missing the view from my window, the neighborhood—specifically my favorite walks there. I'm even missing the weather. I enjoy tropical heat for a time, but part of me comes alive when I feel a stiff breeze coming off the Puget Sound. Homesickness is a fairly broad concept, and it's not simply about missing home.

When kids at camp get homesick, often what they're missing is their parents. But when we become independent adults, we also experience homesickness. Sometimes this experience hits us while on an extended trip. But many of us experience a kind of melancholy longing for the home of our childhood. I remember very specifically as a child playing outside and then coming in from the cold. Our side door opened directly into the kitchen, and because my mom was cooking dinner, the contrast from cold to hot air caused my glasses to fog up.

For some reason, this moment from my childhood has stuck in my brain and causes me to feel a twinge of sadness when I remember it. It brings to my awareness that sobering fact that we cannot go home again. I realize that not everyone has a pleasant childhood to remember, and those who do have memories different from mine. However, I suspect that this occasional longing for childhood home transcends the direct experience of the actual childhood home. It is more often free-floating homesickness that can attach to memories, sentimental movies, classic toys, and whatever else. Its origin is not my warm kitchen and fogged glasses but rather a deep longing for a home lost long ago.

Displacement

When Adam and Eve sinned against their Creator by eating the forbidden fruit, that impacted more than just their relationships. Most significantly, their relationship with God was broken, but they were also removed from a garden perfectly designed for their sustenance and comfort. They were dis-placed.

Throughout the narrative of Scripture, this theme of displacement continues to emerge, usually as punishment or curse:

- When Cain murders his brother, he is sent out as a wanderer.
- When the people of God refuse to trust God's promise regarding the promised land, they are forced to wander in the desert for forty years.

- When the temple is established in Jerusalem, those who are unclean must live outside of the city walls.
- When God's people fail to live up to the covenant God had established with them, they are sent into exile in Babylon.

We all carry some aspect of the curse of displacement within us. This is why, I believe, we often feel that nagging sense of homesickness for some childhood place we never experienced or to which we cannot return. We are all, to some degree, exiles who long to return home. Later in this chapter we see how the gospel fulfills our deep desire to return home.

Place and Embodiment

Before we explore the question of how this displacement is healed and how longing for home is fulfilled in Jesus Christ, we need to consider why place is so important to us. Hints can be found in the creation accounts. God created the world in a particular way. According to the first creation account in Genesis 1, God created over the span of six "days" and on each day took on a different aspect of the created order.

If we map out the days of creation in two columns, an interesting pattern emerges.

We see that the right-hand column involves moving things and the left-hand column involves fixed things. Moreover, if we look at the three rows carefully, an even more specific relationship emerges. The fixed thing on the left can be seen as the field within which the corresponding things on the right move. The sun, moon, and stars move within the field of light and darkness. The birds and the sea animals move within the sky and water. Finally, the land animals and humans move within the field of dry land that was exposed when God gathered the waters together.

This suggests that every creature was not only created by God but also *placed* by God. When we affirm the goodness of creation, then, we

Figure 8

THE DAYS of CREATION

LIGHT AND DARK

SUN, MOON, AND STARS

SKY AND EARTH

BIRDS AND SEA ANIMALS

WATER AND LAND

LAND ANIMALS AND HUMANS

Lee Hardy

affirm the thing itself and also its placement. This goodness of place becomes even more pronounced as we move into the second creation account. Whereas the first creation account allows us to witness the act of creation from the thirty-thousand-foot level, the second act shows us this same thing from the ground level.

God creates a specific place (a garden) perfectly suited for the sustenance of human life. It is set up to meet our needs for both food and beauty: "The Lord God made all kinds of trees grow out of the ground—trees that were pleasing to the eye and good for food" (Gen. 2:9). In this account, God doesn't create humans and then place them in an environment designed for them. God creates humans out of the place itself: "Then the Lord God formed a man from the dust of the ground" (Gen. 2:7).

There is something significant about man here being created from the dust. The narrator derives the name here for man (*adam*) from the fact that he was created from the earth (*adama*). This is all taking place before the fall, and being included in that which the Lord has just declared to be "very good" affirms the goodness of our physical being. Our bodies, in their clunky and messy physicality, are good. God intended us to be embodied creatures.

The goodness of the garden into which our ancestors had been placed can be appropriated and fully enjoyed only by embodied creatures. We affirm the trees' goodness for food by consuming their fruits through our mouths. We affirm that the trees are pleasing to look at by gazing upon them with our eyes. We were designed not for detachment but for engagement and participation with the created order. We were created for attachment to place (see the excursus below). We were later forcibly removed from this ideal place, and we feel restless and long, fruitlessly, to return there. This longing is passed down to the descendants of Adam and is the deep source of a general sense of homesickness.

We struggle to accept the significance of this deep longing. The book of Ecclesiastes, in its existential angst, expresses skepticism about the meaning of our physical existence: "All go to the same place; all come from dust, and to dust all return" (Eccles. 3:20). This language is reflected in our funeral liturgies. But one verse later, the author of Ecclesiastes expresses skepticism of his skepticism: "Who knows if the human spirit rises upward and if the spirit of the animal goes down into the earth?" (3:21).

It turns out that this is a false choice. I will elaborate on this in the next section, but for now I want to touch on the traditional words of committal: "In sure and certain hope of the resurrection to eternal life, through our Lord Jesus Christ, we commend to almighty God our *brother/sister* N., and we commit *his/her* body to the ground, earth to earth, ashes to ashes, dust to dust."[1] When we renounce life on this earth as having an ultimate claim on our life and entrust ourselves completely to God's hands, he gives us new life—life in a physical body prepared for eternal existence in a new heaven and a new earth.

Place and Space

"Place" and "space" are words that we sometimes use interchangeably, but for our purposes I want to keep them distinct. Space can be a geographic designation, but one that isn't particularly distinct. It is a realm of freedom, of possibility. Space is a starting point. Over time, it becomes a place as we settle into our lives there and begin to associate meanings with the place we live.

A good way to envision space and place is to think about a college dorm room. Before a student moves in, it is a space. It has four walls, a desk, a bed, a chair, and a dresser. When a student moves self and stuff in, it slowly begins to be a place. Walter Brueggemann claims that place is "storied space."[2] That is to say, spaces become places as we inscribe meaning and the stories of our lives on their walls and surfaces.

Place is what helps make us feel at home, like we belong somewhere. Place is essential to a sense of belonging. We can't help but turn spaces into places as we spend time in them. This process of turning a space into a place often involves physical changes. We paint a room and place special objects around. But this process can be mental as well. We adopt a favorite coffee shop as our morning spot; a particular route to the store becomes embedded as a pattern. We aren't always aware of our efforts to turn space into place, but after a while a once-foreign geographical region begins to feel like home.

I don't want to give the impression that place is always good and space bad. As much as we need place, sometimes we also need some space. Our lives become too crowded and stressful, so we go on vacation for a little space. Relationships that were life giving become toxic, and we need a little space from someone.

The Bible reveals the significance of place but also shows the importance of space. If Jerusalem is the paradigmatic place in the Bible, the wilderness is the paradigmatic space. Wilderness is where God's people are formed. And it is where prophets hear the Word of God. Jesus is tempted in the wilderness, and he withdraws there to pray. We have no clear depiction of how space might function in eternity, but in our current context, space can play an important role for disciples of Jesus.

Its value can be seen in the spiritual practice of retreat within the Christian community. Amid the crowded distractions of places, it can be difficult to hear the still small voice of God. It can be helpful to go somewhere where we can be less distracted and listen to God for a season.

Space can be positive outside of the discipleship context. In an unfamiliar location, space can feel lonely and oppressive. But once we become settled in and the space becomes place, we sometimes need a break from the places we live and work, to remove ourselves from places that have become too crowded with associations.

Placelessness

Before we get to a more nuanced discussion of place or space, we need to address a related, but much more contemporary, issue. The latter half of the twentieth century saw the emergence of a new concern about the local environment, known as "placelessness." Single-family tract housing developments, shopping areas consisting of big-box stores, and chain restaurants are examples of placeless places. A "placeless place" differs from a space because, though it is filled up with something, unlike true place it lacks any local characteristics. If we were to be set down in the midst of a big-box shopping area, we would most likely not be able to identify what city or even region we were in.

Placeless places present a problem for belonging because they resist becoming places. They are generic by design, for the sake of efficiency. They tend to be cheaply constructed because they need to be replaceable to respond to market shifts. For this reason, those who build placeless places don't usually invest in amenities that could make a stronger connection to the local setting, such as public art or landscaping that utilizes regional species of plants.

If this discussion feels abstract (maybe even elitist), then let me suggest a thought experiment. Imagine you are hosting out-of-town visitors. You've known them a long time, but they've never been to your current place of residence. When they ask for a tour of your city or neighborhood, where do you take them? My sense is that you take them to its places or perhaps to an important space (for example, a desert). You would never think of taking them to your city's placeless places such as Target or Walmart.

Redemption in Place and Redemption of Place

In the New Testament, the history of salvation takes a decisive turn with the birth of the Messiah. Jesus is sent to solve the problem of sin and to undo the curse that has plagued humanity. It should be no surprise that a key aspect of salvation is the redemption of place.

The incarnation itself, if not a complete redemption of place, stands at least as an affirmation of place. Even though Jesus has come to save "the world," he is born in a very specific town in a very specific place. As was common then, he was known by the place he was from. The Messiah is commonly known as "Jesus of Nazareth."

But the significance of place is only hinted at in the incarnation. Jesus later announces to the disciples that redemption will be experienced in place: "My Father's house has many rooms; if that were not so, would I have told you that I am going there to prepare a *place* for you? And if I go and prepare a *place* for you, I will come back and take you to be with me that you also may be where I am. You know the way to the *place* where I am going" (John 14:2–4, emphasis added).

At the very end of the narrative, John paints a vivid picture of redemption as a redeemed place: "Then I saw 'a new heaven and a new earth,' for the first heaven and the first earth had passed away, and there was no longer any sea. I saw the Holy City, the new Jerusalem, coming down out of heaven from God, prepared as a bride beautifully dressed for her husband" (Rev. 21:1–2).

Redemption, then, can be seen as a movement from exile or displacement to place. This affirms that place is good and even essential to our well-being. But as we affirm place, we must also acknowledge that place is not always good; place itself as a conceptual category needs to be redeemed.

As much as we long for place and will experience unease until we inhabit the place God is preparing for us, in the context of this fallen world place can also be experienced negatively. Place can be a framework for exclusion and oppression. When we want to exclude a person or a group, we say that they don't belong in this place, and we express a desire to keep *them* in their *place*.

This sobering reality provides the undercurrent of the second half of Jesus's conversation with the Samaritan woman:

> "Sir," the woman said, "I can see that you are a prophet. Our ancestors worshiped on this mountain, but you Jews claim that the place where we must worship is in Jerusalem."
>
> "Woman," Jesus replied, "believe me, a time is coming when you will worship the Father neither on this mountain nor in Jerusalem. You Samaritans worship what you do not know; we worship what we do know, for salvation is from the Jews. Yet a time is coming and has now come when the true worshipers will worship the Father in the Spirit and in truth, for they are the kind of worshipers the Father seeks. God is spirit, and his worshipers must worship in the Spirit and in truth." (John 4:19–24)

The woman is concerned because she has come to believe that Jesus is truly from God. But as she starts to put the pieces together, she realizes that if this Jewish man is from God, then the Jews are right and Jerusalem is the place where one can meet God. That is bad news for a Samaritan who is not welcome in Jerusalem. If she were to try to worship God in Jerusalem, she would be told to go back to her place.

Jesus affirms that the Jews hold a key to the right worship of God but reassures her that this means inclusion, not exclusion. Jesus lets her know that the true worship of God will not be restricted to one place: "True worshipers will worship the Father in the Spirit and in truth." This could be taken to mean that place is now unimportant to our worship of God. But when we consider how this story unfolds in Scripture, I think it is more accurate to say that there are lots of places to worship God. As disciples gather, they are met by Jesus, who affirms place: "*Where* two or three gather in my name, *there* am I with them" (Matt. 18:20, emphasis added).

There's not just one place to worship God, but we do worship God in a place. The local church is not the whole church, but it is something real and substantial. John is given messages to churches in places: "To the angel of the church in Ephesus . . ." (Rev. 2:1). And if these churches don't repent of their wrongdoing, the consequence has an impact on their place: "If you do not repent, I will come to you and remove your lampstand from its place" (Rev. 2:5).

Jesus not only affirms but redeems place. He chooses Galilee—a place of insignificance and ridicule—as an important base for his public ministry. Many of his disciples, who become the first leaders of the church, are Galileans. And when he gives them the game plan for spreading his message, the redemption of place becomes a key part of his strategy: "But you will receive power when the Holy Spirit comes on you; and you will be my witnesses in Jerusalem, and in all Judea and Samaria, and to the ends of the earth" (Acts 1:8).

We tend to think of these geographic instructions as a set of concentric circles, but they're not. Or we could say all but one are concentric circles. Jerusalem, Judea, and the "ends of the earth" represent a widening footprint for the spread of the gospel. But Samaria is a geographic region much as Judea is a region. The only difference is that Jews considered Judea a favored place while Samaria was a despised place. Jesus wants to make sure that the disciples bring the gospel there, so that churches can be planted there, so that God will be worshiped and meet people in that particular place.

A Secular Gospel of Place

The show *Extreme Makeover: Home Edition* is an example of how this longing for home plays out in secular culture. A worthy family is selected to have their home completely remodeled by a team of enthusiastic experts who can bring about a complete transformation in just seven days.

In one episode, a household consisting of two combined families has been selected. Both the parents in one family had died within a couple of months, leaving four orphaned children. The other family welcomed the kids into their small home and family. The *Extreme Makeover* team determined that a house with enough room for twelve people would be a well-deserved blessing.

The team arrives in the morning and awakens the household with a megaphone outside the front door. This comes as a surprise, but a welcome one. Everyone pours out into the front yard, joyously welcoming the team. The team does a little research on the family to discover their context, their interests, and their desires. Then the family is sent on a seven-day cruise while the team transforms their house.

The team dreams big and comes up with a transformation plan more ambitious and exciting than anything you or I would think up. Then they get started. A massive crew from the local community is deployed. The timeline seems impossible, but as in every episode, they meet the deadline. When the family returns from their vacation, their house is complete.

When the family arrives, the house is blocked from view by a bus. The host of the show, Ty Pennington, yells, "Bus driver, move that bus!" The bus moves, and the family finally gets to see their new house. This is an emotional moment but is only the first phase of the reveal. As the family gets a tour of the entire house, going through the common spaces and then individuals' rooms, they get more excited and exclaim how perfectly the team has understood them and met their needs. It's hard not to get emotional watching this dramatic climax.

Extreme Makeover: Home Edition was a top-rated show for almost a decade, and it's easy to see why. It taps into that archetypical desire that we have to return home. As we see a worthy family receive an incredible gift of a home, we cheer the well-deserved blessing and vicariously satiate our own desire for home. Of course, it's not too difficult to see flaws in the formula. The home that is given and received is significantly shaped by some distinctive American values that are not necessarily kingdom values. The home provides a setting for family life while underscoring values of autonomy, individualism, and consumption.

Such critiques notwithstanding, *Extreme Makeover: Home Edition* celebrates the role that place plays in the experience of belonging. A family is usually chosen because their home's deficiencies prevent them from thriving. The show is essentially about the restoration of place, but it also draws in elements of relationship and story. In the episode outlined above, the rationale for the home transformation was to create more space for the newly forged bonds of familial relationships to strengthen and grow. The house was completely transformed, but in such a way that the stories of both families were preserved. Pictures and the names of the late mother and father were incorporated into the design of the house. The host family was Samoan, and that shaped aesthetic and design decisions.

The Promise of Home

We have learned that place plays a critical role in solving the problem of loneliness by helping friendships to form. Rather than trying to program friendships for people who are lonely, we need to create and support sociable environments that allow people to connect with others regularly in a comfortable setting. In these kinds of settings, friendships (both private and civic) develop naturally and help people feel less alone. Connecting to people in place helps to form friendships, but it also helps us feel a greater sense of belonging. And it is a lack of belonging, not just loneliness, that captures the crisis we face most urgently right now.

In this chapter, we also begin to see how place in itself plays a critical role in our experience of belonging. It's not just alienation from people that causes us to feel a belonging deficit; we also feel alienated from the places we live. This might be because we've had to move from the formative places where so many of our significant life experiences took place. It might be because our home's locale is largely a placeless place crammed with chain stores and cookie-cutter architecture. It might be because there are not interesting and comfortable places to go and enjoy the local terrain, so we spend our evenings and weekends cocooned in the private sphere of home. Many feel little connection to the place where they happen to live, and they long for an experience of home that is deeply rooted in place.

For some the problem isn't a lack of meaningful place but rather that the place to which they have been assigned feels like a prison or is a source of deep shame. These people's longing might be for liberation from a place of shame or oppression and access to a place of freedom and dignity.

For these and many other reasons, the gospel promise of homecoming in place is profoundly good news. Ever since our primeval ancestors were removed from the garden, humanity has carried a deep ache for a return to that place of nurture, fellowship, and rootedness. The gospel doesn't mention a return to the garden, but both Jesus's promise to go and prepare a place for us where we can be with him and John's evocative picture of the new Jerusalem anchor our hope that ultimate redemption will involve place.

EXCURSUS

Place Attachment

The idea of "place attachment" comes from the field of environmental psychology and is used to help understand the process through which people become attached to particular places.

There are *persons*, there are *places*, and there is a *process* that influences the attachment between people and places. This might sound somewhat elementary, but each of these factors opens up numerous other considerations. This tripartite model is depicted in figure 9.

We have considered how a *person* transforms environment from space to place. But often we experience spaces becoming places as part of a group. We become attached to a place not only as an individual but also as a member of a family, friend group, student group, or church. So the question of place often includes the question of groups—how a group is defined, how one becomes included in a group, and how one becomes attached to a place as part of a group.

Place, as we are using the term, always involves a physical realm.[1] The physical realm can be divided up between the natural environment (terrain, flora, fauna, weather) and the built environment (buildings, streets, infrastructure, furniture, public art). Places are not static but are embedded in the flow of time. They feel different at different times of the day and in different seasons of the year. A park that feels like home

Figure 9

Place Attachment:
A Tripartite Model

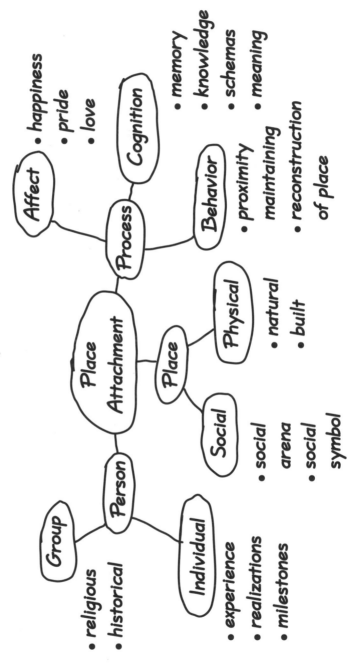

Based on fig. X in Leila Scannell and Robert Gifford, "Defining Place Attachment: A Tripartate Organizing Framework," in *Journal of Environmental Psychology* 30 (2010): 1–10.

on a sunny weekend can feel alien and foreboding if we encounter it at 2:00 a.m. on our way home from a party.

Place has a social dimension as well. The people who live, work, or play in a place have a major impact on what that place feels like, even when those people are not part of one of the groups to which we belong. We experience the people of a place in a distinct way at the social level at a neighborhood coffee shop or dog park. This is different than how we experience people at the public level at a large festival or a sports event.

So, by what process do people become attached to places? We must consider the affective and cognitive dimensions as well as the behaviors that attach us to place. Behaviors might include such activities as decorating a room or organizing the flatware in a kitchen drawer. Rituals often play a vital role. We discover a pleasant coffee shop and find ourselves returning there around the same time a couple mornings per week. The cognitive dimension involves learning and remembering things. We start to recognize interesting features in the natural or built environment.

Place attachment theory tries to account both for how people become attached to places and for the range that exists among people who interact with a place. Why do some people feel at home in a particular place rather quickly while others spend just as much time in the same area and never become attached?

ELEVEN

THE PROMISE
OF A GOOD STORY

Getting to School

Our house is six blocks from the elementary school my son attends for second grade. It's an easy walk on fairly quiet residential streets, and he could well manage it on his own. However, we haven't ever let him walk to school alone. Even if we were comfortable with doing that, other parents and probably the school administration would look down on, and maybe even take action against, us. Everyone knows that walking to school is far too dangerous for a second grader.

The elementary school I attended was about the same distance from my childhood home as this. I walked to school by myself or with friends every day from kindergarten on. What changed between the 1970s and the 2010s that eliminated the practice of walking to school?

The obvious answer is, of course, that things are much more dangerous today than in the 1970s. We don't let our children walk by themselves or with friends because to do so would put them at risk of being threatened, attacked, or even abducted by a stranger.

But would it? Are children actually at greater risk of abduction in the 2010s than they were in the 1970s? According to Lenore Skenazy, the surprising answer to this question is no. Contrary to popular belief, it's no more dangerous for a child to walk alone today than it was then. Skenazy, in her book *Free-Range Kids*, makes the case that things haven't actually gotten more dangerous for kids in the past few decades but rather that *perceived* danger has increased dramatically.[1]

Skenazy attributes this rise to the insatiable need of twenty-four-hour cable news for content and to various programs such as the milk-carton-kid campaign that have made us more aware of relatively unlikely dangers that have always been there. Danger to children may have not changed in the past few decades, but this rise in perceived danger has caused a dramatic shift in behavior. No longer do we feel comfortable allowing our children to roam freely outside. Some parents don't even allow their children out the front door unattended. This increase in perceived danger doesn't affect only our parenting. We ourselves feel less safe alone in public and make choices impacting our daily lives based on this perception of danger.

Story, Freedom, and Enslavement

Skenazy got interested in the subject of children and safety in an interesting way. In 2008, she was in Bloomingdales in New York City and left her nine-year-old son to make his way home by himself on the subway and bus. He'd been asking for weeks for permission to take on this kind of challenge, and she knew he was capable of it. So she decided to let him give it a try. She gave him "a subway map, a MetroCard, a $20 bill, and several quarters," left him at ladies handbags on the second floor, and said goodbye.[2] An hour or so later, he'd made it home just fine.

Skenazy told others about this experience and even wrote an editorial about it in the *New York Sun*. The response she received wasn't what she'd expected. She was taken to task by other parents and various experts for being irresponsible and unnecessarily exposing her son to danger.

She didn't agree, so she began to research danger and children. She discovered that many of the things parents worry about for their children are not nearly as dangerous as they think they are. For instance, she discovered that the rate of childhood abductions by nonrelatives has remained virtually unchanged since the 1970s and that no one has ever been poisoned by Halloween candy. Skenazy shared her discoveries with others and pioneered a movement known as "free-range parenting," which provides an alternative to what she considers the overly cautious approach now normative for US parents.

One way to understand what is going on here is to say that Skenazy and her fellow free-range parents are living their lives as part of one story and those who vehemently criticize her approach to parenting are living their lives as part of a different story. In Skenazy's story, older elementary children are capable of interacting in the adult world with relative independence, and that world isn't filled with people looking for any opportunity to harm children: "I trusted him to figure out that he should take the Lexington Avenue subway down, and the 34th Street crosstown bus home. If he couldn't do that, I trusted him to ask a stranger. And then I even trusted that stranger not to think, 'Gee, I was about to catch my train home, but now I think I'll abduct this adorable child instead.'"[3]

The story in which Skenazy's *critics* live is one in which every public space is likely to include at least one stranger with malicious intent toward children. Every danger that we can imagine presents a risk that must be avoided. And every child is incapable of making good decisions and mitigating risk on her own.

The kind of story we inhabit will have an impact on how we live our lives and the kind of freedom that we can enjoy. Skenazy's story allows her the freedom to leave a precocious child alone in downtown Manhattan. The story Skenazy's critics inhabit tends to restrict options and may lead to a kind of bondage for children who are never allowed to explore their neighborhood.

Of course, stories not only influence our reality through our attitudes and choices; stories are also formulated out of the reality of lived experience. And it's important to note how closely one's story corresponds at some level with reality. If stranger abduction were actually a major problem in New York, and Skenazy was just being naive, then it would be the case that she was a negligent parent. So when I

126

claim that the story we understand ourselves to be living in affects how we live our lives, I'm not suggesting we are free to simply make up whatever story we want. Our life choices will turn out better insofar as the story we understand ourselves to be living in is also tethered to objective truth.

The gospel is a story that is both true and foundational. It begins before all other stories and continues long after all other stories have come to an end. When we receive the gift of forgiveness offered freely through Christ's death on the cross, we are united with Christ, and we begin to experience our stories as connected to that larger story of the gospel. This larger story then shapes the story of our own lives and affects how we live and the freedoms we enjoy. When our lives are deeply founded in and shaped by the gospel story, then we can experience freedom even in the midst of what could be seen as oppressive bondage from the vantage point of another story.

The apostle Paul had his story dramatically subsumed into the gospel story. Although Paul was frequently in chains because of the story he was living in, he understood himself to be fundamentally free. "Now I want you to know, brothers and sisters, that what has happened to me has actually served to advance the gospel. As a result, it has become clear throughout the whole palace guard and to everyone else that I am in chains for Christ. And because of my chains, most of the brothers and sisters have become confident in the Lord and dare all the more to proclaim the gospel without fear" (Phil. 1:12–14).

The story that Paul understood himself to be inhabiting is one for which imprisonment and even death don't pose a significant threat. Although Paul faced the very real prospect of such an outcome, he could rejoice in hope for a glorious future: "I eagerly expect and hope that I will in no way be ashamed, but will have sufficient courage so that now as always Christ will be exalted in my body, whether by life or by death. For to me, to live is Christ and to die is gain" (Phil. 1:20–21).

One way of understanding the good news of the gospel is that we experience the freedom to participate in a good story just like the apostle Paul modeled in his life. Through Christ we are liberated from the bondage of a story in which sin, death, and the devil diminish life, and we

127

are brought into a story in which good wins over evil and in which we are made worthy to be subjects in a kingdom that never ends.

Storied Creatures

Humans are storied creatures. We have been created to experience our identity, to connect with others, and to connect with our environment through stories. We can't help but tell ourselves stories as we strive to make sense of our lives.

We do this so quickly and automatically that we hardly even realize that we're doing it. According research psychologist Brené Brown, we tell a story every time we respond to external stimuli generated by another person.[4] We can observe another's behavior, but there's much we can't observe directly, such as motives. In every interpersonal interaction, we instinctively fill in the missing details by telling ourselves a story.

My colleague comes into a meeting late because

- he doesn't respect me and wants to distract others from my presentation,
- something happened with one of his kids, or
- he put a birthday gift on my desk and wanted to do it while I was occupied.

We'll tell ourselves a story like one of these, and our feelings about the interaction will be based more on our story than on the behavior itself.

According to neurobiologist Robert Burton, we are hardwired to respond to such stimuli by telling stories.[5] Our brains release dopamine as a reward when we connect various experiences and impressions into a coherent narrative. We tell ourselves little stories to make sense of the events of our daily life, but we also constantly take these stories and pull them into the grand narrative of our lives. And as noted, that grand narrative has a major impact on our identity and the choices we make.

This story-making aspect of our humanity also has a strong social and cultural dimension. We connect with others through identification with their stories. We accept certain accounts based on how well they resonate with our stories. We build our own stories from bits and pieces of other stories we hear and find plausible. When we find larger stories especially compelling, we join them and appropriate them as our own stories.

Being part of a larger story can connect us to people we've never met. Connecting via story is distinct from how we connect relationally or geographically. As a US citizen, I am part of a particular story. When traveling overseas, if I meet another US citizen, even though we don't know each other personally and are not presently in our homeland, we have some connection to each other as part of the same story.

Our stories not only shape our behavior and attitudes, they also help us feel a sense of belonging. We feel more settled when we can fit the events of our lives into some kind of coherent narrative sequence, and we experience a greater sense of belonging when we feel some sense of common story with those whom we interact with in our daily life.

A Righteous King

We Christians often think of the story into which we are invited as fundamentally about the forgiveness of our sins and freedom from death through Christ's atoning death and resurrection. But that way of telling the story is highly individualistic. A more complete telling of the story includes other people. A life-changing encounter with Jesus Christ involves not only the freedom of forgiveness of sins but also an invitation to participate in something known as the kingdom of God. When we accept Jesus's offer of forgiveness, we enter into the much larger story of a righteous King who is establishing an eternal kingdom. And participation in this kingdom connects us to a vibrant eternal community known as the people of God.

Throughout Scripture, the righteousness and justice of the King are celebrated, and creation rejoices in anticipation of his eventual reign:

Say among the nations, "The LORD reigns."
    The world is firmly established, it cannot be moved;
    he will judge the peoples with equity.

Let the heavens rejoice, let the earth be glad;
    let the sea resound, and all that is in it.
Let the fields be jubilant, and everything in them;
    let all the trees of the forest sing for joy.
Let all creation rejoice before the LORD, for he comes,
    he comes to judge the earth.
He will judge the world in righteousness
    and the peoples in his faithfulness. (Ps. 96:10–13)

The Lord is the rightful King of all of creation. When the King reigns, all of creation rejoices, because things are as they should be. All of creation experiences belonging. The shalom that characterized the garden of Eden and the sense of belonging that the first humans experienced were largely a function of the fact that the Lord ruled over his creatures as a gracious and loving sovereign.

This story is not simply a static snapshot of hope for a coming king; it is part of a narrative arc that involves lost goodness, heartbreaking errors, flagging hope, and a dramatic restoration. Sin ruptured the vital relationship between Creator and creature, sin led to the humans being removed from the garden, and sin made it impossible for the righteous King to rule his creation as he was supposed to. In rejecting the rightful King, humanity enslaved themselves to a false king and brought suffering upon themselves, ruptured key relationships, and were removed from the place in which they belonged.

From that point of the story on, the absence of the righteous King persists as a crisis in need of a solution. The first attempt at a solution has to do with finding a human king who could potentially alleviate some of the suffering caused by the humans' fateful choice: "In those days, Israel had no king; everyone did as they saw fit" (Judg. 21:25). Of course, no human king is found who can rule the people in a way that measures up to the standard, so the people suffer under various kings.

After centuries of disappointed expectations concerning the desire for a good king, the people of God are given a message that God himself is going to supply a good king for his people: "But the angel said to her, 'Do not be afraid, Mary; you have found favor with God. You will conceive and give birth to a son, and you are to call him Jesus. He will be great and will be called the Son of the Most High. The Lord God will give him the throne of his father David, and he will reign over Jacob's descendants forever; his kingdom will never end'" (Luke 1:30–33). Jesus is a very different kind of king than the people of God were expecting. He is born in humble circumstances and confronts evil not by power but rather by suffering. Nevertheless, his way of overcoming evil is effective.

As the long-awaited righteous King, Jesus blesses the people by setting them free from their captivity: "The Spirit of the Lord is on me, because he has anointed me to proclaim good news to the poor. He has sent me to proclaim freedom for the prisoners and recovery of sight for the blind, to set the oppressed free" (Luke 4:18). Jesus announces himself as King and the coming of the kingdom as both a present reality and a future occurrence. In response to a question from some Pharisees as to when the kingdom would come, Jesus indicated that the kingdom had already come in him: "The coming of the kingdom of God is not something that can be observed, nor will people say, 'Here it is,' or 'There it is,' because the kingdom of God is in your midst" (Luke 17:20–21). However, later in that same discussion, Jesus speaks of a future event when the "Son of Man" (Jesus) will be revealed: "It will be just like this on the day the Son of Man is revealed" (Luke 17:30).

From these and similar passages, the idea developed is that the kingdom of God will come and be fully realized when Jesus returns in glory as the rightful King. However, the kingdom began the process of breaking in through the incarnation and public ministry of Jesus. And Jesus instructed his disciples to pray for the future coming of the kingdom even as they pray for the present reality to become more like the kingdom: "Your kingdom come, your will be done, on earth as it is in heaven" (Matt. 6:10).

The Gospel of the Kingdom

In chapter 9 we explored the gospel as the restoration of a broken relationship and a gift of community. In chapter 10 we explored the gospel as a return home from exile and a gift of the home we've always longed for. In this chapter, we're exploring the gospel as a triumph of the righteous King and the gift of being included in a wonderful story.

This story of the triumph of the King provides the larger context for Paul's freedom from the fear of death and his willingness to put up with suffering and persecution. Knowing that the King is triumphant and that we are included in his victory also frees us from the curse of death and the bondage to sin and fear. We experience that good news in the present possibility of a restored relationship with God through a life-transforming encounter with Jesus the King and in a future reality of participating in the fully realized kingdom of God.

In both of these aspects, we can think about the benefits that a good king can bring and use them to fuel our imaginations as we attempt to pray, wait, and work for the coming kingdom. The account outlined above is not only good news but also a good story. It's a story that unfolds over time and follows a narrative arc of promise, crisis, and fulfillment.

However, our own life experience may or may not make us feel like we are part of a good story. Many people's lives feel random, chaotic, and meaningless. Others feel like they may be part of a story, but one that is evil. Still others may feel their lives were once part of a meaningful story, but now they are disconnected from that story and have little hope for the future.

And as we note above, there is a communal aspect to understanding the gospel as participation in God's righteous kingdom. Taking the gospel as kingdom as our own story can connect us with others who are part of that same story. As participants in the gospel story, we claim Jesus as our King. Upon meeting others who also claim Christ as King, we can acknowledge that we belong to one another as part of the people of God. But because of the invitational nature of the kingdom, connecting through story does not necessarily exclude those who don't claim Christ as King. When we meet another person, we recognize there is room for them in the story, and we do what we can to let them know they are invited into the good story.

But it is not only the Christian story of God's kingdom that builds community in this way. Most compelling stories can bind people together with a common sense of mutual belonging. Nations have origin stories that inspire pride in their citizens and bind them together with a sense of common purpose. Diehard fans of professional sports teams often connect to one another through the shared story of their team's rise from the ashes. And for-profit corporations have recently learned to leverage the community-making power of story to increase sales.

Branding and Belonging

"I'll have a grande decaf soy latte, please." Have you ever wondered why you have to say an Italian word for "large" if you want a medium cup of coffee at Starbucks? The reason is that Starbucks wants to secure your loyalty by making you feel that you are a part of their story. There's no better way to make you part of a story than changing your language to fit the language of the new story. Starbucks doesn't just want you to be a buyer of their products; it wants you to belong to the Starbucks community.

And who wouldn't want to? To belong at Starbucks is to be grafted into a story that goes all the way back to that humble storefront coffee shop in Seattle's Pike Place Market. It's a story about connection and making the world a little more humane, one cup of coffee at a time. Here's how Starbucks tells their story to the world: "From the beginning, Starbucks set out to be a different kind of company. One that not only celebrated coffee but also connection. We're a neighborhood gathering place, a part of your daily routine. Get to know us and you'll see: we are so much more than what we brew. We call our employees partners because we are all partners in shared success. We make sure everything we do is through the lens of humanity—from our commitment to the highest-quality coffee in the world, to the way we engage with our customers and communities to do business responsibly." And in their statement of values the very first one, not surprisingly, has to do with belonging: "Creating a culture of warmth and belonging, where everyone is welcome."[6]

According to business consultant CJ Casiotta, branding was an effective marketing strategy for the latter half of the twentieth century, but "belonging" is supplanting "branding" as a way to secure a loyal customer base. The word itself betrays branding's slightly sinister intent; an identifying mark seared onto skin certainly leaves an impression and also makes clear who is incurring the cost and who is deriving the benefit from a relationship. "Branding," according to Casiotta, "is for cows, but belonging is for humans."[7]

Belonging is less about getting people to buy your products and more about helping people figure out who they are: "Belonging is different. It's about tapping into the identity that already exists in people and creating products, content, and communities that help them express that identity to its fullest potential, which makes their lives more meaningful."[8] Now, it's reasonable to be skeptical about the prospect of a for-profit company simply wanting to help me express my identity without any thought to how that might benefit it. Nevertheless, I think Casiotta is correct at least insofar as companies would be wise to give the impression of caring about their customers as whole people and inviting them to belong to a coherent and compelling story. But those of us who have experienced belonging through Christ should be at least somewhat resistant to this sales strategy that is at best a pale imitation of the kingdom of God.

The Power of the Story

Story plays a critical but elusive role in today's cultural crisis of belonging by helping us escape the stories that restrict our freedom by making us afraid. Story also helps us escape our loneliness and alienation by binding us to others with whom we share a common story. And story provides an avenue for building connections with others as we learn their stories and share our stories with them. Story is an important aspect of the good news of the gospel, because story plays a key role in the crisis of belonging.

The dominant story in our culture seems to be one of vulnerability and danger. This story tells us that unless we are especially vigilant, we run the risk of harm to ourselves, our children, and our property. It tends to overemphasize belonging in the private realm as we look to our family and tribe for protection. This story disconnects us from others in the civic sphere and prevents our experiencing belonging in our neighborhoods and cities.

Many are seeing the crumbling and dissolution of some grand narratives that gave shape and meaning to their lives. Narratives of our country, our institutions, our traditions, and even our genders are all up for grabs, which is causing much disorientation. In some respects this dissolution is a good thing. Many of the narratives that have shaped us need to be unmasked for all of their moral ambiguity. But while old narratives are quickly coming down, new narratives haven't been created to replace them, causing people to feel somewhat uneasy and detached from their environments.

The gospel can serve as a catalyst of belonging by being good news on both counts. By being grafted to the gospel story through confessing our sins and believing in Jesus, we can experience freedom from fear as we find our place in the story of the kingdom of God. Embracing the gospel story builds courage as it binds us to the community of a righteous King. This freedom can help us be open to trusting and connecting with others in our neighborhoods and cities. Though the gospel frees us from fear of death, I don't think we have to take significant risks to our well-being to benefit from less fear of others. Just being open to the difference between real danger and perceived danger can increase our willingness to connect with others.

With regard to the fragmentation and dissolution of stories, the gospel can encourage us to generate and communicate new stories that connect people in new ways. We can connect with others by learning their stories and telling them ours. Learning to share in the story of our neighborhood helps us all feel like we belong. That story may not have formal connections to the gospel, but it may hold the key to helping us all feel a greater sense of belonging to the place we live. Insofar as we can encourage belonging, we "seek the shalom" of the places to which we have been called, since belonging is the subjective experience of shalom.

EXCURSUS

Thick and Thin Language

One important element of discovering and developing a sense of common story is having a strong sense of shared meaning with other people in our life. Part of what we mean when we say that we belong somewhere is that the people in that place "get" us and we "get" them. When people "get us," it means that we have a strong sense of shared meaning.

The philosopher Michael Walzer makes a helpful distinction between thick and thin language. We use thin language when we don't have a great deal of shared meaning with another, and we use thick language when we do.[1]

We can describe the same event using thin or thick language. "A girl kicks a ball through metal bars in a rectangular shape and backed by netting" is an example of thin language. "Senior forward Kelly McDonald scores the winning goal in the final seconds of the game to give the Central High Eagles their first state title in thirty-eight years" exemplifies thick language. To understand the thick description, one needs to understand the rules of soccer, the American high school, and the basic structure of high school sports.

As we explore the connection between place and belonging, we can assert that the ability to use and understand the thick language of a particular locale is key to establishing a sense of belonging. If this is true, then we can begin to think about what is involved with becoming conversant with the thick language of a place.

PART FOUR

A CRISIS OF BELONGING

A longing for belonging intersects with relationships, place, and story in every human culture at every time. But it is my contention that it has reached a crisis state in contemporary American culture for reasons specific to our time and place. We've exacerbated our relationally alienated state with others by embracing innovations in transportation, housing design, and communication that minimize face-to-face interactions. We've forgotten how to build places for civic interaction and have converted existing social spaces in the civic realm into parking lots. And we've embraced a story of accumulation and hurry that has made us feel that we don't have the necessary time to invest in things that help

137

us attain a sense of belonging. In this section we will explore how this crisis of belonging has unfolded over the past half century. We'll discover that the crisis of belonging is connected to our experience of relationships, place, and story; but it all begins with three pieces of glass.

TWELVE

THREE PIECES OF GLASS

The Crisis of Belonging in Relationships

Return to the Table

You're out for dinner with friends. Before ordering, you take a quick trip to the bathroom. As you return to the table, you find everyone not talking, not studying the menu, but staring at their phones.

It's not an unusual story. In fact, it's pretty ordinary. But it feels odd to you. You're not sure why. You've certainly been guilty of the same in all kinds of circumstances, so you can't claim the moral high ground. But if you're honest with yourself, it feels a little depressing, maybe even hurts a bit. If you could freeze that scenario and tease out your feelings, you might be able to gain a little clarity about what's going on.

In the first place, there's relational affront. Normally, in any relational setting, we give a number of nonverbal cues to acknowledge someone, especially a friend approaching. We make eye contact, we shift our chairs, we smile. Your friends don't do any of these things. They're not intending to snub you, but they are distracted by their screens and don't see you coming.

Second, there is something amiss regarding place and embodiment in this scenario. Everyone at your table is ignoring not only you but

139

also one another and the place you are sharing. Each one of them is choosing to engage with someone or something inhabiting a different place. *This* is a special place. You chose it because you enjoy the food and ambiance. These friends enjoy being together enough to put the effort into getting together like this. So why choose to be elsewhere? Their phones can connect them with some fairly entertaining things and people, but they do so via one, perhaps two, of their senses. The encounter captivating their attention is mostly a cognitive, rather than a bodily, experience. It feels a bit thin—literally less than full-bodied.

Third, your friends' decision to pull their attention away from your shared experience and toward shared experiences with others not in the same room changes the story you might be sharing. They are, in a sense, leaving the narrative flow of this scene in the story of your shared lives. They're also pulling out of the narrative they share with others in the restaurant.

They have not only ignored you, they probably have also missed social cues given by the busperson and your server. They, and other patrons who have been sucked into their phones this evening, have exited the civic drama being played out in this particular restaurant on this particular evening. They have (inadvertently) communicated not only to you but also to others in the restaurant that something or someone more important is on the other end of a device. This might sound extreme, but it is not too severe to suggest that phone absorption, when succumbed to by enough people, has reduced the social capital in this setting and in the wider community.

Since you can't really freeze time, all of the foregoing registers only subconsciously, in a microsecond. But it does register. And it just feels a bit wrong. The question is, What does it mean that this doesn't feel right? Is this just a sign that you're getting old, perhaps a bit nostalgic? Or is there more substance to this feeling? How did we get here? Did the emergence of smartphones a decade or so ago so rapidly change how we interact with one another?

My sense is that this is more than nostalgia. Something's going on here, and it's not the way it ought to be. However, I don't believe that it started (at least in the United States) with the smartphone. In the United

States, this type of behavior and the deteriorating impact it has on our personal and civic friendships started long before the smartphone. I believe that for at least a half century, we've been making deliberate society-wide choices to disengage from face-to-face interaction with one another, and what we're now experiencing are the cumulative effects of some of these changes.

We can account for these changes by examining three pieces of glass—the windshield, the TV, and the smartphone—that each represent a major step toward where we are today.

Car Culture

In the years following World War II, we made a significant society-wide shift in North America. We began to create buildings and infrastructure with the expectation that people would get from one place to another only by driving an automobile. This approach differed from any other country's at any time in history. Prior to this, transportation in the modern developed world was always multimodal, which meant you had multiple options to get from one place to another. You could take the train, walk, ride a bike, or (if you were in a rush) take a private car. From about 1950 to 2000 in the United States, we built a society that was highly dependent on the automobile.

For most people today, when considering how to get from one destination to another, the only realistic option is taking a car. In a multimodal transportation system, a car is a convenience. In the second half of the twentieth century, we created a society for which a car became a necessity.

There were good reasons for this somewhat radical experiment. Gasoline was cheap, and driving was enjoyable. Naturally, the car was the preferred mode of transportation. The postwar economy was booming. Young families wanted houses; growing corporations needed to expand and add facilities. Since land was cheap, it made sense to spread out and give everyone what they wanted. As the population spread out, it wasn't necessary to invest in public transit, since most people could drive to their needed destinations.

As we saw in chapter 7, zoning was used not only to separate commercial areas from residential but also to separate housing according to income level. This began a trend to separate everything imaginable. We created sports complexes to pull youth sports out of the neighborhood. We separated commercial buildings so that retail, offices, and manufacturing would be in separate areas. We built special housing projects to keep all of the poor people in one part of town, and we built retirement homes to keep older people in one area.

This spreading out meant that commute times from home to work and then back again became longer. It became normal to live twenty, thirty, even forty miles from one's place of work. But possibly the most significant change was the total number of trips the average American made per day. With everything separated, one had to jump in the car not only to get to work but also to go to a friend's house, to buy an aspirin, to get a cup of coffee, or to get one's child to basketball practice. In 2010 the average US household made 9.6 car trips daily.[1]

A number of intended and unintended consequences arose from this postwar experiment. One of the most obvious was that we spent more and more time behind the wheel of an automobile. Most of this time was spent alone or driving children. This meant less time for civic face-to-face interaction. In a multimodal context, one would run into other people on the bus, on the way to the store, or walking kids to school.

Not only did the task of driving to various destinations leave less time for face-to-face interaction, building design also limited the contact we could have with others. Most houses built during this period included an attached garage, allowing residents to arrive and depart without going through the front door and encountering anyone who wasn't part of one's family.

Many office buildings built during this period included on-site or underground parking, which allowed employees to access the building without meeting anyone who wasn't a fellow employee. Together these design features meant that we could drive from our homes to work without ever breathing outdoor air or having a face-to-face interaction with anyone not a family member or a coworker.

In this environment, we do encounter other people throughout the day, but the way we encounter them changed: encounters are mediated by the automobile windshield. This is the first of the three pieces of glass. When we encounter someone this way, we don't encounter another human being with whom we might connect. We as a driver meeting another driver encounter a competitor—a competitor for lane space and parking spaces.

We can tell that something is off about our relationship with the other driver by the way we treat him or her. We tend to act differently toward other people when we and they are driving cars. We say things and make gestures that are less than polite. We relate in ways that we would not in a million years when encountering a person face-to-face. This leads us, regrettably, to less-than-humane behaviors. This negatively affects our character by eroding some of our instincts for civility.

Another issue is that we have less and less opportunity for normal physical interaction with other human beings. Not only do we act less civilly to other drivers, we are losing touch with some of the common practices of civility in the public realm: our civility muscles are atrophying. We are not disrespectful because we harbor feelings of ill will toward our neighbors; we just have lost any sense of public responsibility for one another.

TV Friends

Let us return to examining the kinds of buildings we constructed after the car became the preferred mode of transportation. Prior to World War II, if you looked at a typical house, you would first notice a front porch, a front door, and a picture window or two.

After World War II, when you looked at a typical house, its most prominent feature would be a two- or even three-car garage. There might be a "curb appeal" front door, but it would rarely be used by the owners. Residents of this style of home typically enter through the garage. You would not see a front porch. Since we were spending more time driving our cars, we were also spending less time taking an after-work stroll in the neighborhood. There would be less interaction between neighbors walking by and those resting on a porch. We used to sit on our front porches, especially in the warmer months to stay cool and because it was too hot to do much of anything else. The advent of air-conditioning led us to abandon the front porch and move indoors.

But guess what? We kind of missed the interaction with the parade of neighbors going by our front porch. As a recent book aptly claims, "Everyone's normal, until you get to know them."[2] In my experience, all people are a little quirky, and when you put them together, those quirks are multiplied exponentially. This is part of the reason that actual neighbors are so interesting. It can be pretty entertaining to get below the surface and find out what makes your neighbor tick, and it's even more exciting when you witness drama among your neighbors in real time.

By driving our cars into our attached garages and going straight into our air-conditioned homes, we miss an opportunity to witness the ongoing drama that is our neighborhood. Do you know what we did to fill that void? We invited a bunch of other interesting people into our homes via a new invention. The television screen is the second piece of glass to consider.

A few years ago, my wife and I were really into *The West Wing*. If you're not familiar with that, it's a TV drama that focuses on the president of the United States and his staff. It's a great show, with a compelling story line and interesting characters. We watched this show faithfully and tracked the characters: Jed, Toby, Josh, Sam, and Charlie.

Around that time, I was invited to speak at a conference in Washington, DC. The host organization was covering my expenses, but I had to take an extra night in DC that would be on my own dime. We didn't want to pay for a DC hotel, so we were brainstorming alternatives. In the middle of our brainstorming, my wife said, "Oh, no problem, we know tons of people in DC you could stay with." She stopped herself in time, but both of us knew that she was about to say, "Josh, Toby, or Sam." We both burst out laughing, but the reality is that we had developed what could be considered quasi-social relationships with the fictional characters of *The West Wing*.

I don't think we are alone in this. I suspect that this tendency has only gotten stronger with the advent of reality TV. Most of us are not going to make the mistake of thinking that our quasi-social relationships with TV characters are real relationships, but I do think we are drawn to them for similar reasons, and they impact us in similar ways.

Because we are created for relationships, we are naturally drawn to other people, and our interest is piqued as their stories unfold before us. In these quasi-human encounters, we tend to be rather passive. We laugh at things that are funny. We cry at things that are terrible or heartwarming. We get drawn into complicated narratives.

But the characters we get to know on TV are unlike the characters in our neighborhood in some important ways. They don't wave back at us or engage us in two-way conversations. They don't ask for favors from us and don't make any relational demands on us. They aren't available to us as potential friends.

This is also true to some extent of the real stories we encounter on TV. The news exposes us to a constant stream of heartwarming and heartbreaking human-interest stories. But again, the people we meet in these stories make no demands on us, because there is usually nothing the viewing public can do to tangibly celebrate good stories or ameliorate the pain of bad stories. We usually passively consume these stories and allow them to foster an illusion that our lives are more exciting than they actually are.

If the automobile causes us to lose civility in our interaction with other humans, the television moves us in another direction. This second screen causes us to become more voyeuristic in many of our relationships.

Mobile Distraction

Between the car and the television, we've virtually eliminated any human interaction with people who are neither related nor known to us. But there are a few gaps in the system. In our daily lives we must remove ourselves from windshield and TV screen. We need to pop out to the store for groceries. We may need to pick up our kids from school. And these excursions may just put us in face-to-face contact with another human being. These situations can make us a bit uncomfortable, because individually and collectively we are out of practice.

The good news is that we have a solution to this problem. We now have these small pieces of glass we can carry in our pockets that can effectively shield us from encounters with other people. We can pull these tiny screens out any time we feel uncomfortable or bored in company.

If my observations are typical, most people do pull out their smartphones instinctively when in a public place. If you're with other people waiting in line at the grocery store or with parents at school waiting to pick up your kids, you're likely to see a high percentage of people staring down at their smartphones.

These portable devices are extremely convenient. They help us stay in touch with people who are important to us, and they help manage our increasingly complex lives. I'm not sure how I would be able to parent or to be a pastor without the benefit of my smartphone.

But just like our cars and our TVs, these devices can have a negative impact on our character. Just as we have an easier time being rude to other people while driving, we can be malicious in our comments about others on social media. And just as we voyeuristically engage the stories of strangers on TV, we can get sucked into little snippets of strangers' lives through social media. All the while, we are oblivious to the people we see around us.

Malformative Practices

The impact of these three pieces of glass, taken together, can be quite malformative. We were designed to be in relationship with others, and the effect of these three developments has been to pull us away from direct life-giving relationships with others. We flourish when we are rooted in place; these devices pull us away from the significant places of our lives. We are meant to understand the story of our lives as connected to the larger story of God's reconciling love for the world, and these devices pull us away from the primary narrative of our lives.

They have a negative impact not only on us personally but also on society. By limiting the time that we spend on face-to-face contact, they tend to erode long-standing traditions of civility. Saying "excuse me" when you have to cut in between two people in conversation, giving the checker at the store your undivided attention, and making brief eye contact when passing another person on the sidewalk are all ways that we affirm the dignity of the people with whom we share daily life. There are also traditions of initiating and cultivating social relationships with the shopkeepers and residents of our neighborhood.

The cumulative impact of the three pieces of glass is corrosion of our relationships. As we noted in chapter 9, our relationships with other people are already difficult because of the corrosive effect of sin. But our windshields, TVs, and smartphones are exacerbating rather than helping the problem. These technological developments have made our lives more efficient in some ways and have provided more options for entertainment, but those things have come at a cost. They have greatly diminished our social capital within the context of the places that we live. The car, the TV, and the smartphone have together contributed to diminish our humanity and deemphasize the civic friendships that are so essential to our sense of belonging in the places that we live.

THIRTEEN

THE DECLINING CIVIC REALM

The Crisis of Belonging in Places

A Devalued Civic Realm

Let's just say that after reading chapter 12, you feel convicted that we face a situation of declining social capital in this country and that you personally recognize a diminished sense of belonging in your own neighborhood. You're inspired to do something about it, so you decide to turn off your TV, forgo your car, and walk to somewhere that you can connect with a few neighbors. You resolve to keep your phone in your pocket and walk with your head up, your attention focused outward so as to send a message that you are open to some civic interaction.

The inside of your home is the private realm, as is the property on which your home sits. The inside of commercial buildings and the surrounding property are private as well. The sidewalk that you now begin walking along, the street next to it, walking trails, any parks that you pass, public buildings (library, post office, or city hall), and any space between the buildings that is not privately owned are all part of the civic realm. The civic realm is where you are free as a citizen to do what you feel like (so long as you're not breaking any laws) without having to be invited in by the owner or to justify your presence by being a paying customer. The civic realm is one of the places where you can meet others and get to know some of the people with whom you share daily life.

Imagine this very possible scenario: For the first couple of blocks, you feel pretty isolated. You're walking along a street consisting solely of single-family residences, and other than a few joggers wearing earbuds, you don't see any people. Eventually you approach a busier street with lots of evidence of activity. There is no shortage of people here, so you are hopeful about your plan for human interaction. As the residential street comes to an end and you enter the commercial corridor, what greets your eyes is a dispiriting sight. The residential street ends abruptly as you encounter a four lane arterial street. You immediately feel exposed and a bit threatened by the fast-moving cars. You scan the chaotic environment for some kind of public setting, or at least a commercial establishment in which you could hang out and get some relief from the fast-moving cars. About two hundred feet away you see a commercial development that kind of fits the bill. A large parking lot is edged on three sides with strip malls housing various businesses. On the side facing the street are a number of oversized signs on large poles advertising some of the businesses to cars passing by. There are patches of grass tucked in here and there and a few berms of juniper bushes separating clusters of businesses. The patches of grass don't appear to be designed for anyone to use as a place of rest but rather seem intended to visually break up the monotony of concrete, cars, and cheap construction with a hint of "nature."

Your heart sinks. This is not a place you want to spend fifteen minutes, let alone the whole afternoon. You can tell immediately that this won't be a good place to meet or converse with any of your neighbors. Any neighbor you might meet isn't going to voluntarily spend time in this public space. So what's wrong with this picture?

The problem isn't the absence of a civic realm. More than 50 percent of what you see here would not be considered private. There is a sidewalk and some landscaped grounds available for public use. There is a wide public street and a parking lot for your use as well. The problem with this setting is twofold. The first is that it wasn't designed primarily

149

for your use—at least in the way that you have chosen to interact with it. Second, it was not designed for your ultimate use—as a final destination. Most of what you see here was designed as a means to help you get somewhere else.

This place was designed primarily for access and use by automobiles. If you were driving a car to this location, you would appreciate things like a designated turn lane in the middle of the arterial and, no doubt, the numerous parking spaces available. Unfortunately, these are some of the very things that make this place particularly inhospitable to pedestrians. If you need to cross this arterial, you are faced with the choice of taking your life into your hands by crossing five lanes of traffic without a crosswalk or walking an extra three hundred feet in either direction to get to the regulated crosswalk.

The other problem is that the part of the picture that can be considered the "civic realm" is really designed for only transitory use. The arterial, the parking lot, and even the sidewalk are designed to help you use your car to gain easy access to the shops and services in that area. The landscaping is there to soften the hard edges of the concrete and to give you something a little bit interesting to look at as you drive by.

When we think about the civic realm, at least in the United States, we can articulate at least two kinds of uses for it. The first is "instrumental." One reason for the existence of the civic realm is to provide a setting for the transport of people and/or goods. We need streets, bridges, and even parking spaces so that we can get to the store to buy groceries and so that we can get to our friends' houses to meet them for coffee. A second reason for the existence of the civic realm is to provide a place for us to go and enjoy the day, to meet a friend, or to get out and be in the company of others. I call this second reason "ultimate," not in the sense that it is the "best ever," but rather that it is an end in itself. It's not leading to something else.

Between these two types of uses for the civic realm, I'm sure that most of us would concede that the first is of primary importance. We need roads, bridges, and parking spots in order to accomplish the tasks of our day. In political conversations about spending tax dollars on "infrastructure," these kinds of things are usually what is meant.

The second reason for the civic realm—as a place to hang out, meet someone, or just enjoy the passing of time—is considered secondary at best. Parks, benches, and walking trails are usually considered nice but not necessary.

From the Commons to the Parking Lot

This way of devaluing the civic realm as an important place for human interaction is a relatively new phenomenon. We have a history of creating civic space that goes back even before our founding as a country. When the Puritans first arrived in New England to set up towns, one of the first things they did was build a meetinghouse in the center of town, a burial ground, and a common field for public use. The commons, as this field was called, was ostensibly for the grazing of livestock, but it also provided a central place for residents of the town to gather and casually interact.[1]

Prior to European settlement, many Native American communities set up their villages with a central ground surrounded by civic buildings that would be used for public meetings and communal ceremonies. American towns that were first settled by the Spanish were usually built according to precise guidelines established by the Spanish throne. The Law of the Indies, as these guidelines were called, stipulated that the town would be built around a central plaza: "The main plaza is to be the starting point for the town. . . . The plaza should be square or rectangular, in which case it should have at least one half its width for length inasmuch as this shape is best for fiestas in which horses are used and for any other fiestas that should be held."[2] The Law of the Indies also required smaller plazas throughout the town, depending on its size and population.

A number of American cities were built around not just one area but a series of smaller squares and common areas. The plan for Philadelphia included a central square of ten acres and four other squares of eight acres each for common use. Similar plans were established for Annapolis, Maryland, and Williamsburg, Virginia. One of the best-loved examples of this type of approach to town planning is Savannah, Georgia, which established a set of wards consisting of a square surrounded by six blocks. As the town grew, it maintained this pattern of wards and now boasts twenty-four gorgeous public squares for each of its wards.

In addition to these patterns of intentionally incorporating public space into towns, Mark Childs, in his book *Squares*, documents numerous other examples.[3] Among these are French examples, which influenced the development of Mobile, Alabama, St. Louis, and New Orleans. Childs also notes the traditional courthouse squares, which were developed in county seats in the Midwest and South. And last, there are universities like Harvard, William and Mary, Princeton, and the University of Virginia that built on and developed earlier precedents of English college designs.

This fairly long-standing tradition of developing coherent public spaces for citizens to enjoy and interact with took a decisive turn with the onset of the automobile. As convenient as cars are, they require a tremendous amount of storage space. As the car moved from luxury item to standard feature of the middle-class household, where to park became increasingly important.

In areas of town that hadn't yet been built out, parking lots became the first priority for any land not dedicated to a building. But for areas already built out, the question became what existing lots could be converted for parking. And in more cases than not, the answer was to convert public squares into parking lots.

In the suburban model of development, this trend became even more pronounced. There was a powerful symbiotic relationship between the suburbs and the automobile. The suburbs needed the automobile in order to work. The only way to sell a house more than ten miles from the breadwinner's place of work and a couple miles from the grocery store was if the family owned at least one car. Over time it became clear to most families that one car wasn't going to be enough. Since the car would be required for most tasks of daily life, it would be preferable for anyone above driving age to have access to their own car. This new reality rapidly multiplied the number of cars in the United States.

Soon planners had to assume that everyone using any building for any reason was going to arrive there by car. In the suburbs it became logical to think of one parking spot per customer at any given time. Planners had to use a different approach from an urban or even a small-town setting, where people can park their car once and accomplish multiple tasks in different buildings.

This new pattern of transportation led to what has become known as site-specific parking requirements in the suburbs. Imagine a typical day in which you go to the gym, to the coffee shop, to work, to lunch, to the bank, to the grocery store, to a bar, and then home. This typical day would require eight parking spots, or roughly 1,296 square feet of land, for one person. If you multiply that number by more than a few people, it really adds up. Of course those spots are going to be used by others throughout the day, but rules for on-site parking are based on the assumption that each building should ideally supply the number of parking spaces that will be needed by all customers on the busiest day. This type of requirement virtually guarantees that at most times of day those parking lots are going to be mostly empty.

While parking requirements in the suburbs were high priority and demanded a lot of land, the suburbs did not consist solely in buildings, parking lots, and private land. There were some requirements for public space in the suburbs. There were two primary forms this requirement took. One was "open space" regulations. Open space regulations involved municipalities requiring commercial developers to designate a certain percentage of their project as open space. Since the requirement was usually some kind of percentage and wasn't specified, often the developer shoehorned the necessary open space into the least profitable parcels of land. These tended to be odd-shaped parcels in inconvenient locations, and consequently they didn't provide great spaces for hanging out or meeting one's neighbors. If you remember the scene I described at the beginning of the chapter, you will note that it included some public space, but it is not the kind of public space that is inviting or convenient for people to actually use.

The other kind of public space that was often required in the suburbs was playground space. As our understanding of the need for spaces for adult enjoyment and interaction has diminished, we have managed to maintain the importance of places for children to play. Even as the automobile took up a greater percentage of surface area in cities and suburbs, we continued to build playgrounds. Of course most playground parks include places for adults to sit, but those seats are usually meant for the parents (or caregivers) of the children playing in the park.

Between the abstract open space requirements and the playground requirements, it seems pretty clear that the need for adults (or even teenagers) to have a place to enjoy the day and have some social interaction isn't particularly high. While this may seem unremarkable to us, if one were to review other countries or other time periods where humans settled on the land, this would seem odd indeed. It seems that at any other time or in any other country, having ample places for people of all ages to enjoy the local setting and to socialize is a high priority. So the question becomes, Why did we start approaching the need for public space in this way? It is to that question we turn next.

Against the City

Some of the impetus for ignoring the need to provide good civic spaces for enjoyment and social interaction can be traced back to a distaste for the city and for civic life, which comes from at least two distinct sources. The first source of this anti-urban bias comes from what has been called the frontier mentality. Before we can understand the frontier mentality, we need to articulate a contrasting perspective.

In the classical tradition, cities and urban life were considered good for the development of one's character. Aristotle considered cities to be essential to our being human. They force us to interact on a regular basis with people who aren't family or close friends. This kind of frequent contact with others inevitably leads to conflict, strain, and misunderstandings. The compact nature of the city forces us to figure out ways of dealing with those people with whom we have conflict or who annoy us.

In working out conflicts with our neighbors, we often learn something about our neighbors that we didn't know before, we learn something about ourselves, and we learn how to be better communicators. These kinds of lessons develop our character and can strengthen the civic health of a place. They explain why words like "civility" and "civilized" have the same root as the word for "city" (*civitas*).

For a variety of reasons, many of the pioneers who founded this country did not stick around to "work it out" with their neighbors in their home countries. Granted, in many cases, their neighbors were not simply annoying to them but were oppressing them and actively bringing them harm. They sought a frontier in the New World that would allow them to worship God and form a new life together in relative freedom. While this was often understandable, it did help to establish a frontier mentality that we have never quite been able to shake.

Of course, the next phase of this frontier mentality was the migration from the East Coast to the West. In this case, the pioneers who led the way didn't flee persecution so much as they sought opportunity. But one can't help but also pick up on a desire to escape the confines of human community in this impulse to seek the frontier. For many, no doubt, the East Coast felt crowded and confining—physically crowded by the number of people but also perhaps socially crowded by formal, confining East Coast manners and customs.

This frontier mentality may also have been part of the draw of the suburbs. What made the suburbs attractive was not just the newer homes but also the lower density and the location at the edge of town. The suburbs felt decidedly less crowded than the city. For many, moving to the suburbs felt like moving to the country, because the adjacent land was often undeveloped. As noted in chapter 12, the suburbs instigated new housing designs, in which the house was oriented toward the backyard. The suburban house was often considered a retreat from civic life and a refuge from society.

Because the frontier mentality was fundamentally about putting distance between oneself and one's neighbor, there was not much interest in advocating spaces designed for adult social interaction. It is not the case, however, that there was a complete lack of interest in public amenities in the suburbs. There was little interest in squares and plazas, but as just noted, there was great interest in playgrounds for children.

There was also a high regard for unspoiled wilderness, although not always enough to prevent its succumbing to the insatiable appetite for land endemic to the suburban model of development. To understand the interest in these two kinds of public space, we need to turn to the second source of distaste for the city.

This second source can be traced to eighteenth-century England, especially to the influence of a group of evangelical Christians. Until then, a typical London merchant operated his business in the same building as his private home. Over the course of the eighteenth century, this pattern began to change. It was long-standing practice among the aristocracy to own an estate separate from one's primary domicile. But in the eighteenth century, some merchants had sufficient resources to purchase a country home of their own. These homes were nowhere near the scale of the aristocratic estates, but they did allow some members of the middle class to emulate some aspects of upper-class life.

As this practice spread, some merchants flipped the arrangement. They moved their families to the country. They maintained a home at the business site but used it only during the week. A typical pattern was for a merchant to spend weekends at the country home and weekdays in the city home.

Eventually, this transformed to the family maintaining one home, located in the country, and the merchant traveling to the city for work. This, of course, is a very early example of what has become a standard pattern in the American suburb. However, one specific instance of this arrangement either influenced or represented a significant shift in thinking about public life: the Clapham community.

Clapham was a residential community about five miles outside of London. It was initiated by the Thornton family, who were wealthy members of the evangelical movement. Over time, the community became a residential enclave of influential evangelicals, including John Shore (president of the Bible Society), John Grant (chairman of the East India Company), and antislavery activist William Wilberforce.

According to Robert Fishman, the Clapham community blended Christian conviction with this newly emerging residential model in such a way as to redefine civic and private life.[4] In particular, the evangelicals had concluded that city life had a corrupting effect on one's spiritual life. As Fishman puts it, "The evangelicals never tired of repeating that, if all urban social life must be rejected, the truly godly recreations were family life and direct contact with nature."[5] He then quotes the poet William Cowper:

> Domestic happiness, thou only bliss
> Of Paradise that has survived the fall![6]

> God made the country and man made the town:
> What wonder then that health and virtue, gifts
> That can alone make sweet the bitter draught
> That life holds out to all, should most abound
> And least be threaten'd in the fields and groves?
> Possess ye, therefore, . . .
> Your element.[7]

If the urban life of London was to be rejected, then Clapham would have to substitute by providing a setting for maximal exposure to family life and nature. Its houses were organized around a central commons developed in a style imitating unspoiled nature. The individual houses likewise were landscaped in a naturalistic style to create a suitable Edenic setting for the family.

The homes included a "library" that was really more of a family room. It usually opened into the garden in back. In addition to serving as an access point to the world of "nature," the library was the center of family life, a place of music, reading, poetry, and conversation. This was meant as a replacement for public life in the city: "The library and the garden outside of it were the Evangelical substitute for all of the plays, balls, visits, and coffee houses of London. Here the closed domesticated nuclear family became a reality. The social activities of London did not suddenly cease. Instead the social graces were directed inward toward the mutual education and moral betterment of the family itself."[8]

What we see beginning in Clapham for evangelicals is a growing division between the private domestic life of home and the public civic life of the city. God is seen as more present in the domestic realm, and the civic realm is mistrusted as evil. Men, of necessity, must leave the protection of the private realm and steel themselves as they enter the civic realm to do business. At day's end, they can return to the safe haven of the domestic realm to be nurtured and built up again. The women's job is to act as managers over this spiritually nurturing domestic realm. And within the domestic realm, children are given access to nature and are protected from the corrupting influence of the civic realm.

Between the frontier mentality and the spiritualization of the domestic realm, we begin to see some of the foundational values that undergird the suburban development patterns of the second half of the twentieth century. The suburban house with garage door in front and orientation toward the backyard reflects the frontier mentality by keeping each family unit cordoned off from contact with any outsiders. Very little attention or investment was given to public space for adult social interaction because the evangelicals had abandoned civic life as irredeemable. Where there was investment in public amenities, parks for children and wilderness lands got support from various groups who, like evangelicals, desired to protect and nurture children and had a strong preference for Edenic settings.

Erasing History

At around the time the automobile was radically reshaping our cities and neighborhoods through its insatiable need for space, an intellectual revolution was taking place within institutions and among thought leaders that would have a dramatic impact on the built environment. This intellectual revolution was a pervasive and multifaceted movement known as Modernism, which took shape through a series of meetings in the 1920s and 1930s and led to the creation of a document called the Athens Charter.

Modernism is too broad to be adequately described here. However, we can point to a couple of general tendencies within this movement that had a significant impact on the civic realm. The first of these tendencies was a deliberate break with history. The leaders of the Modernist movement

158

tended to see history as too messy and capricious to serve as a helpful guide for the future. They had a disdain for tradition in general and for the traditional forms of civic life. Modernists saw themselves as making a heroic break with thousands of years of misguided impulses and replacing them with rational and efficient plans for the city of the future.

Another major impact of Modernism on civic life was the tendency to look at the city from thirty thousand feet. This led Modernists to put a lot of stock in master plans and models that looked neat and intelligible on maps and in scale models. Unfortunately, after they were built, these projects looked very different when the people who had to interact with them on a daily basis experienced them on the ground.

The Danish architect and planner Jan Gehl has done a great job of exposing the problems of Modernist city planning. Gehl was trained as a Modernist but soon became convinced that most of his training was not helpful in creating spaces that people would enjoy using. He started spending time doing research by hanging out in the civic realm just noticing how people used (or didn't use) civic space. Gehl was convinced that people generally knew what they liked and that when a good space was provided for them, they would choose to spend time there. Gehl wasn't impressed with architectural renderings of formally beautiful spaces and people enjoying those spaces if real people didn't choose to spend time there.

The legacy of the Modernist movement for civic life is different than that of the automobile. The latter caused existing civic space to disappear and diminished the amount of civic space that would be built in new developments. The Modernist movement ensured that whenever civic space did get built, it would be underutilized and ultimately unsuccessful in encouraging people to gather and enjoy time engaging one another and the places that they live.

Appropriating Eden

In chapter 10 we noted that all of us carry within us a vague deep-seated awarenss of alienation from some good and satisfying place in which we can feel at home. Some attempts at leaning in to that impulse have been more successful than others. The slow march of human history has led to the development of traditions in town planning and construction of civic space that have been relatively useful in developing spaces that draw people in and provide places of respite. Interestingly enough, it has been in the last one hundred years or so in which we seem to have lost our ability to create satisfying civic settings.

We do have in this country some examples of settings for public and social interaction. Perhaps there are places like this near you. In many cases, those places were built in cities before the onset of automobile-oriented development. I've been fortunate to live most of my life in neighborhoods that were developed prior to World War II; consequently, I have enjoyed good places for public interaction close to my home.

Over the past decade or so, interest in building places intentionally for civic interaction has increased. Many cities are taking scenic waterfronts that had become automobile oriented and redeveloping them for pedestrian use and civic interaction. But for the majority of people, there are not good spaces for public and social interaction within walking distance. It's hit or miss.

Interestingly, people seem drawn to environments with good civic spaces even if they are very different from what they've experienced.

One of the more popular vacation destinations in this country is Disneyland. What makes Disneyland so enjoyable is the picture it evokes of old-school civic interaction, with its Main Street USA and its absence of automobiles. Americans also enjoy traveling to Europe and are charmed by the cities' plazas and walkable streets. But as much as people are drawn to vacation in destinations with good civic spaces, they don't generally believe that these kinds of spaces could exist where they actually live, as part of their everyday lives.

The reasons we currently lack good civic spaces lie in a few waves of dominant thought patterns that swept our country at times and strongly influenced how we stewarded (or failed to steward) our civic space. At one point we became enamored of the automobile and thought that the future belonged to this form of transportation. At another point we believed that we could "fix" thousands of years of accumulated wisdom with a more rational and scientific way of organizing the city. And a particular wing of the Christian community became convinced that civic life was irredeemably evil and that God was more present in private life and in nature than he was in the civic realm.

Some perspectives that shaped many of the decisions behind our lack of good civic space are no longer influential. However, their legacy continues to shape our daily lives through the ways they have impacted the physical shape of our cities and neighborhoods. As perceptions and perspectives about the relative value of public space change, we can respond in various ways. We can note our disappointment and withdraw further into the various screens described in chapter 12. Or we can fan the flames of our disaffection and begin to imagine how things can be different. My hope is that we will risk trying to recover the long-standing heritage of civic life that has been part of civilized society for thousands of years. In part 6 we explore concrete ways to pursue this goal.

FOURTEEN

BUSY

The Crisis of Belonging in Story

How We Are

"So, how are you?"

"Great, I'm just super busy right now."

"Oh yeah, me too. It's just crazy."

How many times have you had this conversation? Being busy seems to be the new normal for lots of people.

Most of us have come to accept this as a reality of contemporary life. And busyness seems to be a major factor in our belonging deficit. For many, there just isn't enough time to squeeze everything in. When we get home from working a full day, we face another set of tasks on the home front. Kids need to be picked up from school or practice; dinner needs to be prepared, lunches made, and dishes done; kids need help with homework; and bills need to be paid. After we get everyone settled for bed, we barely have enough energy left to get ourselves to bed. We watch a few minutes of our latest show and fall asleep. This unceasing daily grind leaves almost no time for the kinds of activities and involvements that might help us experience a greater sense of belonging to the places where we live.

So the question needs to be asked: Why are we so busy all the time? It certainly isn't an obvious outcome of current conditions. We have access to an incredible number of devices specifically designed to save us time and effort. We have machines to quickly clean our clothes and our dishes. Sending an email is quicker and easier than typing a letter. Writing a memo or a report on a computer is much easier than creating a physical document. We have lawn mowers to cut our grass and furnaces to warm our homes.

If we could travel back in time and describe to our great-grandparents all of our time-saving innovations, they might picture our lives as being very different than they actually are. They might picture us working three days a week. They'd likely assume we'd have time to take a leisurely stroll with our families, shoot the breeze with our neighbors, or get involved with a model train group or some other volunteer organization. They might think that our biggest problem would be figuring out what to do with all of our free time.

If we tried to explain to our great-grandparents that we actually might be more busy and more harried than they were, they would have a hard time believing us. How could we possibly have less discretionary time with all of these time- and labor-saving devices?

Denying Death

In chapter 11 we discovered that the story we believe we are inhabiting can have a significant influence on our behaviors and choices. In that chapter we noted that it is common within our culture to live within a story of fear in which the lives of our children and our lives are constantly in danger. This story of ubiquitous danger can lead us into a condition of bondage in which we drastically restrict the kinds of activities we allow our children and ourselves to participate in. Against that common cultural refrain, we noted how the gospel can be powerfully liberating with its story of a returning King and his victory over death.

In this chapter, we consider the possibility that inhabiting this story of fear and danger may also be connected to the common state of busyness that we are experiencing. Underneath the story of danger and fear perhaps lurks the unspoken fear of death. It has long been noted that Western civilization in general, and American culture in particular, is characterized by a strong impulse to deny our own mortality.[1] One way that we have responded to our unspoken fear of death is to attempt to eliminate every real or percieved risk for our children and ourselves. Another aspect of this strategy to deny our mortality may also involve keeping ourselves so busy that we don't need to think about such morbid topics.

Regardless of whether a fear of death is behind the busy condition of each and every one of our lives, most of us do live in and participate in a culture that keeps us too busy to think about much beyond managing our increasingly harried schedules. And the aggregate trends that have led to these cultural habits may very well find their origin in a denial of death. Some of the more direct causes of this culture of busyness involve fragmentation, consumerism, and an obscure monastic malady known as acedia.

Fragmentation

One reason for this lack of discretionary time is that our lives have become more spread out and fragmented, thanks in large part to the first piece of glass—the automobile windshield. As we saw in chapter 12, the automobile-oriented style of development put a windshield between us and our neighbors. But it did something else as well. Auto-oriented development has parceled out nearly every activity outside of our homes into different geographical locations. And even when we don't absolutely have to drive a great distance for a particular activity, we often will drive anyway, because driving a lot has become normal for us. This fragmentation and the time spent in our cars is eating up quite a bit of our discretionary time.

We purchase our homes to achieve maximal square footage, desirable features, and access to good schools or good hospitals; we give only a little thought to how far our home is from our work or our spouse's.

No longer do our kids automatically go to neighborhood schools, so we often have to drive them across town. And sports have moved from the neighborhood park to the massive sports complex in the industrial part of our city. Driving twenty to thirty minutes to church is not considered excessive. We may have a grocery store a few miles away, but we drive the extra distance to Costco because the food is cheaper there.

Depending on the size of our family and our obligations, this fragmented, driving-oriented lifestyle can feel like a three-ring circus. One spouse picks up one kid at school and then rushes her across town to drop her off at soccer practice, only to rush off to another school with a different dismissal time. The other kid needs to be driven to Target to get a display board for a school project. Meanwhile, the other spouse is rushing to finish the grocery shopping in time to pick up the first kid from soccer practice. They rendezvous at home with just enough time to eat some Bagel Bites and a premade salad before one kid needs to be driven back to school for play practice.

This type of fragmented life is largely driven by the design principles of postwar suburban development. But it's not entirely accurate to blame fragmentation on the suburbs as a general concept. The concept of the suburbs goes back further than our postwar version, though earlier types of suburban arrangements didn't have this kind of fragmentation. Around the late nineteenth and early twentieth centuries in the Northeast, "streetcar suburbs" were fairly common.

"Streetcar suburbs" was the name given to neighborhoods and small towns that sprouted up around streetcar stops along the lines that connected to major metropolises like Boston and New York City. Typically, the breadwinner used the streetcar to travel to and from his (rarely her) workplace in the city. The rest of the family spent the weekdays quite happily in the streetcar suburb without ever having to get into a car.

Everything needed for daily life was within walking distance of home. Within a mile or two, one would find schools, grocery stores, parks, a library, a hair salon, a hardware store, and a church. The car, if the family had one, might be used on the weekend to drive into the country or back to the city to enjoy a cultural event. Life in a streetcar suburb was simpler and much less busy than life in the typical postwar American suburb.

Consumerism

The postwar era witnessed a rapidly expanding economy and good job prospects for returning GIs. The postwar suburbs combined with government-sponsored home loans to allow more people than ever to achieve the American Dream of homeownership.

Corporations jumped on this opportunity and began making an important shift in their advertising strategy. No longer were corporations selling their products to target a need identified by potential customers. Advertisers now began to create needs that consumers didn't know they had, leading to a growing culture of consumerism. The consumerist narrative held that the acquisition of stuff was a marker of the good life, and that more things led to more happiness.

The house in the suburbs with the white picket fence was a key part of the consumerist narrative in two ways. It was a consumer product par excellence, but it also served as an ideal container for consumer items. Farther away from the city, lots and houses could be larger. Filling one's house with the newest and best products became a national pastime.

As houses got filled with stuff, consumers realized that they needed larger houses. House size in the United States has been increasing steadily since the 1950s, while family size has been shrinking. In 1950, the average new single-family home was 983 square feet, and the average family size was 3.37 members. In 2017, the average house size had expanded to 2,599 square feet, while the average family size had declined to 2.54 members.[2]

As this cycle of consumerism continued in the second half of the twentieth century, corporations helped accelerate its growth by becoming more sophisticated in their marketing. By updating and improving products every year, they caused consumers to become dissatisfied with earlier models.

Of course, larger houses, more stuff, and the latest models of things all cost money. And Americans found themselves working harder and for more hours to pay for this lifestyle. For this, and a number of other reasons, it became increasingly common for both parents to work outside of the home, which made juggling children's needs and other home responsibilities increasingly complicated.

Acedia

With all of this busyness, it is interesting that the core issue may have something to do with a concept related to sloth. There are more than a few cultural observers who claim that the pressing sin of our time is acedia. *Acedia* is a Latin word that literally means "an inability to care" but eventually became translated as "sloth." This seems a contradiction to everything we've said so far, but acedia is a much more complex concept than is normally captured in the popular understanding of sloth.

Acedia is not about chronic inactivity but rather about a deep failure to care, which we try to fix through frenetic activity. Acedia can be thought of as a failure or an unwillingness to engage in the place or activity to which one is called. Monks knew it as the "noonday demon." During work or in prayer, time may seem to pass so slowly it feels as if the sun is stuck halfway through its course.

Kathleen Norris discovered this word through a book from the fourth-century monk Evagrius Ponticus:

> The demon of *acedia*—also called the noonday demon—is the one that causes the most serious trouble of all. He presses his attack upon the monk about the fourth hour and besieges the soul until the eighth hour. First of all he makes it seem that the sun barely moves, if at all, and that the day is fifty hours long. Then he constrains the monk to look constantly out the windows, to walk outside the cell, to gaze carefully at the sun to determine how far it stands from the ninth hour [or lunchtime], to look this way and now that to see if perhaps [one of the brethren appears from his cell]. Then too he instills in the heart of the monk a hatred for the place, a hatred for his very life itself, a hatred for manual labor. He leads him to reflect that charity has departed from among the brethren, that there is no one to give encouragement. Should there be someone at this period who happens to offend him in some way or other, this too the demon uses to contribute further to his hatred. This demon drives him along to desire other sites where he can more easily procure life's necessities, more readily find work and make a real success of himself. He goes on to suggest that, after all, it is not the place that is the basis of pleasing the Lord. God is to be adored everywhere. He joins to those

reflections the memory of his dear ones and of his former way of life. He depicts life stretching out for a long period of time, and brings before the mind's eye the toil of the ascetic struggle and, as the saying has it, leaves no leaf unturned to induce the monk to forsake his cell and drop out of the fight. No other demon follows close upon the heels of this one (when he is defeated) but only a state of deep peace and inexpressible joy arise out of this struggle.[3]

Acedia is about not being able to be fully present in whatever task is at hand. It can sometimes manifest as lethargy, but in our culture it more commonly takes the form of frenetic activity. We don't feel meaningfully engaged in our work, so we pack more work in, subconsciously hoping that an increase in quantity will increase meaning. In an interview with the *Los Angeles Times*, Norris put it this way: "We appear to be anything but slothful, yet that is exactly what we are, as we do more and care less, and feel pressured to do still more."[4]

What is interesting about acedia is how the word has come in and out of use since the fourth century. For a time it was rarely used; then it returned around the same time as many of the other changes we've been looking at in our study of belonging. "The timeline in Oxford English Dictionary online is phenomenal for this word. The most interesting part was that [acedia] was marked as obsolete in the 1933 OED, but after World War II it was back: Why did we need this word again?"[5]

I suspect that the twentieth-century return of acedia is connected to the automobile and consumer culture that we've been discussing. Both the logic of extreme mobility made possible by the automobile and the impulse to seek happiness through consumption have to do with pulling our attention away from the contingencies of the places where we live. We're not monks with trowel in hand wondering what better settings might await us on the other side of the distant hills, but there may be something similar at play as we rush off to the Apple Store to secure the latest version of the iPhone.

As we saw in chapter 10, we are creatures wired to desire beauty, and each of us has been placed in environments in which we can experience shalom. But pursuing beauty and seeking peace within the constraints of the places we live (and in the company of the others who live there) takes work and patience. Rather than seeking to soothe our acedia through activity, we may have to slow down and pay more attention to the people and the places close to home.

Laziness

Eugene Peterson claims that busy pastors are lazy because they let everyone else tell them what they are supposed to do rather than do the hard work of deciding what they are called to do.[6] This idea has had a profound impact on how I understand my work as a pastor over the years. But I don't think that the wisdom of this notion should be restricted to pastors.

I suspect that much of the busyness we experience currently stems from a combination of personal and cultural laziness. In the name of rationality, we've allowed so-called experts to break apart the natural form of the neighborhood and chop up our daily life into a geographically diffuse system of activity zones. We've allowed ourselves to be persuaded by profit-seeking corporations that happiness can be had only if we get the latest upgrade. And we've been unwilling to put much work into seeing beauty and seeking peace in the places we live, choosing instead to flit here and there, seeking the latest trend and the most compelling distraction.

As I suggest above, it may be that this laziness, at its root, comes from a deep-seated impulse to deny our own mortality. If that is the case, then those of us who claim to be citizens of God's kingdom can begin to break this cycle by remembering that we are part of a story in which death has been defeated by a righteous King. Claiming this larger truth won't automatically make our lives less fragmented, quash our consumeristic impulses, or allow us to dwell comfortably in place. But if properly understood, it will give us an important and necessary foothold to do the hard work of cultivating lives that are defined by more than frenetic activity.

Fixing Busy

The next time someone asks you how you're doing in a casual conversation, pay attention to how you answer. If the first thought that pops into your head is "busy," let me encourage you to not treat that condition as a function of modern-day forces beyond your control. Consider the possibility that our lives don't have to be always busy. Busy is a denial strategy more appropriate to those who have reason to fear death.

Busy also is an enemy of belonging. And, while a little more elusive, belonging is much more satisfying than busy. If we accept that basic premise, we can choose to lean in to a different set of values both individually and at the societal level that prioritize belonging over busy.

These choices are neither simple nor easy. In many ways they are countercultural and often feel counterintuitive. Part of what's countercultural about pushing against our busy culture isn't just the choices themselves but the overall structure of the choice. We need to push past the range of choices presented to us. It may be helpful to think of this next step like an alcoholic sitting at a bar and deciding she has been drinking too much beer. She has a lot of alternatives to beer available in the bar, but most of them are bad ones. To address her problem she needs to physically leave the bar and join a group of others committed to helping one another form a community of care as together they resist the temptation to drink.

In thinking about busyness and belonging, we've been conditioned to think of our choices only in terms of individualistic consumer choices. And we've been conditioned to think of making choices primarily as something we do only with our brains. To break the cycle of busy, and to find our way back to belonging by connecting with the people and places of our lives, we must broaden our understanding of what it means to make choices. We explore this idea in the next section.

PART FIVE

THE **SHAPES** CHOICES TAKE

There is a well-known parable about a man looking for his keys at night under a lamp-post. When asked if he is sure this is where he dropped them, he confesses that he thinks he may have dropped his keys somewhere across the street. When asked why he's not looking over there, he answers, "The light is better here."

This parable is used to illustrate the foolishness of utilizing methods based on their case of use rather than their effectiveness. As we turn our attention toward solutions to the crisis of belonging, we need to acknowledge that some of our first impulses will involve methods that are easy or comfortable but not necessarily effective.

In the following chapter, we explore the limitations of solving the crisis of belonging through individual consumer choices. The subsequent chapter disabuses us of the notion that the development pattern we've followed for the past seventy years in this country resulted from individual free-market choices. The final chapter of this section demonstrates some of the problems with seeking Cartesian solutions—trying to get our thinking right.

FIFTEEN

COMMUNALLY
SHAPED CHOICES

Solutions as Consumer Choice

The range of problems that can be addressed with a credit card is astounding. Unfair child labor practices can be solved by purchasing clothing that is certified "sweat free." Purchasing cruelty-free makeup will prevent animals from being mistreated anywhere. Picking up a few cans of dolphin-safe tuna will ensure that no dolphin is ever unnecessarily killed. And of course the entire environmental crisis can be solved simply by plunking down a chunk of change for a shiny new Prius.

At some level, we all know that purchasing an item that doesn't contribute to an intractable problem is quite a long way from solving that particular problem. But lots of people are still drawn to this kind of "ethical shopping" as a way of responding to the difficult realities of this increasingly harsh world. Opportunities to do the right thing with one's credit card are popping up in just about every conceivable arena. This fact alone signals the increasing interest in this practice. Ethical shopping represents a significant market. And I don't think that this practice is just a public relations stunt dreamed up in corporate "community relations" departments. If there wasn't a market for it, these opportunities would eventually dry up.

Please don't hear me as being critical of such practices. This kind of response to global problems makes some sense. The kinds of situations we are confronted with every time we open a newspaper or browse our preferred newsfeed are unspeakably heartbreaking. Since there is very little that we can actually do to solve these problems, the least we can do is to avoid contributing to them by being a little careful with how we spend our money. And ethical shopping isn't completely useless. Our purchases in some cases do help support an alternative economy that can be a huge blessing to a few folks. The success of farmers markets has had a significant impact on the food industry and has allowed many small farms to thrive. And being deliberate in our consumer choices and using everyday objects as "conversation starters" can help raise awareness of the issue to other people within our circle of influence.

While all of this is true, I also believe that there is something particularly revealing about the attractiveness of these kinds of solutions for contemporary Americans. What makes ethical shopping a preferred kind of solution for us is that it doesn't require us to make any significant changes and doesn't challenge any of our unspoken cultural values. It doesn't impinge on our individualism or require anything other than a modest financial sacrifice. We don't have to cooperate with others, adjust our schedule, or change our lifestyle in any way to participate. We make a basic consumer choice, pay for it, and get on with our day with little or no perceptible difference in how our day would have gone had we made a different choice.

Abraham Maslow famously quipped, "I suppose it is tempting, if the only tool you have is a hammer, to treat everything as if it were a nail."[1] And I think this is somewhat true of how we tend to see large-scale problems in our culture. At some level, we understand that buying a sweat-free T-shirt isn't going to end exploitative child labor practices, and yet we can't really imagine what else we could do to help solve that particular problem.

Actually, if we put a little time into it, we probably could think of some more-effective strategies for addressing a problem such as exploitative child labor practices, but the solutions that we would likely envision would be costly, messy, and risky to us personally. And so we end up preempting any such thought experiment and focusing on "what I can do." And while buying that sweat-free T-shirt doesn't solve the problem, it does alleviate some of our guilt.

In chapter 17 (spoiler alert) we will explore the possibility that walking to work, school, and worship impacts the way that we look at and experience the world. For many people, however, that realization will be nothing more than an interesting thought experiment, because for many people walking as a form of transportation to any destination is all but impossible. The only realistic way to get to work, school, or the ball field is to take a car, because each one of those activities is likely to be out of walking distance from where we live. Waking up one morning and deciding to start walking to places is not tenable, because it cannot be facilitated by making a simple purchase at a store. It's nearly impossible to repackage walking in terms of some kind of ethical shopping issue, and therefore for most of us it's hardly worth thinking about.[2] From what we know about our preference for solutions that involve making a simple consumer choice, it should not surprise us to discover that many people think of the idea of walking to work, shop, play, or worship as a somewhat attractive but quaint idea with no possibility of being accomplished by an ordinary person in the "real world."

Ad Hoc and Fundamental Choices

If we look at this issue a little more closely, we discover that one would be able to choose walking as a regular form of transportation simply by making one purchase. That one purchase is not a pair of walking shoes. The purchase I am referring to is . . . wait for it . . . a house. Yes, I'm talking about the decision to purchase a house—four walls, a roof, and maybe a yard that you spend most of your adult life paying off. The important thing is that the house one purchases is in a walkable neighborhood (i.e., has a high Walk Score; Walk Score is a popular online tool for determining the walkability of a particular neighborhood).[3] Alternatively, one could buy a condo or rent an apartment in a walkable neighborhood.

While it's true that one cannot put a house on a credit card, a home is technically a single consumer purchase. As such, it is an especially impactful consumer decision. If one were to buy a house in a neighborhood that includes a mix of building types (residential, commercial, recreational) within a one-mile radius, one could walk to many destinations quite easily and conveniently.

But buying a house is quite a bit different from other consumer choices that we might make, such as buying a T-shirt, some laundry soap, or even a car. Buying a house is not only more of a major investment than other purchases; the purchase of a house will likely also impact our schedules, our relationships with others, and our lifestyle. Buying a house can be called a "fundamental choice" and is very different from more simple choices we make throughout the day.

According to the field of moral philosophy, we can divide the ethical choices we make between "ad hoc" and "fundamental." Ad hoc choices involve a single decision that is relatively self-contained. Buying a sweat-free T-shirt or a Prius can be considered ad hoc ethical choices. Other kinds of ad hoc ethical choices include the decision to give a homeless person some money, the decision to not exceed the speed limit, and the decision to say something when a cashier gives too much change.

Unlike ad hoc choices, fundamental ethical choices involve a single decision that will significantly influence one's subsequent choices. Deciding whether to have a baby is a fundamental ethical choice, for example. Prior to having a baby, a couple could make relatively simple decisions about how to use their discretionary time based on a cost-benefit analysis. The question of how to spend one's evening is a relatively uncomplicated decision for someone without a child: Do I want to go out or stay in for dinner? How will these options affect my budget?

After having a baby, these choices become more complex, as one must now consider the needs of the child as well as the capacity each parent has for caring for that child. Choosing whether to have a child is a fundamental ethical choice, but that fact is not altogether surprising. They may not know exactly how, but most couples understand that having a baby will radically change their lives and have a major impact on how they use their discretionary time.

Choosing where to live is also a fundamental ethical choice. Unlike the choice of whether to have a baby, making a choice about where to live is for many people a surprising kind of fundamental decision. That is to say, the way choosing where to live impacts subsequent choices is often not expected and sometimes not even perceived by the person (or persons) making the choice. This is especially true when the home purchaser is following our culture's standard script for how to make such a decision.

When choosing a house in which to live, many people consider square footage, amenities, view, and (depending on one's age demographic) proximity to good schools or medical care. One might give slight consideration to the distance between one's home and place(s) of work, but if that distance is under twenty miles, it won't usually be a major consideration. In any case, many buyers wouldn't consider the idea of buying a home close enough to walk or bike to work a realistic goal.[4]

Nor would all buyers think about the impact of the location of their home on the quantity of automobile trips in their day. In the early part of the twentieth century, a person living in one of the streetcar suburbs surrounding Boston might choose to commute via car (as opposed to the train). But that trip would likely be the only car ride from that household on that day. Everything else (trips to the store, the park, and the bank) could be accomplished on foot.

In the twenty-first century, the average American takes close to four separate car trips per day.[5] The fact that each member of the family has no option but to drive to go out for coffee, get groceries, get a haircut, or see a friend is likely not a consideration in purchasing the home.

Purchasing a single-family detached home surrounded exclusively by other single-family detached homes (as opposed to commercial businesses and apartment buildings) is a fundamental ethical decision because it will have a major impact on each and every decision regarding form of transportation. Even though people shopping for a home might grasp the implications of making this choice, it may feel like an exercise in futility to analyze this decision so critically when there seems to be only one realistic option for many people.

177

But is living in a neighborhood where driving is required really the only option? There are, in fact, neighborhoods in which one could live and be able to walk to school, shop, work, play, and even worship. The neighborhood I live in is one. From our house my wife and I can both walk or bike to our separate places of work, to the bank, and to get coffee, and our kids have been able to walk or bike to their preschool and their elementary, middle, and high schools. This is true of the home we live in now, and it has been true of every home and each of the four neighborhoods that we have lived in as a family. Living in a walkable neighborhood is important to our family, and we know of other families who have made similar decisions.

Those committed to living in a place where walking and biking are viable forms of transportation discover a couple realities pretty quickly. The first is that most walkable neighborhoods tend to have been built before about 1950, although more and more homes in walkable neighborhoods are being built in the twenty-first century. The second is that walkable neighborhoods can be quite a bit more expensive than their automobile-oriented counterparts in the suburbs.

These two realities are not unrelated. From about 1950 until quite recently, for reasons discussed below, the dominant neighborhood style was the automobile-oriented suburban style. This meant that the supply of suburban houses (especially new houses) was much more plentiful than the supply of homes in walkable neighborhoods. According to simple economics, an increase in supply tends to be correlated with a decrease in price. Once the suburban style had become fully entrenched, purchasing that sort of home was the cheapest and most convenient option for most home buyers. If you want maximum square footage and amenities for minimal price, buying a home in an automobile-oriented suburb is the most obvious choice. That means most people will choose to purchase a single-family detached home surrounded by other single-family detached homes and won't be able to walk or bike to many destinations.

Earlier we considered the difference between ad hoc and fundamental ethical decisions for individuals. As we think about why a home in an automobile-oriented development has been the cheapest and most convenient option for the past half century, we approach a different category of decision that exponentially ramps up the concept of a fundamental ethical decision. We are talking here about policy decisions made by our government at the national and the local levels. Some of the policy decisions that we have made in this country concerning zoning, lending practices, and infrastructure investment have had a significant influence on millions of fundamental ethical decisions for households throughout the country. Below we examine a few of those policy decisions.

SIXTEEN

POLICY-SHAPED CHOICES

When I say we need to seek approaches to problems that are communal as opposed to individualistic/consumeristic, I'm not suggesting something new or radical. We've been making choices like this for as long as we have existed as a country. These kinds of choices are made at the societal level and are known as "policy." We don't always think of policy in terms of choice, because policy is decided by policy makers and experts often outside of our purview. And once a policy is determined and established, it just becomes part of the reality that we deal with when building a house or starting a new business. Policies tend to remain in place in perpetuity regardless of their efficacy or relation to common sense.

The United States embraces a free-market economy, which leads people to think that most decisions are made by rational consumers via a simple cost-benefit analysis. That is not strictly true, because the cost and the benefit of certain decisions have been significantly shaped by policies adopted years before the consumer choice is made.

As noted in chapter 15, many people choose to purchase homes in automobile-oriented suburbs because they tend to be cheaper than homes in walkable neighborhoods. And we know from Economics 101 that the cost of a house has a lot to do with supply and demand. But the supply of houses in automobile-oriented subdivisions has been largely determined by policies. Most people choose to bring their children to school in a car. But driving is the best (or only) option for transporting a child to school because of policies. Here, we will look at a few policies that have had a significant impact on the choices that shape our experience of belonging.

Zoning

The first policy that has had a major impact on belonging has been zoning. As noted in chapter 7, zoning is a policy tool that divides land into separate zones in order to allocate buildings into distinct geographical areas according to their use. In its early form, zoning separated commercial from residential buildings, but over time the separations became more fine-grained and complex. Residential was divided up according to housing size (gigantic, large, medium, small, condos, and apartments). Zones for commercial were divided between retail, manufacturing, and office. And there were specialized zones for medical facilities, recreation, and so on.

Zoning in the United States technically began in New York City in 1916; in this first case, it was used to prevent skyscrapers from blocking out too much sunlight from the streets. By the end of World War II, zoning shifted into a heavy-handed tool used by municipalities to separate types of activity into different geographical areas. Zoning in its heyday wasn't applied primarily in city centers such as New York but rather in the newly developing areas on the fringes of historic cities. During the latter half of the twentieth century, it had become an almost universal mode of land-use regulation for just about every municipality in this country and was used to create the contemporary suburbs.

A watershed event for zoning, however, was a Supreme Court case in 1926, *Village of Euclid v. Ambler Realty Co.*, in which the court ruled that cities did have rights to restrict land uses according to functional zones. Prior to this decision, land use *was* regulated. But it was done primarily through nuisance laws. If someone was planning to build something in your neighborhood that was dangerous, noisy, or smelly, the city could deem that project incompatible with the residential character of the neighborhood and prohibit it.

The Supreme Court case came about when the Village of Euclid (a suburb of Cleveland) passed a zoning law prohibiting commercial buildings and apartment buildings in a particular residential zone of the town. A local real estate company (Ambler Realty) owned land in the newly designated residential section and planned to develop some of that land for commercial purposes. The owners of Ambler Realty believed that the creation of an exclusively residential zone made its land less valuable and therefore constituted an unfair violation of their land-use rights.

The court decided in favor of Euclid primarily on the basis of public safety—particularly the safety of children. Justice Sutherland, who wrote the majority opinion, made the claim that having buildings for commercial use in the midst of a residential neighborhood would be unsafe for this vulnerable population: "Some of the grounds for this conclusion are promotion of the health and security from injury of children and others by separating dwelling houses from territory devoted to trade and industry."[1]

This, of course, makes sense when we think of commercial as a cement factory or a tannery located in a residential neighborhood. But "commercial" is a pretty broad brush; it includes such things as hair salons, coffee shops, and corner groceries. Considering the full range of "commercial," it becomes a bit harder to see what the public safety issue is.

In chapter 7 we saw that prohibiting a coffee shop in a residential neighborhood had more to do with banishing strangers from the neighborhood than protecting public safety. We can continue the conversation by asking why a residential apartment building should be prohibited from existing in a neighborhood that includes single-family detached residences. Or, to be more specific, how does the presence of apartments pose a public safety threat?

The real reason has nothing to do with public safety. The fundamental issue for this particular part of the zoning decision had to do with income segregation: "Very often the apartment house is a mere parasite, constructed in order to take advantage of the open spaces and attractive surroundings created by the residential character of the district. Moreover, the coming of one apartment house is followed by others, interfering by their height and bulk with the free circulation of air and monopolizing the rays of the sun which otherwise would fall upon the smaller homes."[2] Let's examine the logic behind this statement. On the one hand, it does seem to fall in line with one of the original applications of zoning (the zoning laws in New York City preventing tall buildings from blocking the sunlight).

But take a moment to read the statement more carefully. The apartment building is described as a "parasite"—that is, "constructed in order to take advantage of the open spaces and attractive surroundings created by the residential character of the district." Are not apartment buildings also "residential"? And given everything else that has been said about children, one critic of Euclid quipped, "Does Justice Sutherland know that apartment buildings contain children as well?"[3] It appears that when Justice Sutherland uses the word "residential" here, what he really means is "for residents wealthy enough to buy single-family detached homes."

Under the guise of maximizing sunbeams (for health reasons?), which fall upon the detached homes, then, *Euclid* cemented what would become the rather intractable practice of keeping people of differing income levels separated from one another. On some levels, this is a normal, even acceptable practice. People of means will often pay for the privilege of being surrounded by people of their own socioeconomic class; it's part of the rationale for exclusive country clubs. But what we see in *Euclid* is a legal precedent that encourages municipalities not just to allow but to promote large-scale segregation of a population based on socioeconomic status. The fact that it does so under the guise of the health and well-being of children makes it slightly more insidious.

Another aspect of the story of residential development patterns in this country involves excluding racial minorities from certain neighborhoods through a lending practice known as "redlining." Fortunately, this practice was deemed illegal and was effectively ended by the 1970s.

We are justifiably proud of the fact that it is no longer legal to exclude someone from buying a house in a particular neighborhood because of their ethnic or cultural background. However, we take it for granted that people should cluster together according to very fine graduations of price points they can afford. Or to put it another way, we consider it a fundamental right to exclude everyone of a lower economic status from our neighborhood. This has historically not been the case in the United States, and it is not typically the case in other countries today. The neighborhood I live in consists primarily of single-family detached homes, but on just about every block there also exists an apartment building and/or condominiums.

Please don't read me here as being more radical than I actually am. I have no particular qualms about individuals owning larger and more luxurious homes than their neighbors if they can afford them. My concern has more to do with the practice of excluding all but one social class from a particular neighborhood. And to be quite honest, some of my concern stems not just from a heart for the destitute. A wider variety of housing options in a neighborhood is often a prerequisite for maintaining a lively and diverse population including young professionals, the elderly, artsy bohemians, craftsmen, teachers, police officers, and the like. To take just one example, I think that it is advantageous for the teachers of our children to live in the neighborhood if possible. But that will rarely occur if the school happens to be located in an upper-class neighborhood where all the houses are on five-acre lots.

Euclid became a landmark case for land-use policy. The practice of establishing particular zones for particular uses is sometimes referred to as Euclidian zoning. Once *Euclid* established the precedent that municipalities could restrict private land uses into geographical zones, most cities pushed to adopt their own zoning laws. Euclidian zoning evolved into a kind of bizarre planning impulse to segregate and consolidate every kind of activity and worked against the more organic and complex way that cities and neighborhoods had historically come together.

During the second half of the twentieth century, these zoning practices were extended and applied in multiple areas of life. As that happened, we quickly dropped even the pretense of connecting them to public safety. Not only did residential houses get separated by price, but neighborhood sports fields became clustered into massive sports complexes. Poor people were clustered into zones of projects or other low-income housing areas. Even the elderly were clustered into retirement homes, away from the young.

We now can hardly imagine daily life before zoning. No retirement homes: a person could be too old to drive and still live in relative independence in a walkable neighborhood. No "soccer moms": kids generally could walk to a local park for practice and might need a ride to a game across town. Now a person too old to drive must be shipped off to a retirement home, and a youngster who wants to play sports is lucky to spend as much time on a field as she does in the back seat of a parent's car.

Lending

Zoning wasn't the only factor pushing twentieth-century culture toward automobile-oriented development. In addition to the political change brought about by *Euclid*, other institutional factors contributed to and even accelerated our shift in this direction. One of these factors was homeownership policies.

In 1934, the National Housing Act was enacted to help energize the housing market following the Great Depression. From this act the Federal Housing Administration (FHA) was created. The FHA provided long-term low-interest mortgages for middle-class families. This program has been wildly successful in encouraging homeownership; however, during the postwar era, it helped create an institutional culture that had a corrosive effect on the traditional neighborhood.

For a home to qualify for an FHA-supported loan, it needed to be new construction. From the perspective of minimizing risk, this was a sensible stipulation. However, the impact that this had on the housing market was to divert a huge number of potential homeowners away from older traditional neighborhoods into the suburbs. If one

wanted to purchase a home in a walkable pre–World War II neighborhood, one would most likely not qualify for an FHA loan. But if
one wanted to purchase a newly constructed home in an automobile-
oriented suburb, one would be more likely to qualify for a loan. The
FHA has since made adjustments to such policies, but the impact of
bias during decades of home building has left an indelible imprint
on the landscape.

The FHA virtually guaranteed ongoing investment in the suburbs
while simultaneously starving the inner cities and older residential
neighborhoods of new investment. This policy-level change, perhaps
more than any other, is responsible for the fact that purchasing a home
in the suburbs is the least expensive and most convenient option for
most home buyers today.

Infrastructure

Another factor leading to automobile dependency was how we invested
public funds. In short, we developed a habit of spending lavishly on
roads and highway construction while limiting investment in public
transit.

A major influencer of postwar development patterns was the Federal
Highway Act of 1956. This act was initiated by President Eisenhower
and over ten years authorized $25 billion for construction of forty-
one thousand miles of roadway—the largest public works project in
American history.

Around the same time, not only was investment in public transit
being decreased but deliberate efforts were made to dismantle the public
transit that was already in place.

From the 1920s to the 1950s General Motors operated a subsidiary
corporation that existed to acquire and convert rail companies to bus
companies in municipalities across the country. The purpose of this
endeavor was to increase the demand for motorized vehicles. Over this
time, they managed to convert over one hundred streetcar systems in
Los Angeles, St. Louis, Philadelphia, Baltimore, Salt Lake City, and

other cities. A federal grand jury found them guilty of conspiracy, and they were fined $5,000 for their activities.[4]

Such substantial federal investment in road infrastructure and disinvestment in public transit established a pattern for development that would persist for the rest of the twentieth century. Development decisions were made with the assumption of universal adult automobile ownership. This in turn meant that people could purchase houses farther and farther from their places of work and their other destinations.

What wasn't considered in pursuing a more spread-out automobile-oriented development policy was its additional costs. Roads are not the only infrastructure for which municipalities are responsible. And the more spread out a population becomes, the more expensive it becomes to supply the needed infrastructure. Under the ground, water and sewer systems need to be expanded. Above ground is electrical, phone lines, and cable. Municipalities need to supply emergency services such as police and firefighters as well as maintenance services such as street sweeping and landscaping.

Public transit is particularly challenging. Besides fewer resources for public transit in general in automobile-dependent areas, the dispersed population in the suburbs requires a more extensive system to be adequately serviced. Given these constraints, many areas just allow their public transit to remain grossly inadequate.

For these and a host of other reasons, Charles Marohn has described automobile-oriented suburban development as a kind of pyramid scheme.[5] Municipalities are drawn to the suburban model because it is popular with developers and the up-front costs are relatively minor. In the suburban model, the municipality can require the developer to build many of the roads and provide many of the parks. Because suburban development was supported by policy, it was easy to attract projects and get them completed. This led to quick tax revenues for municipalities. But over time, the additional infrastructure and service costs pile up, and the municipality starts to lose money on the development. This often leads to pursuing more tax revenue through more suburban development, which only pushes the cash flow problem out further—for one's successors to deal with.

The Possibility and Limit of Policy

It is important to know that even in a market economy, many of our decisions are not based on a simple cost-benefit analysis but are very much shaped by policy. This can initially be a frustrating realization, because most of us are not in a position to directly influence policy. We go to buy a house and discover that the price of a home in a walkable community is twice that of a house in the suburbs because of policies that were adopted eighty years ago. We would love to see a coffee shop near our home, but find we can't because of zoning restrictions. And we want to develop a commercial property in an underinvested part of the city but discover that excessive parking requirements make it all but impossible.

As individual citizens, we can't usually create or even change policy on our own, but we can weigh in as policies come up for review or a vote. Because of the work of organizations like Strong Towns (which provides a bracing analysis of the long-term costs of municipal policies)[6] and because of an increased interest in walkability, many policies are shifting from the older automobile-oriented approach. When these issues come up, we can vote in favor of policies that encourage belonging, and we can support leaders who challenge the midcentury approach.

Good and wise policies are important to support decisions that encourage belonging. But policy alone cannot create community or engender a sense of belonging among residents. It should also be noted that community can't be created by making fundamental ethical choices that support belonging. Buying a house in a walkable neighborhood won't build community if you don't walk in your neighborhood. In the next chapter, we explore strategies that can truly build community and encourage a sense of belonging. The strategies I am referring to are called "practices" or "liturgies." We need to learn to see the practices or liturgies we are already engaged in so we can consider the possibilities of new ones.

SEVENTEEN

LITURGICALLY SHAPED CHOICES

Cartesian Solutions

In chapter 12 we highlighted some of the problems associated with widespread smartphone use. Smartphones provide a too-convenient distraction, pulling us away from spontaneous face-to-face interaction with the people we encounter in everyday life. Smartphones erode precepts of civility and can diminish our humanity as we make unkind comments about others on social media. And smartphones direct our empathy and instinct for connection toward people we'll likely never meet in person while causing us to ignore those with whom we could enjoy a real relationship involving risk, trust, and shared intimacy.

Making these kinds of claims against smartphone use doesn't make me a radical. I don't think that they even would be considered very controversial. Lots of people have real concerns about the impact of smartphone use on us individually and societally. You don't have to be very old to remember a time when you could walk into a room and see people with their heads up, engaged in conversation or signaling a readiness for it. Now, more often than not, when people share space together, most if not all are slouched down looking at a screen.

So, here's a question: Despite growing concern about it, why is smartphone use continuing and even growing? Or to put it another way, Have you ever been concerned about someone else's smartphone use and told them to try to limit it? If so, how effective was that conversation? Or have you ever been concerned about your own use and tried to self-regulate? If so, it's likely you slowed down your use for a day or so and then returned to your normal patterns.

Why is it so hard to change behavior even when we know that the behavior is not good for us? The smartphone dilemma illustrates some of the limitations of cognitive solutions to problems. We cognitively know that too much smartphone use is not good for us individually or societally, but we continue it almost unconsciously or out of force of habit.

Secular Liturgies

In his book *Desiring the Kingdom*, James K. A. Smith claims that our common understanding of what determines behavior is mistaken.[1] We tend to believe that we form convictions with our minds, these convictions inform our decisions, and decisions guide our actions. Smith calls this way of understanding behavior "Cartesian," because it is based on an understanding of human behavior put forth by René Descartes.

Descartes understood cognitive processes as being the highest and most essential function of the human person. This can be seen clearly in his most famous quote: "I think therefore I am." Smith contends that Descartes doesn't account nearly enough for the way our bodies and our habits influence our behavior and even shape our thinking. Throughout the day, we take thousands of actions. We turn off the alarm, go to the bathroom, brush our teeth, choose an outfit, get dressed, go downstairs, make coffee, and so on.

The majority of such actions are guided by habits, bodily needs, desires, and preferences rather than some kind of cognitive decision-making process. If pressed, we could probably provide a cognitive rationale for most of these actions. But the question can be asked, Which came first: the cognitive decision or the action? Smith believes that in more cases than we care to admit, it is the behavior that leads to the conviction.

The reason Smith makes this point is to draw our attention to deeply influential forces in our culture that shape our thinking, not through cognitive persuasion, but rather through behavior. He calls these forces "secular liturgies." Secular liturgies are habitual cultural practices that shape our behavior and our thinking.

One example of a secular liturgy is the common practice of visiting the shopping mall. Smith's four-page description of the mall as liturgy is worth the price of the book, but for our purposes I will quote one passage near the end of his account:

> After time spent focused and searching in what the faithful call "the racks," with our newfound holy object in hand, we proceed to the altar, which is the consummation of worship. While acolytes and other worship assistants have helped us navigate our experience, behind the altar is the priest who presides over the consummating transaction. And this is a religion of transaction, of exchange and communion. When invited to worship here, we are not only invited to give; we are also invited to take. We don't leave this transformative experience with just good feelings or pious generalities, but rather with something concrete and tangible, with newly minted relics, as it were, that are themselves the means to the good life embodied in the icons who invited us into this participatory moment in the first place. And so we make our sacrifice, leave our donation, but in return receive something with solidity that is wrapped in the colors and symbols of the saints and the season. Released by the priest with a benediction, we make our way out of the chapel in a kind of denouement—not necessarily to leave (our awareness of time has been muted), but rather to continue contemplation and be invited into another chapel. Who could resist the tangible realities of the good life so abundantly and invitingly offered?[2]

According to Smith, going to the mall is a secular liturgy that shapes not only our behavior but also our beliefs. The mall teaches us that redemption can be ultimately achieved through consumption. This message is not normally appropriated in its full force but rather through the more benign idea that if we're bored, upset, or disappointed, a trip to the mall for some "shopping therapy" will set us aright again. Ultimately, the message communicated at the mall is rooted in a picture of "the good life." Insofar as we accept this picture, we respond positively to visiting the mall, and those visits strengthen our feeling of well-being.

Of course none of these messages are explicitly stated, but they come across loud and clear in the form of this place and the patterns that are enacted there. Obviously, redemption through consumption is antithetical to the gospel. But if this is indeed what is being communicated, Smith challenges us to consider how best to counteract these heretical convictions. We could offer a Sunday school course on Christian worldview with the explicit purpose of exposing this false teaching and clarifying the truth about redemption found in the Scriptures. Smith contends that this wouldn't be very effective, because secular liturgies influence us through our bodies; therefore, teaching our minds is of limited use.

The best way to oppose the false teaching of secular liturgies, Smith maintains, is not just to teach truth to minds but also to employ Christian liturgies. Smith makes a persuasive case for how baptism, the Lord's Supper, and regular gathering for worship can form behavior and conviction around gospel truth. Christian liturgies are based on a picture of the good life (shalom) as portrayed in Scripture. Insofar as Christian liturgies shape our behavior and our convictions, they will draw us toward this picture.

The Liturgy of Driving

I believe that Smith is absolutely right about the power of liturgies to shape behavior, conviction, and ultimately our picture of the good life. My only critique is that his argument seems to draw too sharp a distinction between Christian and secular with regard to liturgies. I agree with him completely that explicitly Christian liturgies like baptism and the Lord's Supper are good, and we would do well to ramp up our thinking about and our investment in them.

I want to extend Smith's argument by considering how all secular liturgies might not be equally antithetical to the gospel. A superficial reading of Smith might suggest he is saying that all secular liturgies are antithetical to the gospel and all sacred liturgies are in line with it. I don't believe that Smith's helpful interpretation of secular liturgies needs to be read like that.

Seeing shopping as liturgy is important both because of the values that so clearly undergird the experience and also because of its impact on people's lives. Almost everybody shops at the mall occasionally, and some people do so frequently.

But if mall shopping is important because of the values it supports and the numbers of people who engage in it, driving should be considered even more so. A high percentage of the population drives, and those who drive do so daily. It is how most people get to almost everywhere they need to go. On average, Americans spend just under an hour a day driving.[3] That works out to about 365 hours per year, almost nine forty-hour weeks.

Driving is so common we don't often think about it as a particular activity. But the reality is that every time we turn the key in the ignition and press our foot to the gas pedal, we enact a ritual that is deeply formed by certain values and impacts our experience of belonging.

If driving is indeed a kind of liturgy, the question we need to ask is, What picture of the good life is suggested by this liturgy? In particular, how important is belonging in this vision of the good life? We already began to answer this question when we noted that driving can be malformative to our personhood. When driving, we say things and make gestures to other drivers that we would never do face-to-face on a sidewalk.

But driving as liturgy also fits within a distinct picture of the good life that is at least somewhat different from what we see in Scripture. A culture based on driving values individualism, autonomy, and convenience. A society that prioritizes driving as a mode of transportation doesn't value community or belonging very highly. As already noted, an automobile-oriented culture encourages us to engage in different activities with geographically dispersed people. This makes it hard to form deep relationships with the people who live near us. And it makes it hard to form connections to the place in which home is located.

I wouldn't go so far as to say that driving is absolutely antithetical to the gospel, but I do believe that its effects on us individually and culturally seem to be moving us away from the good life (shalom) as depicted in Scripture. As we've been considering the impact of three pieces of glass in this book, I think we could make similar claims about the liturgies of television and smartphone use so prevalent in our culture.

Liturgies of Belonging

If it is true that driving moves us away from the good life, then perhaps we can consider transportation liturgies that align more closely with the values we find in Scripture. At least we could find secular liturgies of transportation that conflict less with biblical values. While these liturgies aren't likely to replace driving as the dominant way to get from point A to point B, some participation in them can begin to shift our imagination toward a world where community and belonging are more highly valued.

The first practice that comes to mind as an alternative to driving is, of course, walking. I'm talking here about walking not as a form of exercise but rather as a form of transportation. Walking to school, to the store, to a friend's house, or to a coffee date are examples.[4]

Throughout history, walking has been, for most people, the default transportation for daily living.[5] Now, in many contexts, walking this way is all but impossible. I happen to live in a fairly walkable neighborhood (Walk Score: 76),[6] so for many errands I can choose to walk, bike, or drive. I realize that many people cannot realistically choose to walk to many necessary destinations (for reasons we've noted in the previous chapter). But since, for me, walking (or driving) is a choice that I *can* make, I can easily consider the outcomes of either of these choices.

When I choose to walk to work, it is a very different experience from when I choose to drive. Either choice gets me to my destination within a reasonable time frame. But the values that are expressed and reinforced by each of these two forms of transportation can be quite different.

Whereas driving encourages us to think and act as an autonomous individual, walking is more communal. When I pass another person walking, we almost always make eye contact and usually greet one another and sometimes engage in conversation. When I'm walking and someone I know is walking the same direction, we often end up spontaneously walking together and chatting.

Walking to work helps me pay attention to and form connections with the distinctive particularities of the place I live. The faster our bodies move through a space, the fewer senses we utilize and the less detail we perceive. Streets for automobile travel utilize symbols and signs to communicate mostly with our eyes using language and logos to convey information. Driving along a multilane arterial, one is likely to see a lot of "lollipop" signs. A lollipop sign is an oversized message mounted on a single pole—they are so ubiquitous that you probably don't think about them (Charles Schwab, Starbucks, Payday Loans, etc.).

That is why so many of our contemporary public settings are so ugly and disjointed. Signs point to a reality that exists somewhere else. Looking at a sign that says "beach" with an arrow is completely different from standing somewhere with sand between our toes, salty air in our noses, and the roar of waves in our ears. Looking at a sign that says Starbucks and is mounted on a pole is different from walking by a coffee shop and smelling coffee and fresh-baked pastries.

This is true not only with how we experience commercial establishments. When I drive to work, my mind is occupied with reading signs and symbols (Speed Limit 30, double yellow line, Left Turn Only, green light). When I walk to work, I'm immersed in a world of real things. I notice subtle signs that spring is coming. I see a new walkway being built at a neighbor's house. I hear two squirrels chasing each other up a tree trunk. I smell freshly cut grass, and I feel a shift in the wind indicating impending rain.

I walk to work about once a week (the other days I ride my bike), and I'm amazed that each time I walk, I notice dozens of small details I didn't notice before. That is partially because the landscape of my neighborhood is constantly changing, but it is also because such plentiful sensory input is impossible to grasp driving at 25 miles per hour. As a Christian walking this route, I am constantly reminded of the abundant creativity of the God whom I am privileged to call Father.

My point in making this comparison is not to extol walking as the only acceptable form of transportation but rather to highlight the way that the liturgies of ordinary life present us with choices that can draw us toward or away from kingdom values. I especially want to make the point that the distinction between a kingdom-affirming and a kingdom-denying liturgy cannot be made simply on the basis of whether the liturgy in question comes out of the life of the church. I believe that within the secular realm itself, we are constantly presented with liturgies that are more or less kingdom affirming.

I use the phrase "common-grace liturgies" to describe secular kingdom-affirming liturgies. I introduced the concept of common grace in chapter 3 when we were talking about kingdom belonging. "Common grace" is used to describe nonsalvific forms of blessing that God uses to bless humanity as a whole; and when common grace blessings are administered through human agents, those agents are not necessarily members of the Christian community. I believe that walking as a form of transportation can be considered to be a common-grace liturgy. When we walk this way, kingdom values such as community identification, engagement with nature, and attention to particularity are reinforced within us.

A Multiplicity of Liturgies

I'm not suggesting that driving is altogether bad or that it automatically forms us in ways contrary to the kingdom of God. If it were, the Christian community in the developed West would be in a perilous state. Certainly we can think of numerous examples of mature disciples who drive a lot. The reason that driving isn't deadly to faith is that it is but one of a great many formative activities in which we are engaged.

The activities in which we engage at home, at work, with our Christian community, and with non-Christian friends are all formative in their own ways. If we focus attention on Christ as our Lord and allow the Holy Spirit to form us and work through us, our engagements will serve as crucibles and help form us in the image of Christ.

Our transportation choices may be one of numerous faith-formative practices in our life. What I suggest here is that a disciple who drives often may well be a mature disciple but may also struggle with a certain kind of loneliness or lack of belonging as a consequence of spending an inordinate amount of time in an automobile.

The Christian disciple, then, participates in a common cultural practice and experiences the consequences of that practice along with other members of society both Christian and non-Christian. Think back to the shopping mall as cultural liturgy. A Christian disciple who goes to the mall somewhat regularly will likely continue to be a mature disciple and an effective contributor to God's mission in the world. However, the mall's foundational values such as redemption through consumption will have a persistently corrosive effect on the disciple's Christ-formed self-understanding. The extent of the corrosive effect depends on how much the disciple wholeheartedly participates in this liturgy.

My assertion is a bit more involved than this, since the current crisis of loneliness and belonging is caused primarily by larger cultural trends arising from societal decisions to focus on driving. If we drive less and walk more, we may still experience loneliness and lack of belonging, because our private choices cannot always override larger cultural forces. Another person might decide to start walking to work on a regular basis but find that because they live in an automobile-oriented neighborhood, they rarely see another person on their route to work and that there are no good places to stop and enjoy some social interaction.

My point is that our mode of transportation can be seen as a kind of liturgy that shapes us either toward or away from some kingdom values. If we want to address the problem of loneliness and belonging within our own lives and at the larger societal level, we need to consider how we get from place to place. This is not the only question that we need to consider, but it is an important one that is easily overlooked. When we consider mode of transportation as a formative liturgy, we need to consider this question at multiple levels—ad hoc moral choices, fundamental moral choices, community collaboration, and policy. We explore these levels in the next section.

PART SIX

ENCOURAGING BELONGING

In this section, we turn our attention to the more hopeful question of what can be done to solve or at least push back against the crisis of belonging. We begin with a discussion of the kinds of help that can be generated through design solutions: walkability, thresholds, third places, and squares. In the next chapter we introduce the concept of proximity, which is not a tool per se, but rather a conceptual framework that helps orient our thinking toward belonging. Following is a discussion about placemaking as a communal process that both creates spaces for relational and environmental

199

engagement and also builds communal ties through a collaborative process. Finally, we discuss the way that we encourage belonging through the work of local culture, which is essentially the generating, cultivating, and transmitting of the stories of our lives and the stories of the community.

EIGHTEEN

BELONGING BY DESIGN

We've noted how a lack of adequate settings for casual social interaction among neighbors contributes to the problem of loneliness and belonging. We may be persuaded that too much time engaged with the three pieces of glass (windshield, TV, and smartphone screen) has prevented us from enjoying face-to-face contact with friends and neighbors. If we decide to forgo them and head outside, we're likely to be disappointed with what we discover. Rather than being rewarded with meaningful interactions with neighbors, many will find settings hostile to human navigation and not encouraging of interpersonal connection. We've spent the second half of the twentieth century building what can be best described as inhospitable neighborhoods separated from equally inhospitable commercial districts. We have built neighborhoods for fast, efficient automobile travel and have not focused on how people might engage these spaces for enjoyment.

Most of us have a pretty good idea of what an inhospitable neighborhood looks like. More important, we have experienced what they feel like. We now consider some alternative arrangements that draw people out of their homes and encourage them to enjoy the neighborhood. Some of these arrangements require significant investment of public funds that might be driven by policies beyond the scope of ordinary citizens. But many can be instigated by individual residents or by a community of neighbors working together.

As we consider the sociability of neighborhoods, keep in mind the various levels of belonging (introduced in chap. 1). In particular, we are looking at the ways neighborhoods can encourage civic belonging (social and public). This is important, because when we talk about "interacting with others," it should be clear that we're not talking about an expectation that you need to have deep conversations with every person you meet in every neighborhood setting. That would be a nightmare for the introverts among us (and may even be a bit much for the extroverts).

Settings for public belonging are places you can enjoy being with others who live in your community with no expectation for sustained conversation. People-watching is a typical activity in these kinds of settings. Settings for social belonging encourage a little more social interaction with neighbors, but the expectation can be pretty minimal. These kinds of settings encourage what we explored in chapter 2 as civic friendship. It requires no more than a simple recognition of another person as someone you see regularly in a place. It may also involve knowing each other's names and maybe a few basic details of each other's life.

Walkability

I realize that walkability might sound like a niche concept—that is, of passionate interest to a specialized group but of little concern to most people. I consider thread counts in bedding a niche concept. My wife and I recently caved in and upgraded from our queen-size bed of twenty years to a new king-size bed. This involved buying new bedding. I imagined the sheets would be an afterthought, a quick grab on our way out the door.

We knew we needed a king sheet set—white or maybe blue. Since the bed was a significant investment for us, I made the mistake of searching "bed sheet reviews." I had no idea there was a difference between

Egyptian, pima, and Sea Island cotton. And speaking of cotton, many reviewers think bamboo is the way to go. Then we had to decide on thread count. In any case, we did a little research to buy the best sheets we could for our budget. But honestly, after the first couple of nights, while some reviews we read were impassioned, we really didn't notice anything distinguishing our new expensive sheets from our old sheets. My skin just isn't that finely tuned.

I think this is probably how many people feel about walkability. It seems to be a somewhat obscure concept that a few people are passionate about but most normal people wouldn't really notice if they happened to stumble upon a "walkable" neighborhood.

But this is not actually the case. In the first place, you would notice you were in a walkable neighborhood, because you would actually feel like walking from one place to another. Jumping into your car to go somewhere a quarter mile away would seem absurd, even though people do that all the time to get from Target to PetSmart. And you wouldn't be the only one who felt like walking around; you would likely see other people walking around. It would seem more alive.

You can gauge the significance of walkability with a simple tool known as Walk Score. Walk Score ranks every zip code in the country according to how walkable it is; 100 is most walkable, and 1 is least walkable. A score above 70 is very good, and a score above 90 is a "walker's paradise" where you can easily get by without owning a car.[1]

Walkability is not just a niche interest but a condition that has significant economic impact for a neighborhood. Recent surveys of home sales show that an additional point in a Walk Score can increase a home's value by close to 1 percent or $3,000.[2] Neighborhoods in the same city can easily have 30–40 points of difference in Walk Scores.

The American Planning Association claims that 56 percent of millennials and 46 percent of baby boomers prefer to live in a walkable neighborhood over a traditional suburb. Realtors are finding significantly less interest in traditional "prestige" homes with high square footage and nice views if those homes are located in an automobile-dependent neighborhood. Many buyers now eschew size and views to live in a walkable, vibrant neighborhood.

So what makes a neighborhood walkable? According to Jeff Speck, there are four fundamental laws of walkability.[3] In Speck's book *Walkable City*, he says that walkable neighborhoods must be useful, safe, comfortable, and interesting.

To understand walking's usefulness, we must learn a new term—"pedestrian shed." That is the distance a person will generally choose to walk rather than take a car. In many contexts a pedestrian shed is about a quarter mile. There must be a variety of amenities within the pedestrian shed for people to have a reason to walk.

A good mix of services and stores is required. Access to transit is helpful. I happen to live in a **useful** neighborhood (Speck's first necessity). The distance between my home and my church is .7 miles, and traveling between the two, I walk by a grocery store, a bank, a pharmacy, an auto repair shop, a dentist's office, a financial planner's office, an accountant's office, four salons, a massage therapist's office, a chiropractor's office, two dozen restaurants and pubs, and three coffee shops. I can live happily for weeks without ever getting into a car.

Permeability can be an important factor in a useful walk. Pedestrians must be able to easily get to and from places that are close to each other. Permeability is a given in a neighborhood consisting of a regular grid of blocks. But many newer neighborhoods were built with a disregard for permeability. Things that get in the way of permeability are cul-de-sacs, institutions like hospitals that take up multiple blocks, and limited-access roads such as freeways that cut through neighborhoods.

The second principle is that a walk must be **safe**. Pedestrians must not only be safe from cars; they must also *feel* safe. The biggest issues here are streets that are too wide and rounded street corners that allow cars to speed through a neighborhood. Allowing cars to parallel park is helpful; it provides a buffer between pedestrians and fast-moving traffic. It's helpful if the neighborhood is safe for bicycles as well. When more bikes are around, everyone tends to be safer. When drivers expect bicyclists, they tend to drive slower and more attentively, making it safer for bicyclists, pedestrians, and other drivers.

The third principle is that a walk must be **comfortable**. The buildings in a neighborhood are critical to the comfort of a walk. It is actually the *space between* the buildings and how the buildings shape the public realm that's important. The most important element of comfort is enclosure. Street enclosure is achieved when the height of the buildings and the distance between them creates a kind of outdoor hallway or, for plazas, an outdoor room.

When the buildings are too low and the streets or parking lots too wide, one feels exposed, and walking is not pleasant. Good trees that add to the sense of enclosure as well as adding shade and rain protection contribute to a comfortable walk. Think of the walk between strip malls for a picture of an uncomfortable walking environment.

The fourth principle is that a walk must be **interesting**. It is never interesting to walk by a large parking lot or a long blank wall. Yet in many neighborhoods this is exactly what pedestrians must endure. Shops at the street level, front yards with low fences, and restaurants with outdoor tables or windows that open to the sidewalk all contribute to an interesting walk.

Living in a walkable neighborhood is a significant amenity for many people. But the walkability of a neighborhood isn't only something that is enjoyed when one is walking. A walkable neighborhood is usually also a good neighborhood for getting around on a bike. And a walkable neighborhood can provide better settings for casual interactions with one's neighbors as they are attending to daily tasks within the neighborhood.

Thresholds

Now that we've considered how a neighborhood can be more hospitable at the macro scale through walkability, we turn our attention to how the private home or business can contribute too. To begin, we consider a case study brought to my attention by James Rojas, who undertook a study of a largely Mexican American neighborhood in East Los Angeles.[4]

Rojas noted that this particular neighborhood had been built largely by white middle-class residents of a prior generation. It was now populated mostly by Mexican Americans, who made certain adaptations to their homes. One of the major adaptations had to do with adding fences to the front yards.

The first-generation residents of this neighborhood did not put fences around their front yards but kept the front open. One of the first things that the Mexican Americans did when they purchased one of these homes was to enclose the front yard with a low fence. These fences might be picket, wrought iron, or chain link, depending on the homeowner's socioeconomic status. You might think that fencing the front yard would be a step away from hospitality in the neighborhood. According to Rojas, you'd be wrong. The low fence in the front yard was a highly hospitable move.

To understand this, go back to the layout of the original houses. The front for the original residents consisted of a well-manicured lawn, a walkway, and a few steps leading to the front door. The front yard was not a social space, but a showpiece to demonstrate values such as responsibility and conformity. A stranger wanting to interact with a resident of one of these homes undertook a difficult task of crossing the property line, walking up the walkway, ascending the steps, and knocking on the door. The resident opens the door and immediately assesses whether the person knocking at the door is a friend or a stranger. If it is a friend, she immediately relaxes and ascertains the nature of the visit. If it is a stranger, she remains in defensive mode and thinks, "What does this person want from me?" The conversation will likely be short and tense, not conducive to forming new friendships.

By putting a low fence around the front yard, the Mexican American residents instigated two very important changes. The first is that they created a social space in the front yard. The fence establishes what is known as defensible space; the private space of the yard is clearly marked, so that strangers know they aren't supposed to enter unless invited. This allows the residents (including the children) to feel more comfortable hanging out in the front yard. The Mexican Americans in this neighborhood referred to this space as *la yarda*. *La yarda* signifies more than just a Spanglish version of the word "yard"; it represents a totally different concept. *La yarda* allowed the residents' personality to be expressed in this space. A typical *yarda* would include some seating area, some children's toys, and even a shrine. However, this defensible space also allows easy visual and auditory communication to and from the public realm of the sidewalk.

The other thing that is accomplished has to do with the gate of the fence. In the original layout of the yard, the threshold for the house was the front door—not a very hospitable threshold. The Mexican Americans made the gate the threshold and moved it out to where it abutted the public realm of the sidewalk.

Making the gate a threshold instead of the front door turned out to be a very hospitable move. It was not unusual for a resident to just hang out in *la yarda* by leaning on the gate, making it easy to talk to folks as they walked by. This was a comfortable space for interaction. Rojas noted people meeting people for the first time in this setting, and he noticed people who knew each other standing within a few feet of each other and going five minutes or more without saying a word. Can you imagine standing across from someone at your front door and not talking for five minutes?

Rojas noticed that residents could signal what kind of social interaction they were up for by how they used their yard. They leaned on their front gate if they were open to talking with people on the sidewalk. They moved back to the sitting area if they felt like being left alone. And they gravitated to the side yard if they wanted to share gossip with a neighbor.

This case study of Mexican Americans in East Los Angeles suggests some ways that an individual homeowner can make the home a more hospitable place for the neighborhood. Achieving defensible space by adding a low fence and a gate is one thing. One can even utilize one's front yard more for the purpose of engaging one's neighbors. I've heard numerous stories of people bringing chairs, swing sets, or picnic tables to the front yard to engage with neighbors and people walking by.

My family lived for three years in a small first-story apartment in Pasadena. We had a low cinder-block wall that defined the five-foot pathway to our front door. Because there were five of us living in a small apartment, that little enclosed pathway usually included some spillover from our apartment. We were a little embarrassed about the messiness of it.

After reading Rojas's study, we started thinking about it differently. We brought out four chairs we'd found in a dumpster and started referring to our walkway as *la yarda*. On Friday afternoons we set up a table and made drinks for our neighbors as they made their way home at the end of the day. It started as a kind of joke, but over time it became a beloved tradition, and we had neighbors sitting on those dumpster chairs throughout the week.

Thresholds are important not only for our residences but for commercial spaces as well. The reason a walk along a main street is more interesting than walking along a big-box store is that the street has significantly more thresholds per block. Each store or restaurant has a door (and sometimes windows) acting as a threshold that invites you to enter. We may hardly notice these thresholds, but they keep us engaged as we walk by.

Liminality

The concepts of *la yarda* and defensible space help us understand how the single-family detached home can be hospitable, but there is a similar dynamic at play in attached homes like apartment buildings and condominiums. In 1973 a psychologist named Andrew Baum conducted a study of students in two different kinds of dormitories at Stony Brook University that demonstrated how design can significantly impact our social interactions.[5]

One dorm had individual double rooms laid out on each floor along a long corridor. Each floor had a common lounge. The other dorm had rooms laid out on each floor as a series of suites. In each suite were three bedrooms connected by a common lounge. Each dorm accommodated roughly the same number of students per floor, who were randomly assigned to one dorm or the other.

Baum found that the two groups had very different experiences. The students in the dorm with rooms along the corridor felt more crowded and irritated in day-to-day life. They were less likely to make friends with the people on their floor than were the students in the suites. The latter reported being happier and more settled in their environment. They made friends with and were more helpful to one another. These differences could be seen outside of their dorms as well. The researchers called some of the students into a meeting for which they had to wait in a hallway outside the meeting room. The students from the suites sat closer to others and engaged in more conversation than the ones with rooms along the corridor.

The problem with the rooms arranged along the corridor is that there is no liminal space where a student can feel comfortable while deciding whether and how to engage with others socially. The student has little control over whom they run into and when. They go from the private realm of their room into the public hallway without any transitional space. If they're feeling a bit social, they might head down to the floor lounge, but rarely do people actually do this. For one thing, they don't know who else is down there. Also, as we've noted, many of our daily decisions are made noncognitively. This is especially true for social decisions. We often don't decide to be social and then go seek others; rather, we run into people we know and then get drawn into social engagement.

This connection between housing design and social connection is true not only for college students; adults and children living in apartments and condominiums also find it easier to connect with their neighbors when good liminal spaces are provided for them. As more people decide to live in cities in search of walkable environments, many move into high-rise apartments. Unfortunately, many of these apartment buildings are laid out in the corridor style. And for many, this makes it difficult to form relationships with their neighbors. But much more sociable housing models are being used.

Charles Montgomery tells the story of a man in Vancouver, British Columbia, who moved from a high-rise tower to a townhouse on the same block.[6] The hallway of the high-rise wasn't a place to hang out, and so many people used the elevator that he rarely saw someone he knew. When some friends moved into an adjacent townhouse, this man

209

sold his high-rise condo and bought a townhouse as well. In doing this, he gave up a spectacular view but gained a home that was much better situated for making friends. The townhouses were arranged facing a courtyard with a volleyball court. And each townhouse had a little balcony from which residents could interact socially with people in the courtyard or withdraw socially. While living in the high-rise, this man had not made friends with any of his neighbors. But within a few weeks of his move, he had gotten to know all of his neighbors and his social life was transformed.

Hospitable Spaces

In addition to walkability and more sociable thresholds, hospitable spaces are key to the friendliness of a neighborhood. They invite people to stop and engage with the physical environment of a neighborhood or perhaps to engage with other people.

Hospitable spaces can take a variety of forms. They might be something formal such as a park, plaza, square, or playground. Or they might be something more organic, like a cluster of mailboxes, stairs to an apartment building, or a street corner on the way to a common destination. Regardless of what form these hospitable spaces take, it helps if they include seating, shade, and access to public streets.[7]

As mentioned above, the engagement encouraged in hospitable spaces may be at the public or social level. Hospitable spaces geared for interaction at the social level are places we visit fairly frequently, and while we're there we're likely to recognize a few familiar faces. We might know people's names, and casual conversation feels comfortable. Hospitable spaces geared for interaction at the public level tend to be places where we can be with other people but with less expectation of social interaction. People-watching is a typical activity in these kinds of places.

Every hospitable neighborhood should have at least one good place for social interaction. That is to say, every resident should have a good place for social interaction within about a quarter mile of home (i.e., the pedestrian shed). Places for public interaction don't need to be present in every neighborhood. But there should be enough of these kinds of places dispersed in a city or town so that all residents have relatively easy access to them. Below, I make these concepts a little more concrete with more-specific examples of places for social and for public interaction.

Third Place

A neighborhood third place is a classic setting for social interaction. "Third place" is a term coined by Ray Oldenburg to describe places that we find ourselves visiting on a fairly regular basis.[8] Oldenburg believes that third places provide an important counterbalance to the more structured and demanding settings of work and home. If your home is your first place and your work is your second place, you need a third place that is distinct from them. A third place can be a coffee shop, a pub, a barber shop, or anything that works for you and for others in your neighborhood.

There are countless kinds of third places, and each one operates according to its own rules. By definition, third places are not subject to a strict set of operating principles. Third places provide a comfortable setting for neighbors to interact with one another. They also provide a place for newcomers or visitors to feel less alienated and to more quickly establish a sense of belonging.

One reason third places are so important is that our homes tend to be unsuitable for connecting with people casually or for forming new relationships. Inviting someone into your home involves a significant social risk for you and for your guest. Most people tend to vet others pretty thoroughly before inviting them into their homes. Also, we rarely spontaneously invite people into our homes, because they aren't clean enough for company. This is partially a consequence of most adults working outside the home, a factor that also makes coordinating schedules difficult.

Third places are important because they can greatly extend the range of people we can get to know and increase the frequency of contact we have with people we already know. At a neighborhood coffee shop we can talk about sports with someone we'd be unlikely to invite into our home, and over time we can develop a casual friendship. We can also chat with a neighbor for five or ten minutes on a daily basis at a third place. Regular unplanned contact with others is a key element of forming friendships.

The fictional setting of Cheers, with which we began this book, is a classic third place. Patrons use this neighborhood bar as a place to blow off some steam and connect with others between their work and their homes. In this bar, significant friendships provide the grist for the narrative arc of each episode. But the background is saturated with the comfortable din of civic friendships. That iconic "Norm!" greeting is testimony to the power of civic friendship.

Squares

We need hospitable spaces for public, as well as social, interaction. They don't need to be quite so prevalent in each neighborhood, but each city or town should have enough of these kinds of places for all residents to have easy access to one or more of them. Squares are a common type of place for public interaction, but many other types of places can serve this purpose equally well.

We envisioned walkable streets as outdoor hallways. If you think of a city or town as a large house with the roof removed, the streets can be thought of as the hallways. Squares are the rooms formed by the buildings surrounding and enclosing them. We could be a bit more precise in describing some of these places as plazas, forecourts, and so on, but "squares" works as a good general term (the shape doesn't need to technically be square).

Whereas the walkable street or urban hallway invites movement, the square invites people to stop and rest. Therefore, a successful square should have well-arranged places to sit as well as some shade. Good squares often include some kind of statue, water feature, or tree to provide visual focus.

Planners attuned to the human element of cities and towns have developed a host of principles for making a successful square. We won't go into the details here but will note a simple evaluative criterion used by Jan Gehl for determining whether a public place works.[9] Gehl claims that when people choose to stop and sit in a place, it is a successful public space. Many situations in everyday life, such as the line at the post office, force people to congregate. But there are also numerous examples of places where people choose to sit and read, enjoy an ice-cream cone, chat with a friend, or just bask in the sun. Those places are often successful squares.

On the other hand, we've all seen squares and plazas that are oddly devoid of people. A developer might be granted some concession from the city (additional height for a building) in exchange for including some kind of civic place on-site. These places are usually poorly designed and rarely used. There is also a strange tradition of using the traditional language of plaza to describe some kind of commercial development consisting of low buildings surrounding a parking lot. Suffice it to say that no one voluntarily chooses to hang out in these places.

Squares are the classic example of places designed for the purpose of public interaction, but there are numerous other forms that serve the same purpose. In his book on squares, Mark Childs provides helpful descriptions of some of these other forms, such as civic coves, forecourts, courtyards, civic lots, civic grounds, campuses, and urban frameworks.[10]

Civic Hospitality

Those with the gift of hospitality often have an innate sense for how to design the interior elements of their homes to make people feel welcome and to encourage easy interaction. This is not entirely different from the ideas presented in this chapter. We've been examining design elements in the civic realm that help people (including strangers) feel welcome and encourage the kind of social interaction that is appropriate within social and public settings.

Such elements are extremely important for encouraging a sense of belonging, but these design elements only work when there are enough people out and about in a neighborhood to interact in these kinds of settings. Of course, a reliable test of good civic design is whether it draws people into civic spaces. But design can't usually engender lively civic interaction on its own. As we have noted, there are strong forces at work within our culture that encourage people to live various aspects of their lives in separate geographical areas. In order to push back against this tendency, we need to encourage people to invest time and energy in the geographical areas that are close to where they work, live, or worship. We'll take up this topic in the next chapter.

NINETEEN

BELONGING
THROUGH PROXIMITY

Hardware and Software

Over the past twenty years or so, we have seen a complete reversal of
thinking with regard to the physical layout of US cities and neighborhoods. The automobile-oriented development that was the dominant
mode for new construction has slowed down considerably and has
completely fallen out of favor in many regions. Single-family residential
neighborhoods designed around a cul-de-sac or arterial street arrangement are less common. Shopping malls are dying. Even sports stadiums
are moving away from being islands in the middle of seas of parking
and now are being built within urban neighborhoods.

Some new neighborhoods look and feel like neighborhoods did
before the automobile became dominant. Mixed-use neighborhoods
that include single-family homes and apartment buildings on the same
block are being built again. Separating residential and commercial is no
longer a given, and we're seeing a return of neighborhood coffee shops
and corner grocery stores. People are rediscovering pre–World War II
neighborhoods that already include these elements and are choosing
to buy homes there, reinvigorating those neighborhoods.

These developments are both exciting and hopeful in terms of helping to relieve rampant loneliness and encourage belonging. However,

these changes also reveal something about the challenge we face. The automobile-oriented style dominant from 1950 to 2000 showed that community ties could be negatively impacted by building in a way that encouraged social isolation. But what we have learned since 2000 is that human community can't be restored by buildings alone.

We now know how to build a more hospitable neighborhood, but that doesn't mean that people who live there will automatically start acting more neighborly. The problem is that by building neighborhoods that encouraged social isolation during the second half of the twentieth century, we not only caused those who lived there to feel more lonely but also discouraged the traditional patterns and practices of neighborliness. Sitting on the front porch and talking to neighbors out for an evening stroll is but one example of numerous little traditions that helped knit together a particular neighborhood. Of course, even in a highly automobile-oriented suburb, certain highly motivated individuals have been able to maintain some neighborly practices; but the overall trend has been for each household to become increasingly isolated, insulated from the houses around them. The term "cocooning" has been coined to describe this phenomenon.

Thus, when we consider how to break the cycle of loneliness and to encourage belonging, we need to think in at least two modes—hardware and software. "Hardware" is the physical layout of the neighborhood. We've noted how houses, streets, sidewalks, and gathering spaces can encourage or discourage face-to-face interaction. "Software" comprises the patterns and practices cultivated and enacted by the residents of a particular neighborhood that actually create those moments of social connection. In this chapter we explore some of the software necessary for breaking the cycle of loneliness by making connections with our neighbors.

Parish

As we think about the software question of practices that encourage belonging, we need to recover the concept of parish. A "parish" is a territorial unit that constitutes the jurisdiction of one particular church, over which one priest exercises spiritual authority. "Parish" can also refer to the active congregation of a particular church, but in many cases the geographical aspect of this term is quite strong. A resident of a particular parish may think of herself as connected to the parish church even though she doesn't attend worship services there. Likewise, many parish priests and congregants think about the needs and concerns of the people living within their parish regardless of whether they come to church.[1]

"Parish" is a helpful term that can expand our thinking beyond the confines of a church building or a private residence while still respecting the importance of geography. To recover this term in a way that will be useful, we need to first acknowledge the ways that it no longer applies. Christianity is no longer the dominant religion in most contexts, and even in contexts where Christianity is well represented, churches represent a wide spectrum of denominational expressions. For these reasons, the idea of a majority of residents in a particular geographical area thinking of themselves as part of one parish no longer applies.

That said, I do think that it is a good idea for the leadership of a church to think of their mission and ministry in terms of parish.[2] A church concerned only with the needs and wishes of those on its membership rolls and/or who participate in programs within the church building can be described as an insular church. If a church wants to avoid insularity, a common alternative is to try to shift its focus to a more global perspective. The problem here is that the world is a pretty big place. Apart from the occasional mission trip, translating global perspective into concrete action can be difficult, and it's hard to invest in personal relationships with global neighbors.

A parish mentality is a better alternative to the insular church. A church with a parish mentality thinks of the geographic area around the church as a significant focus of its ministry. A parish church exhibits care for the people within its parish whether or not they participate in the church's programs. A parish church cares about the natural and built environment around it. And the parish church cares about the history, the symbols, and the culture around it.

From a neighborhood-design standpoint, certain kinds of churches are better designed and situated to embrace the parish concept. These churches are usually located in walkable neighborhoods and are situated within the fabric of the neighborhood. The front doors of these churches usually come right up to the sidewalk, and if there is a parking lot, it is located in the back. I describe these kinds of churches as embedded churches. Most churches built prior to World War II were embedded churches. During the second half of the twentieth century a suburban church model emerged that was better suited for an insular-church mentality. These kinds of churches are usually surrounded by large parking lots, and the front doors are set back from the public streets and buildings in the neighborhood.

It can also be helpful to think of our homes in terms of parish. A Christian household can be thought of as a minichurch where God is worshiped, discipleship is nurtured, and the gospel is demonstrated. I see the Christian home not as a replacement for the church but rather as a kind of annex that extends the mission and ministry of a local church spatially and chronologically. If a Christian household is a kind of church, then a Christian household as church can adopt a parish mentality by showing concern for the neighborhood as a whole, and not just for the members of the household. Churches that are more insular in their relationship to their own neighborhood often leverage the parish concept by encouraging their members to be more intentional neighbors where their homes are located.

The Art of Neighboring

> "Teacher, which is the greatest commandment in the Law?"
>
> Jesus replied: "'Love the Lord your God with all your heart and with all your soul and with all your mind.' This is the first and greatest commandment. And the second is like it: 'Love your neighbor as yourself.' All the Law and the Prophets hang on these two commandments."
>
> Matthew 22:36–40

According to Scripture, loving our neighbor is a fundamental obligation of disciples of Jesus. Yet, as we have seen, we live in a culture where neighbors hardly know, let alone love, one another. While it's true that Jesus's command to love our neighbor can include anyone we encounter who is in need, we cannot lose sight of the fact that loving our neighbor at least should include the people who live near us.

This embarrassingly simple insight was part of the impetus for Jay Pathak and Dave Runyon to do some serious thinking about what neighbor love involved for their communities. This revolutionized their approach to ministry and led them to write an excellent book called *The Art of Neighboring*.[3]

Before providing practical advice about how to be a better neighbor and encouraging neighborliness in one's neighborhood, Runyon and Pathak offer a simple tool for evaluating one's current level of neighborliness. The test is quite simple. First draw a tic-tac-toe board and draw a house in the middle square. That is your house, and the open squares are the eight households that are physically closest to yours. This works with detached single-family homes or apartments. Take a moment to decide which addresses or apartment numbers go into each blank space.

Then try to answer the following three questions for each of the spaces (I'm paraphrasing Pathak and Runyon's original questions):

1. What are the names of the people who live here?
2. What is one detail about the lives of the people living here that couldn't be determined by looking at the outside of their home (where they are from, what they do for a living, etc.)?
3. What is one thing about a resident of this home that would be known only to someone they trust (something they hope for, something they fear, their spiritual beliefs or practices)?

After filling out the grid to the best of your ability, you are ready to tally your score. You get one point for each answer you are able to give. How you actually tally your score isn't terribly important. For most people, just the exercise of filling out the grid reveals a lot about their neighborliness.

In my experience in walking people through this experiment, most people are convicted that they are not as good neighbors as they ought to be. The good news is that Runyon and Pathak spend most of the book providing encouragement and practical tips on how to improve one's score by becoming a better neighbor.

One idea they offer is to host a neighborhood potluck. This is not new or revolutionary, but they address some of the common roadblocks we face when attempting something like this and provide some helpful advice on how to work around them. They note that some neighbors are not initially interested in gathering for social reasons but can be persuaded to get together for the purpose of safety. Getting together to exchange contact information and to encourage keeping an eye on one another's homes can be a great first step in certain neighborhoods.

"Location, location, location" is a common adage in real estate. In thinking about location, potential home buyers or renters typically think about the physical characteristics of the neighborhood and/or access to schools, medical facilities, and so on. But in many cases, the quality of life in a particular neighborhood has a lot to do with attributes that are not physical characteristics. The culture of a neighborhood, or the level of social capital generated by the neighbors, is what makes a neighborhood great and gives the neighbors a strong sense of belonging.

The good news is that while the physical characteristics of a neighborhood can be difficult or even impossible to change, its culture can be changed by a few neighbors. Working on the art of neighboring is a practical way to improve the culture of a neighborhood.

Localism

The approach described in *The Art of Neighboring* is a specific example of prioritizing the proximate, an idea also called "localism." One thing that each of the three pieces of glass has in common is the eradication of distance. The automobile allows us to hold together lives that consist in pieces geographically separate from one another. Television allows us to enter into fascinating, beautiful, and heartbreaking stories that have nothing to do with our local context. Our smartphones allow us to stay connected with friends and strangers regardless of where they are. That eradication of distance, while seductive, has been a major force in making us feel lonely, alienating us from the places where we live.

If the seductive promise of eradication of distance is behind our crisis of belonging, then perhaps a renewed focus on the local can be a critical part of the solution. Localism is an increasingly popular concept—for example, in eating locally sourced food. The explosion of farmers markets is but one result of this growing local-food movement. There is quite a bit of interest in shopping locally as well. Many are weary of the impersonal nature of big-box retail and are willing to pay for the personal service of a local retailer.

The drive toward localism is largely taking place outside of the church, but it is, I believe, an area where the local church might find common ground with its neighbors. As I mentioned in chapter 3, a local gathering spot can function as a foretaste of kingdom belonging, even if it is not part of a church. And I believe that embedded churches are especially well suited to connect with people who value localism, so long as these kinds of churches also have a parish mentality.

A strong draw of the localist movement is relationships. A popular localist slogan is "Know your farmer." The kingdom of God also is about relationships, albeit relationships rooted in God's covenantal love. But we can identify in the localist movement values more in line with kingdom values than the transactional "bottom line trumps all" approach of the typical national chain.

Prioritization of the Proximate

Localism can mean slightly different things when talking about food, consumer goods, or politics; when thinking about loneliness and belonging, the localism described by the pedestrian shed (introduced in chap. 18) can frame the issue.

Our church has recently been conducting an experiment utilizing the pedestrian shed. Our neighborhood has substantially changed over the past five to ten years, and more changes appear to be coming. In short, our neighborhood is increasingly popular. Over the past few years, we've seen a number of apartment buildings being constructed and new restaurants opening up. Lots of new people have come and will be coming to our front door, and we want to be ready to connect with them. We are fortunate that our church was designed and placed as an embedded church and is well suited for making organic connections with our neighbors.

We had spent a few years talking about our need to be less insular and more tuned into things going on outside the church walls. We wanted to adopt a parish mentality. Everyone seemed to like this idea, but it was a little too general and vague to inspire significant change. So we decided to try something different. We called our campaign For Tacoma, but it was really more about our immediate neighborhood.[4]

We took an aerial photo of our church and the surrounding community and drew a circle to circumscribe the pedestrian shed around our buildings. Because of the density of our neighborhood and some other factors, our circle was about 1/8 of a mile in radius, and it was more oblong than circular. We marked it up and determined that there were ninety-nine distinct entities (besides the church) within our pedestrian shed. An apartment building counted as one entity, but each business counted as a separate entity, whether they had their own building or shared a building with others. In addition to residences and businesses, we had an urban park and a few buildings for which we didn't know the purpose. We researched online and on foot and identified the name and address of each entity.

We created a booklet that contained a simplified map of our pedestrian shed, labeled with letters for each entity, with names and addresses to go with the letters. The rest of the booklet was dedicated to explaining the For Tacoma campaign, which involved assigning everyone in our church an entity that they would pray for throughout the year. We printed four hundred of these booklets and then went through and highlighted one entity in each.

We announced the For Tacoma campaign to the congregation and informed them that they each were going to be assigned their own entity in the neighborhood. One Sunday we distributed booklets to everyone present. Immediately after worship we sent our people out into the neighborhood to find their assigned entity.

We discouraged anyone from doing anything aggressive or weird; we just told people to go visit their entity and provided some questions for them to ask themselves as they observed:

- Who are the people who utilize this building?
- What is their role here (residents/employees/customers)?
- What do they care about?
- What might they need prayer for?

Since that kickoff Sunday, we have featured a different entity each week in worship. We display a picture of the entity on the cover of our bulletin, include a little write-up about the business, and pray for them in our congregational prayer time.

The campaign has been helpful in directing our members' attention outside our particular church. We don't have any dramatic stories of floods of neighbors coming to Jesus or even coming to our church as a result of this campaign. We recognize that the changes that have been taking place in our neighborhood and will continue to take place are uneven from a kingdom perspective.

It's exciting to see a fancy apartment complex being built or a trendy new restaurant in our neighborhood. But we also know that rents are rising dramatically, many people can't afford to live here, and others are being priced out of a neighborhood they've lived in for years. Some of the residents who move into the new apartment buildings will experience loneliness here and will struggle to feel like they belong.

Faithfulness in Place

As a church and as individuals embedded in this neighborhood, we are trying to discern what it means to be sign, instrument, and foretaste of the kingdom in this place at this time. We are also trying to pay attention to secular gathering places that act as foretastes of the kingdom.

223

We recognize that the three pieces of glass—our cars, our TVs, and our smartphones—will continuously pull our attention from the tangible challenges of this neighborhood and direct our energies to an endless number of far-off issues and events. For us, then, a prioritization of the proximate can help to push back against this cultural tendency and to seek to be obedient to God's call on our lives right where we are.

Much of this chapter took the conditions of our parish or neighborhood as a given and focused on how to engage the neighborhood and its residents in meaningful and helpful ways. But as already alluded to, the conditions of most neighborhoods are not given, are not static. They are changing all the time. Some of those changes are aligned with God's kingdom and bring shalom. Some of those changes are contrary to the values of God's kingdom and bring alienation, strife, and loneliness. In the next chapter, we explore how churches and individuals can influence the ways a neighborhood develops through a conceptual tool known as placemaking.

TWENTY

BELONGING
BY PLACEMAKING

The Necessity of Place

In chapter 10 we looked at place as a key component of shalom. The goodness inherent to our creation has to do not only with the fact that Adam and Eve were created by God in his image but also because they were placed in a particular environment that had been designed for their flourishing. For this reason we carry deep within us a longing for place attachment that will never be fully realized until God establishes his kingdom on earth. However, it also means that we have a strong need to make connections to, as well as create meaning in, the provisional places in which we find ourselves. A sense of being rooted in place is essential to our sense of belonging.

We noted that we have a natural tendency to transform generic spaces into places within the private spheres of our life. When we move into a new home, we immediately begin inscribing our identities on the walls and filling the rooms with meaningful objects. We do the same if we get a job that allows us to maintain an office. In this chapter, we explore what that particular impulse can look like in the civic realm as opposed to the private.

In the private realm, we have words and phrases to describe this impulse, such as "nesting," "homemaking," "setting up an office," and so on. Here, I introduce terms for this kind of activity in the public realm, such as "placemaking" and "tactical urbanism." These words might be unfamiliar, because the act of transforming space to place seems more complicated and difficult in the civic realm than it does in the private realm.

This is so for a couple of reasons. The first has to do with a contemporary phenomenon known as placelessness, discussed in chapter 10. Placelessness describes an environment consisting of generic buildings constructed by large corporations that fail to incorporate any significant local identifying markers. Placeless places occupy space by their physical presence, but they fail to provide place.

One reason that this is such a problem in contemporary life is that the deck has been stacked in favor of placeless places. These large corporations have significant financial and organizational resources to build quickly and efficiently. For many years, they also enjoyed the benefit of policies and even tax incentives to encourage their approach to building things. In this context, trying to build something with local significance can feel like David taking on Goliath.

Another reason that creating place in the civic realm feels challenging is that we cannot accomplish it as individuals. Creating place in the civic realm involves working with our neighbors and often partnering with our local government entities. As noted, Americans have a strong preference for solutions that can be pursued as individuals, and we especially like problems that can be solved through making some kind of consumer purchase. Creating place in the civic realm is almost always a communal activity and as such is likely to stretch us and make us uncomfortable at times.

Last, creating place feels challenging because our imaginations have atrophied over the past few decades. Many of us have traveled and have experienced successful places that seem to enrich the lives of those fortunate enough to live near them. Visiting a quaint park in France, a vibrant paseo in Mexico, or a tree-lined square in Savannah, Georgia, can be inspirational.

Then we return home—to some atrocity called Tremper Plaza, which is an ugly parking lot surrounded by strip malls and big-box retail stores. We are shocked by the contrast but soon adjust to our disappointment and start planning our next trip to an interesting, life-giving place. We never dare to entertain the notion that we might be able to create a meaningful place in our own city or neighborhood. We never consider the fact that those interesting places that we visited didn't fall from the sky but were imagined and built by ordinary people not completely unlike us.

Placemaking

Placemaking involves investing in—and sometimes creating—meaningful public places that work for our community. We can probably all think of public places that don't work, such as dead and uninviting plazas. Placemaking strives for better—much better. Placemaking aspires to make public places

- that people choose to spend time in when they don't have to;
- that invite people to sit and enjoy a respite in their day; and
- that are often filled with people of all ages.

Placemaking can be seen as the process by which a community collaborates around a successful shared space in their neighborhood.

The term "placemaking" has become trendy in recent years, causing all kinds of projects and initiatives to lay claim to this descriptor. We focus here on the placemaking that involves a great deal of community collaboration, omitting top-down "placemaking" projects usually initiated by for-profit corporations. This is not to say that such are meritless, just that they are not as helpful to our larger concern of creating a sense of belonging as community-driven projects can be.

Placemaking begins with a shared understanding of what makes a successful public place. The Project for Public Spaces identifies four key attributes of a successful place.[1]

227

1. Access and linkages: A successful public space is easy to get to and get through; it is visible both from a distance and up close.
2. Comfort and image: Comfort includes perceptions about safety, cleanliness, and the availability of places to sit.
3. Uses and activities: Activities are the basic building blocks of a place. Having something to do gives people a reason to come to a place—and return.
4. Sociability: When people see friends, meet and greet their neighbors, and feel comfortable interacting with strangers, they tend to feel a stronger sense of place or attachment to their community—and to the place that fosters these types of social activities.

The placemaking movement is fundamentally about challenging the common impulse that some people are just fortunate enough to live in the vicinity of successful public places. Placemaking challenges the residents of a community to ask, "Why can't we have something like that here?" Creating a successful public place isn't as difficult as it seems. Before our half century of automobile-oriented development, placemaking was a well-understood common practice.

This means that we have thousands of successful public places to learn from and emulate. As placemaking has gotten more popular, we're seeing many contemporary examples to follow as well.

An Elevated Respite in the City

In the heart of the meatpacking district of New York City is a 1.45-mile-long elevated walkway that has to be seen to be believed. The meandering path takes visitors through beautifully landscaped terrain interspersed with inviting places to sit and fascinating public art pieces. Between 2009 and 2014, High Line trail was opened to the public in three stages and now attracts millions of visitors per year. It has spurred a renaissance of the district, and property values adjacent to the High Line have skyrocketed.

In the 1980s the High Line was an abandoned elevated train track covered with weeds and graffiti. The elevated track was constructed in the 1930s to move goods into and out of the district out of the way of pedestrians below. Over time, the work done by trains was taken over by trucks, and in 1982 the final train ran down these tracks, which sat unused for seventeen years. In 1999 they were acquired by the CSX Transportation Corporation, which initially looked at restoring a train line to the High Line. But they later commissioned a study that determined that their best use would be as a public park. The corporation began pursuing partnership with the city for this purpose.

Around the same time a group called Friends of the High Line was formed, and they hosted a design competition for the site and pursued options for turning it into a public space. They faced significant obstacles. Initially, the planning department was unsupportive. Joseph Rose, the city planning commissioner, claimed, "That platform has no right to be there except for transportation, and that use is long gone."[2] Rose claimed they had studied this property for a decade, and that demolition was the only feasible solution. The project also experienced pushback from a local residents' group called Chelsea Property Owners.

Friends of the High Line refused to give up and instead worked to develop a network of support and interest. They commissioned an economic feasibility study that demonstrated that the city would gain more in increased property taxes in the area than the cost of renovating the High Line. In 2001, Michael Bloomberg was elected Mayor of New York City. Bloomburg was an advocate of public parks, and he authorized the High Line to be preserved from demolition and refurbished for pedestrian use. The city also pledged $61 million in revitalization funds. The city then had to negotiate with the Chelsea Property Owners and traded some development rights in exchange for support of their plan.

By 2004, with all obstacles out of the way, a design team was selected and started fleshing out the plan. The following year, the private developer donated the land to the city, which worked with Friends of the High Line to organize construction. In 2009 the first section was opened, and the whole project was completed in 2014. The High Line is a public amenity for residents of and visitors to New York City, as well as a living testimony of the power of ordinary citizens to overcome obstacles and create an attractive respite out of thin air.

An Urban Oasis

Immediately adjacent to my church in Tacoma is another beautiful example of placemaking. Wright Park is a twenty-nine-acre urban park containing a walking path, a pond, hundreds of varieties of trees, a conservatory, and a lawn bowling court. Wright Park was donated to the City of Tacoma in 1889 and has been a jewel in the heart of Tacoma and a great source of local pride. Unfortunately, as Tacoma's economy stalled in the latter part of the twentieth century, Wright Park suffered from neglect and lack of investment. The facility was looking run down, the overuse of motorized vehicles had compromised the paths, and the park was frequently used for illegal activity. It was not considered a good place to take children, and everyone avoided it at night.

In 2004 the City of Tacoma made a commitment to make Wright Park a great public place again and initiated a process toward developing and implementing a master plan. Unlike in earlier years, when a municipality would let bureaucrats and "experts" drive the early stages of the plan and invite community input only late in the process, the Wright Park planning process was community driven from the beginning. The city identified a broad list of stakeholders and held private meetings with them to hear their concerns and ideas. Three different community meetings were held to get feedback at every stage of the process. And a steering committee was formed from various institutions and agencies to guide the process.

The steering committee articulated eleven design principles that would provide direction for the eventual plan. Then they devised an ambitious plan to make the park safer, more accessible, and more useful to the community while maintaining its historic character. It then broke down the project into three phases and created a plan for the timing and funding of these phases.

All three phases have been completed, and I can personally attest to the fact that Wright Park has become a highly successful public place right in the heart of my community. It is continually filled with people of all ages who reflect the racial and cultural diversity of Tacoma.

My children each enjoy different aspects of the park. My older son loves the botanical conservatory and collecting chestnuts in the fall. My older daughter loves to use the park for photo shoots. My younger daughter's high school cross country team uses the park as their home course. And my younger son loves to play on the playground and to watch the ducks on the pond. I regularly use the park for a "walking meeting" if I need to get out of my office for a bit.

The Wright Park Master Plan process can be considered a place-sensitive placemaking process, meaning that it was initiated by a public entity (the City of Tacoma) but was led in such a way as to respect the geographical, social, and cultural context of the site. The place-sensitive approach represents an improvement on some of the top-down, concept-driven approaches to shaping public places of the past.[3]

Charrette

The easiest form of placemaking to envision involves taking a particular piece of land or corridor and turning it into a place of significance. In many cases, however, the context is a little messier. There is a church in Richmond, Virginia, that is located in the center of a small neighborhood. The neighborhood is compact and contains all of the necessary components of a thriving community, but it lacks cohesion and sufficient public space. This neighborhood would benefit greatly from a good network of walking corridors and a central gathering space. The problem is that any land that might be used to develop these kinds of amenities is owned by different stakeholders who have different interests and priorities. Normally, this would mean that very little could be done to improve the neighborhood, since getting the various stakeholders to agree on anything would be all but impossible.

However, in this case, the church was able to get the community to agree on a plan by utilizing a planning tool known as a "charrette." A charrette is a multiday event in which all stakeholders for a particular area are brought together to work out a creative solution that everyone can agree on. The facilitators of a charrette are careful to put together a collaborative planning event that avoids all of the pitfalls of public forums. Participants in a charrette are required to remain in the conversation all the way to the end in order to discourage the "read an angry speech, then storm out of the room" move so common at public meetings.

Charrettes also include experts in many fields so that technical questions can be answered on the spot. Participants in a charrette are organized into groups around tables, where they work with a diverse group of people from their community. Last, charrettes usually involve architects and planners prepared to sketch out the ideas people come up with. At various points during the week, the community is invited to see renderings of some of the best ideas that have been generated and to give feedback.

In some public meetings about a particular project, most of the project has been planned before the meeting, so attendees are rightly skeptical about the role of their input. But in a charrette, participants see their ideas fleshed out on paper in real time. Usually, after hearing the project's goals and parameters, each working group gets to work on a plan and share it with the group as a whole. After all plans have been shared, people can say what they like and don't like about them. New plans are created out of the first round of plans. Members of the community who weren't part of the charrette are invited in to give feedback on these. Then there are more meetings to devise one plan that everyone likes.

It is this kind of process that restores trust in a community and often causes stakeholders to let down their guard and consider compromises and out-of-the-box solutions they wouldn't have considered before. A charrette is an effective tool for putting together a master plan that meets multiple goals for a neighborhood. Some residents want to see more housing options; others want to see an increase in retail and services.

Some want walkability to improve, and others want to see good places to gather. Rather than wait for individuals to pursue their own agendas and see others as rivals or potential blockers, a charrette encourages the residents and stakeholders of a neighborhood to work together and create a community that works for everybody.

Tactical Urbanism

Many of these approaches to placemaking are inspiring but also a little daunting. If the idea of getting one stakeholder in the room seems like a long shot, how is one to get all of the stakeholders there? If raising $20,000 to get the high school choir to a national competition seems like a stretch, finding $60 million for revitalization seems impossible.

Placemaking can seem like the kind of thing that other, more powerful people do. This is why another form of placemaking known as "tactical urbanism," or "DIY urbanism," has emerged. Tactical urbanism is an experimental or incremental approach to making changes to the public space in a neighborhood that utilizes low-cost materials and out-of-the-box thinking.

A group of neighbors might determine there is a need for a good gathering spot in their neighborhood. There is some underutilized land where a few streets come together at an odd angle, and the group starts to envision a minipark or plaza in this spot. With traffic cones, some cafe tables, a few benches, and planter boxes made from old tires, they can build that plaza over the course of one afternoon. Then they can invite the rest of the neighborhood to a party with music, games, and food.

Tactical-urbanist projects can be short-term experiments that simply expand residents' imagination. But tactical urbanist projects can also be an important first step in bringing permanent change to a neighborhood. Rather than waiting for the city to initiate some new amenity, tactical urbanism allows the residents of a neighborhood to take the initiative and show the city what they want for themselves.

This is a very fluid and organic concept, and as you might imagine, there is a broad range of approaches under this umbrella. Some such projects are technically illegal and result in fines for the instigators. But many other projects are accomplished within the bounds of legality or even in partnership with city officials. The emergence of tactical urbanism over the past few years is but one example of a more grassroots, participatory approach to neighborhood development.

Place and Shared Meaning

We have a strong need for a connection to place in order to maintain a sense of belonging to the particular environment in which we live. Some people are fortunate to find themselves living in an area that has a strong sense of place. Others, however, find themselves in a largely placeless environment where it is difficult to form strong connections within the surrounding environment.

Placemaking represents an important tool for recovering place in areas lacking this key amenity. However, placemaking is really just a physical expression of a more general phenomenon. In developing spaces for residents to gather and interact, placemaking is establishing settings where local stories can be generated and shared. And local stories are one of the forms that shared meaning can take among residents of a city or neighborhood.

Place, therefore, can be a catalyst for shared meaning among residents. Place is usually not the shared meaning itself but a forum and container for the shared meaning. In the next chapter, we explore further this idea of shared meaning and what role it plays in securing a strong bond among residents and encouraging belonging.

TWENTY-ONE

BELONGING
AND LOCAL CULTURE

Thick Language

An earlier excursus introduced the idea of thick language, the language we use when we enjoy sufficient shared meaning with others. In settings where thick language is appropriate, we can let down our guard and "be ourselves." If we are able to use thick language and be understood, then there is a good chance we feel a strong sense of belonging in this place.

Most of us have had the experience of being able to use thick language with others but perhaps haven't thought about how that particular condition came about. Some questions might help us make sense of this phenomenon:

- How does the meaning we share with others get generated?
- How does our thick language get shaped over time?
- How is thick language passed on to newcomers in our community?
- What kinds of experiences tend to build a robust story in a community?

Local Culture

In an essay called "The Work of Local Culture," Wendell Berry uses an old galvanized bucket to illustrate a fundamental task of human community. This bucket hangs on a fence post in the woods near his home, and he likes to observe it when he is out walking. You or I might walk right by that bucket without giving it a second thought, but for Berry, "what is going on in that bucket is the most momentous thing I know, the greatest miracle that I have ever heard of: it is making earth."[1]

Berry describes how this happens. Leaves from the trees fall in the bucket, absorb moisture from the rain, and begin to rot. Animals visit the bucket to eat and leave behind shells and droppings. Insects visit the bucket to help break down the organic material, and some die in the bucket. Over time, the result of all this activity is a few inches of good soil in the bottom of the bucket. And that is, for Berry, "the greatest miracle that [he has] ever heard of."

A good case could easily be made that because we are all dependent on food, we are all dependent on soil. And this could be why what is going on in the bucket is so important. Berry makes that specific point in some of his other writings, but that is not why he is so interested in this bucket. In the soil-making work of this bucket, Berry sees a metaphor for the human activity of "making" local culture.

Like soil, local culture is the productive medium needed for the growth of all kinds of other things necessary for a flourishing human life. Later in the essay, Berry notes that the activity of gathering in the evenings to share stories had been the quintessential way of making local culture, at least in rural Kentucky. For Berry, then, local culture can be thought of as the accumulation, distillation, and transmission of the stories generated by the people of a particular place.

According to Berry, "A human community, then, if it is to last long, must exert a sort of centripetal force, holding local soil and local memory in place."[2] Our job, then, as residents of a particular place is to gather and hold the materials necessary for the thing that needs to be made. For the bucket, those things are leaves, rain, shells, droppings, and carcasses, which become soil. For local people, the job is to hear, tell, and (to some degree) generate local stories that become the stuff of local culture.

From here, Berry launches into a sobering argument about how our educational system is geared toward preparing children to leave home and sever local ties rather than to stay and invest in the local culture from generation to generation. Berry worries about long-term cultural effects of sending agricultural goods and young people from the country to the city and then having the city return cheap manufactured goods and packaged entertainment to the country.

I don't disagree with Berry's larger thesis, but I want to take his bucket metaphor in a different direction. What Berry is describing here is the process by which people who live in proximity to one another cultivate and share thick language. Earlier, we described thick language as the kind used when people have a lot of shared meaning. Thin language is used among people who don't know each other very well and aren't part of the same story. What Berry contributes to this discussion is the notion of how people develop the ability to use thick language with one another. To take this notion a bit further, I want to consider how choices we make can move us toward or away from developing the thick language with others that is a key aspect of belonging. The question I want to explore is how the people of a particular city and/or neighborhood can know and contribute to the local culture whether they are third-generation citizens or temporary residents.

Shared Meaning in Tacoma

Let me provide a couple of examples from my local context to help make this more concrete.

Beautiful Angle

For the past fifteen years, Tacoma has been the unwitting host to a guerrilla art initiative known as Beautiful Angle. It's a fairly simple concept. About once a month, two local artists, one a writer (Tom

Llewellyn) and the other a graphic designer (Lance Kagey), create a poster and print 120 copies of it on an old-fashioned letterpress machine. In the middle of the night they post one hundred of the posters throughout Tacoma using wheat paste as the fixative. Over the next day or so, members of the community enjoy the posters, and some pull them down and add them to their collections. The wheat paste makes it very easy to do this. The time the posters are up has grown increasingly short as the collecting community grows. The remaining twenty posters are available for purchase, and the revenue from sales is used to support a local charity.

The concepts and themes for the Beautiful Angle posters are all over the map, but they tend to combine local issues, creative wordplay, and a fairly free use of religious language and imagery. One example, "Olmstead Anthony," is reproduced here. It both employs and disseminates a great deal of shared meaning for the residents of Tacoma.[3] To understand this poster, you need to know a few salient details about our fair city. First, the famous American landscape architect Fredrick Law Olmstead (who designed Central Park in New York City) was commissioned in 1873 to create a master plan for the city of Tacoma that would take advantage of its hilly terrain and sweeping views of Commencement Bay. When the plan was completed, it was considered and then roundly rejected forty-three days later. Many feel that this was a watershed moment for Tacoma. Had Olmstead's plan been adopted, Tacoma would have been established as a shining jewel at the edge of the wilderness. The other thing you need to know is that famous bowler Earl "the Pearl" Anthony was born and raised in Tacoma.

These two figures represent what Tacoma could have been and what Tacoma ended up being. The rejection of the Olmstead plan can be seen simply as a missed opportunity for this struggling "day late, dollar short" town or as a heroic moment of a city holding on to its roots and refusing to try to become something it isn't just to impress the swells. This tension is picked up visually by one character literally speaking flowery language and the other speaking bowling lanes. Olmstead gives voice to the archetypical regret and shame carried around

HISTORY IN THE MAKING.

Frederick Law Olmsted and Earl Anthony met at a bar in heaven.

"Tacoma should have selected my urban design," said Olmsted, twisting his cocktail napkin into graceful curves, "then it would be a world-class city, and not the lumberjack village it became."

"You always were a pompous East Coast jerk," said Earl, tapping two fingers and one thumb on the edge of his beer glass. "World-class cities never have enough bowling alleys."

Beautiful Angle

Figure 10. "Olmstead Anthony" by Tom Llewellyn and Lance Kagey subconsciously by Tacomans, but those residual feelings are dealt a mortal blow by Anthony's dismissive rejoinder and by calling out Olmstead as an "East Coast jerk." This is an appropriate role for Anthony, who was a dominant force in professional bowling for decades but was known for his no-nonsense crew cut and nerdy glasses.

But the text and imagery of this poster represent just the top layer of shared meaning communicated by it. The medium also conveys a significant message. To see this other message, one has to know a bit more about the history of Tacoma: the rejection of the Olmstead plan is not just an isolated incident. At the beginning of the twentieth century, Tacoma was emerging as a prominent up-and-coming city in the Northwest. As the terminus to the rail line from Chicago, it was wealthier than Seattle, just forty miles north. But during the twentieth century, Seattle surpassed Tacoma as the economic and cultural hub of Washington State, and Tacoma developed a reputation for being Seattle's blue-collar, gritty cousin.

Because of this, among Tacomans there is some resentment about our neighbor to the north, and for most of the twentieth century it felt like Tacoma wanted to be Seattle when it grew up. However, over the past fifteen years, Tacoma has experienced a local renaissance and the emergence of a thriving arts community. The feeling is now that Tacoma has found its own groove and isn't interested in becoming like Seattle. However, one can see vestiges of Tacoma's past and its Seattle envy in the way the artistic renaissance is playing out.

The two forms of art that Tacoma is most known for are glassblowing and letterpress. Both of these art forms have a gritty or industrial feel. This specialization is connected to the tension between Tacoma and Seattle. If you want to be an artist in Tacoma, you can't do "sissy art" like they do in Seattle. To be legit here, you have to be able to mangle yourself with your art.

So the fact that the Olmstead Anthony poster is an artistic piece created on massive industrial letterpress machine, affixed to a telephone pole with wheat paste, and then offered without charge to the Tacoma community communicates something important about our shared history with respect to Seattle. The form of the poster aligns with its message. It says, "We don't need fancy galleries, commissions, and pretense, because our art speaks for itself."

The Olmstead Anthony poster is a tangible example of the citizens of Tacoma telling their story, healing wounds, and working out their emerging identity. It is meaningful to long-term Tacomans because it draws together threads of a narrative that goes back over a hundred years. It also plays an instructive hospitable role. Putting this poster on display throughout Tacoma helps newcomers (like myself) get oriented to the narrative in which we have been inserted. Seeing this poster and laughing at the punch line was one of my first moments of feeling like I belonged in Tacoma.

Monkeyshines

Another example of utilizing and developing a thick language of place is the Monkeyshines tradition in Tacoma. Monkeyshines is basically an annual adult Easter egg hunt. Every year, in preparation for the Chinese New Year, the glassblowing community in Tacoma blows hundreds of glass balls that are then stamped with the Chinese zodiac sign for that year (the first year was the monkey). Some time around the official Chinese New Year (the exact date is always a secret) in the middle of the night, the glassblowing community and friends distribute the balls, which are hidden throughout Tacoma.

Eventually someone finds one of the balls and posts it on social media. As you might expect, word spreads quickly, and soon all of Tacoma is crawling with flashlight-wielding Monkeyshines hunters before the sun comes up. This tradition began as a grassroots initiative and was very much off the radar. It was not a city program, nor did it have any recognizable institutional support. There was no Monkeyshines announcement or any official explanation of how it works or why we do it. Someone found a glass ball, someone else found a glass ball, and eventually people figured out that this was a thing.

For those who know about Monkeyshines, it's kind of a big deal. Many who search year after year have yet to find their first ball. People come from out of state to look for balls when the word gets out. Yet lots of people in our community have no idea this is going on. As a relative newcomer to Tacoma, I was fortunate enough to find out about Monkeyshines in my first year, and every time I meet a new resident, I like to tell them about Monkeyshines. It would still be fun and useful if it had been conceived and managed by the City of Tacoma, but the fact that it is an underground movement makes it even more useful for establishing a sense of belonging.

Shared Meaning and Making Local Culture

The Beautiful Angle project and the Monkeyshines tradition are two examples of the kinds of things that establish and instruct a community in the thick language of shared meaning. Through participating in these traditions (or taking a leading role in them), one is in fact strengthening the local culture as well as establishing for oneself a stronger sense of belonging.

These two examples illustrate a small set of a larger category of elements that express and carry many of the meanings shared by a local community. This larger category includes a variety of things:

- local stories
- icons and imagery
- traditions (annual, monthly, weekly, daily)
- sports teams
- lexicon
- food
- music and local bands
- local characters and celebrities
- important sites
- jokes and shared humor
- major institutions (corporations, nonprofits, colleges)
- natural features (bay, mountain, cherry blossoms, etc.)

242

Many of the elements of shared meaning can be pretty minor. For instance, when you visualize a children's play structure that includes things like swings and a slide, what do you call it? In some places I've lived, they call it a "play area" or maybe a "jungle gym." In Tacoma, everyone calls this kind of thing a "big toy." I don't know why, but everyone calls it that, and as soon as I moved to Tacoma, I started calling it that as well.

Through the Beautiful Angle project, Monkeyshines, and less formalized ways (big toy), people who live here have all sorts of opportunities to establish and strengthen a sense of shared meaning. But is this anything like the rich storytelling practices of the tightly knit agrarian community whose demise Berry lamented in his essay?

In a city of 120,000, it is not feasible for the community (or even a good representation of the community) to gather after dinner to share stories. The scale is simply too large. We also are faced with the challenge of the transitory nature of our community. Lots of our children grow up and move to larger cities to find work. On the other hand, we do have enough of a local economy that some of our children are able to find work and stay in Tacoma if they so choose. And we are a growing city; many people choose to move to Tacoma from other locations.

This last point raises an important issue about making local culture in contemporary society. Berry rightly extols the virtues of after-dinner storytelling in a small rural community in Kentucky as a way of making culture. It would be good for all of us if there were more settings like this, where these kinds of practices were maintained. Small rural communities can be a good setting for cultural transmission from generation to generation, but this works mostly within the strong bonds of extended family and long-term members of the community.

Small rural towns don't always do a great job of accepting new people, especially if they represent a different demographic. Similarly, small towns don't tend to do a great job assimilating short-term residents into the shared meanings of the community.

In this regard then, a city like Tacoma can do a better job of making local culture with a more transitory and diverse population than a small town in Kentucky might be able to do. Telling a new resident about

Monkeyshines and then inviting them to come look for glass balls on a random day in predawn January can make the new resident feel like a local pretty quickly.

This is where it can be helpful to think about making local culture in terms of all of the ways that shared meaning is created rather than just restricting ourselves to telling stories. Learning to say "big toy" is a small but not insignificant step toward feeling like a local in Tacoma.

According to Wendell Berry, "A human community, then, if it is to last long, must exert a sort of centripetal force, holding local soil and local memory in place."[4] If Berry is right, it is extremely important that we have a good understanding of place and its importance to local culture. We can build up our local culture by learning the things of our community that constitute our shared memories and teaching them to others.

Merging Stories

Continuing with Berry's bucket analogy, we can think of placemaking as a matter not only of learning, ruminating, and passing on the stories of our community but also of connecting the stories of our own lives to the larger and longer stories of our community. Collected within that bucket hanging on a fence post on Berry's walk are a random set of elements that happen to be bound together by the geographical constraints of a galvanized bucket. Wherever those elements came from, they are now being formed into a common substance that is rich and vital.

In 2007 we were called to Tacoma so I could become the pastor of a church that was 134 years old. Whenever I am called to a new location, I like to invest a good amount of time and energy in learning the stories of the church and the local community. With the church, I had to be a little more proactive than I'd been in learning Tacoma stories.

Early in my tenure, I called a meeting of the past and present elders. I arranged seats in a large circle and had them sit in order of the date they had joined the church. Beginning with the elder who had been at the church the longest, I had each share a memorable story from the era during which they'd joined. Through this simple method, we were able to put together a basic narrative of at least the past half century at First Pres. I learned a lot during that hour, and I think everyone there learned something about the church as well.

While it is extremely important to learn the story of a church, eventually the time comes when our personal story begins to merge with the larger story of the church. Of course, this happens from the moment we begin to engage with a particular church community, but the more momentous occasions in our lives can become significant connecting convergence points where narratives come together.

For us, the birth of our fourth child (a caboose) was one of those events. Most of the pastors who had preceded me were quite a bit older, so the members of the congregation couldn't remember a senior pastor ever having a baby in their midst. Some of our older members couldn't remember the last baby shower they had attended. As for us, our three older children had all been born in Missoula almost ten years before. We'd thought we might be done with having kids. It was quite memorable to be thrust back into the baby vortex in this relatively new setting. Having a child in this community provided countless opportunities to bond with the members of the church and the larger community of Tacoma by learning to say "big toy" when we were looking for a place to get some wiggles out.

Events

Everything we experience in our community becomes woven into our story with a particular group of people in a particular place. However, the experienced significance of certain things can vary considerably depending on their nature and our approach to the situation.

We can use the term "events" to describe these kinds of experiences, but I also like the Japanese phrase *ichi-go ichi-e*, which literally means "one time, one meeting," to convey this idea. The idea is that every time we gather with a group of people, it is a unique event. This is true even if we gather with the same group of people more than one time, because each time it is different.

As mentioned earlier, my wife is a high school theater teacher, and every spring she puts on an incredible musical with about 150 students. They perform eight shows over two weekends. As a devoted husband and loyal supporter of the arts, I try to make it to every single show. This practice has reinforced for me the truth of *ichi-go ichi-e*. Every performance uses the same script, the same score, and the same group of kids, and every night the event is different.

The run of a show has a particular pattern. Opening night is energetic and exciting, but sometimes kids forget a line or two. The second night is often the sloppiest, because the kids get overconfident from a successful first show. After this, they start to get into a groove, and the show jells. Characters become more clearly focused as actors learn about their characters through audience response. Closing night is usually a very emotional show.

I have become especially aware of the impact of the audience on the cast as a whole. The way an audience reacts to what's happening onstage has a huge impact on the feel of each show. I've come to believe that in many cases an audience gets the show they deserve. A rowdy audience that responds to the jokes gets an especially funny show. A sentimental audience gets an emotional show. And an audience that watches politely but doesn't respond audibly gets a flat show.

And then of course there are the major incidents that become part of the lore. At one production of *Hairspray*, the lead (Tracy) was recovering from a bad cold but thought she was able to perform. She almost made it through the first song when she lost her voice. She opened her mouth, and no sound came out. Fortunately, she didn't have another song until the next scene.

The assistant stage manager knew the part from all the rehearsals and was told she'd have to finish the show with less than ten minutes to prepare. The problem was that she didn't fit the costume of the lead, and there wasn't time to fix her hair into the iconic "Tracy hairdo." The costumer converted a dress into a costume, a wig from a lobby display was retrieved, and by the second song, the lead had been replaced and finished the show with only a few missed lines. The entire cast had to work together to make it work, since the new Tracy hadn't learned any of the blocking. Many in the audience had no idea that something was different, but for the cast and a few other insiders it became the stuff of legend.

Because of its event character, live theater performances have a tendency to get embedded as memorable parts of the story in a particular place. This is markedly different from watching a show at home on Netflix. There are some amazing TV shows and movies now that tell captivating stories. Those stories make significant impressions on us, but because they are not tethered to any particular time or place and because there is no actual interaction between the actors and the audience, Netflix shows don't tend to make significant contributions to our story in a place. Of course, there are ways to augment the "eventness" of a Netflix show. For example, we can invite a group of friends to come over for a themed show-watching experience. But I'll take live theater over Netflix any day.

Belonging as Knowing the Story

Belonging involves a sense of fitting in with a particular place, a particular group of people, and/or with the ethos or narrative of a place. To feel as if we belong somewhere, we have to have a network of relationships at the intimate, private, social, and public scales. We have to feel some sense of attachment to the place where we live, work, worship, and play. And we have to know enough of the story to feel included in the local conversation.

We've explored some of the processes by which that story is generated, shaped, and passed on. Of course, these three elements mutually reinforce one another. We need institutions to build and activate successful public spaces for people to gather. We need to gather to generate and share those stories with one another. When these three aspects come together in the right way, we usually experience a satisfying sense of belonging.

247

Unfortunately, the hope of this kind of belonging isn't always enough to help us resist the powerful forces of the three pieces of glass that work in the opposite direction. Even as we long to belong, most of us spend an inordinate amount of time driving our cars and feeling angry at other drivers. Most of us still choose to binge-watch a Netflix series instead of heading out the door to interact with our neighbors. And of course, we can't go more than a few minutes without pulling out our phones and checking for updates.

Fortunately, solving the crisis of belonging isn't just up to us. As disciples of Jesus, we believe in a God who gets the last word and has invited us into his story. In this life, we can try to be more intentional about pursuing belonging for ourselves and for our communities, but we know that our efforts will fall short of the belonging we will experience when Christ returns, reconciles all things to himself, and draws the threads of our stories together.

At the conclusion to his Chronicles of Narnia series, C. S. Lewis depicts heaven not only as the end of all stories but also as the beginning of the real story:

> And as He spoke, He no longer looked to them like a lion; but the things that began to happen after that were so great and beautiful that I cannot write them. And for us this is the end of all the stories, and we can most truly say that they all lived happily ever after. But for them it was only the beginning of the real story. All their life in this world and all their adventures in Narnia had only been the cover and the title page: now at last they were beginning Chapter One of the Great Story which no one on earth has read: which goes on for ever: in which every chapter is better than the one before.[5]

As we experience triumphs and failures in our attempts to offer signs and instruments of belonging, the fact that the reality of God's belonging is breaking through and drawing us in gives us hope. As we live out our story and connect it to the stories around us, we can take comfort in the fact that all of our stories are being gathered together into his story.

CONCLUSION

Belonging to the God Who Knows Your Name

Whoever has ears, let them hear what the Spirit says to the churches.
To the one who is victorious, I will give some of the hidden manna. I
will also give that person a white stone with a new name written on it,
known only to the one who receives it.

Revelation 2:17

OK, let's just acknowledge up front that there are a few things in this
passage from Revelation that we don't fully understand. Nonetheless,
I'm going to utilize it as a counterpoint bookend for my opening story
about Norm walking into Cheers as a foretaste of kingdom belonging.
I'm seeing this evocative image as a kind of eschatological fulfillment of
Norm's experience of opening the door to his favorite bar. I am making
this connection because there seem to be some overlapping elements.

In both pictures, there is a threshold. Norm's is a door to his favorite
bar. When he opens it, he enters the space and experiences belonging
in the social space of Cheers. In Revelation, the threshold is fellowship
with Christ, who is depicted as entering through a door: "Behold, I
stand at the door and knock" (Rev. 3:20 ESV). Transformed through
Christ, disciples participate in his victory over death and experience
belonging in God's kingdom.

Norm enters his social space with the expectation of a glass of beer and some pretzels. These things are not insignificant, since eating and drinking with others is an important aspect of forming attachments to people and places in our lives. As Norm drinks and eats with others in this setting, they are doing the work of local culture by sharing stories and generating stories together.

In Revelation, those who cross the threshold are promised manna, the food that sustained the people of God on their journey through the wilderness. Manna is an actual thing, but it is also a symbol of God's provision for the physical needs of his people. Elsewhere, that sustaining food is depicted as a lavish feast: "Let us rejoice and be glad and give him glory! For the wedding of the Lamb has come" (Rev. 19:7).

Norm's belonging is affirmed as he is greeted by a crowd of regulars calling out his name. The passage from Revelation describes the belonging of God's people affirmed through the presentation of a white stone with their name written on it. Except this will not be the name that they were called throughout their earthly life; it will be a new name. Throughout the Scriptures, God sometimes gave those whom he called a new name to signify their true identity in him. Abram became Abraham, Jacob became Israel, and Simon became Peter.

The name on the white stone will be new, but it will be recognized by us. It will resonate with us as more true to who we are than the name we formerly used. Hearing and recognizing our name is portrayed in John's Gospel as one of the more intimate ways we experience belonging: "The gatekeeper opens the gate for him, and the sheep listen to his voice. He calls his own sheep by name and leads them out. When he has brought out all his own, he goes on ahead of them, and his sheep follow him because they know his voice" (John 10:3–4). Near the end of his Gospel, John shows that this is not just a beautiful image but a concrete reality when he depicts Mary encountering the resurrected Jesus for the first time. She doesn't immediately recognize him by sight, but when he says her name, she instantly knows him and greets him with a joyous and intimate greeting. "Jesus said to her, 'Mary.' She turned toward him and cried out in Aramaic, 'Rabboni!' (which means 'Teacher')" (John 20:16). John here captures a beautiful moment of belonging for a disciple of Jesus.

Each element of the promise in Revelation 2 picks up an aspect of belonging. The "one who is victorious" establishes our belonging in the place of God's kingdom. The new name represents our relational belonging to the God who knows our name. And the manna represents our belonging to the story of salvation, as we too are sustained in our physical needs by the God who loves us.

And the white stone? Among biblical scholars, there is not a clear consensus as to what role this stone plays in the image. So I'm not even going to try to legitimize this interpretive move, but when the Spirit promises to "give" the stone, I'm picturing him throwing the stone. Yep, the Spirit cranks it back and lets that sucker fly right at us. And we all know what is especially vulnerable to thrown stones. Glass houses.

We live in a culture that is experiencing a profound crisis of belonging largely because we have insulated and isolated ourselves from people, place, and story by encasing ourselves behind three pieces of glass—windshields, TV screens, and smartphones. We desperately need something or someone to break through these elements of our self-imposed exile and draw us in to the belonging that we most desperately want. Why not envision the Spirit breaking through this glass-encased existence we have built for ourselves? It wouldn't be the first time he's done something like this. Paul depicts him breaking down the dividing wall of hostility between Jews and gentiles. And why not picture the church as an agent of Christ, helping to break this self-imposed exile to which so many have been condemned?

Ultimately, this work will be completed when Christ returns and reigns in glory. When Christ's kingdom is fully realized, our longing for belonging will be met. This belonging will not play into our autonomous individualistic tendencies but will involve relationships, place, and story. I suspect in some ways it will feel very familiar and unremarkable. Remember the delightfully ordinary picture of shalom from the book of Zechariah: "Men and women of ripe old age will sit in the streets of Jerusalem, each of them with cane in hand because of their age. The city streets will be filled with boys and girls playing there" (Zech. 8:4–5). But in other ways it will be unspeakably beautiful and awe inspiring: "The city does not need the sun or the moon to shine on it, for the glory of God gives it light, and the Lamb is its lamp. The nations will walk by its light, and the kings of the earth will bring their splendor into it" (Rev. 21:23–24).

These are delightful promises, and they fill us with hope. But I do not believe that it is God's intent that we just sit around waiting for this belonging fulfillment. We are meant individually and as churches to act as sign, instrument, and foretaste of belonging for those inside and outside the community of faith.

Jeremiah's instruction to the exiles that they are to seek the shalom (belonging) of the city to which they have been called makes this perfectly clear. Jeremiah's charge reminds us that we must seek belonging not only in the private realm of family and friends but also in the civic realm of neighbors and fellow citizens. Our experience of belonging and their experience of belonging are inextricably connected: "Pray to the LORD for it, because if it [experiences shalom (belonging)], you too will [experience shalom (belonging)]" (Jer. 29:7).

To bring this full circle, we want Norm to experience true belonging in God's kingdom in his current situation and in his eternal existence. At the same time, we can appreciate that he has found a place where he can experience belonging within his local civic realm. We can also pray for Norm and millions of other neighbors that they would find relief from the loneliness and alienation that so plague our society. We can pray and work to strengthen our neighbors' connections to people, place, and story right where they live. And we can pray and work that we too would experience connection to people, place, and story right where we live.

NOTES

Chapter 1 What Is Belonging?

1. Jane Jacobs, "The Kind of Problem a City Is," chap. 22 in *The Death and Life of Great American Cities* (New York: Vintage Books, 1961).

2. Joseph R. Myers, *The Search to Belong: Rethinking Intimacy, Community, and Small Groups* (Grand Rapids: Zondervan, 2003).

3. Myers, *The Search to Belong*, 50.

Chapter 2 The Special Need for Civic Belonging

1. Peggy A. Thotis, "Personal Agency in the Accumulation of Multiple Role-Identities," in *Advances in Identity Theory and Research*, ed. Peter J. Burke, Timothy J. Owns, Richard T. Serpe, and Peggy A. Thotis (New York: Kluwer Academic, 2003), 179–94. Cited by Charles Montgomery, *Happy City: Transforming Our Lives through Urban Design* (New York: Farrar, Straus & Giroux, 2014), 127.

2. Montgomery, *Happy City*, 127.

3. Montgomery, *Happy City*, 128.

4. John Helliwell and Christopher Barrington-Leigh, "How Much Is Social Capital Worth?," in *The Social Cure*, ed. J. Jetten, C. Haslam, and S. A. Haslam (London: Psychology Press, 2010), 55–71.

Chapter 3 Signs, Instruments, and Foretastes of Belonging

1. Lesslie Newbigin, *The Gospel in a Pluralist Society* (Grand Rapids: Eerdmans, 1989), 232–33.

2. "Who We Are," Hilltop Artists, accessed July 10, 2019, https://www.hilltopartists.org/who-we-are/.

Chapter 6 The Shape of Kingdom Belonging

1. *Babette's Feast* (*Babettes gæstebud*), directed by Gabriel Axel (Panorama Film A/S, 1987).

2. Celeste Heiter, *A Culinary Homage to Babette's Feast* (Love Bites Cookbooks, 2012), 1.

Chapter 7 Strangers and Kingdom Belonging

1. Christine D. Pohl, *Making Room: Recovering Hospitality as a Christian Tradition* (Grand Rapids: Eerdmans, 1999), 14.
2. See David T. Lamb, "Racist or Hospitable?," in *God Behaving Badly: Is the God of the Old Testament Angry, Sexist and Racist?* (Downers Grove, IL: InterVarsity, 2011), 76–80.
3. Village of Euclid et al. v. Ambler Realty Co., 272 U.S. 365 (1926).
4. Michael Southworth and Eran Ben-Joseph, "Reconsidering the Cul-de-Sac," *Access* 24 (Spring 2004): 29, http://www.accessmagazine.org/spring-2004/reconsidering-cul-de-sac/.
5. Pohl, *Making Room*, 95.

Chapter 8 Kingdom and Covenant Belonging

1. Mike Breen, *Covenant and Kingdom: The DNA of the Bible* (Pawleys Island, SC: 3DM, 2010).
2. Timothy Keller and Katherine Leary Alsdorf, *Every Good Endeavor: Connecting Your Work to God's Work* (New York: Penguin, 2016).
3. Personal conversation with Jeff Vanderstelt, October 8, 2014.
4. Alan Hirsch and Ed Stetzer, *The Forgotten Ways: Reactivating Apostolic Movements*, 2nd ed. (Grand Rapids: Brazos, 2016), chap. 8.

Part 3 The Gospel and Belonging

1. Timothy Keller, *Center Church: Doing Balanced, Gospel-Centered Ministry in Your City* (Grand Rapids: Zondervan, 2012).

Chapter 9 The Promise of Community

1. This woman's name and some personal details have been changed to protect her privacy.
2. Miller McPherson, Lynn Smith-Lovin, and Matthew E. Brashears, "Social Isolation in America: Changes in Core Discussion Networks over Two Decades," *American Sociological Review* 71 (June 2006): 353–75, cited in Jacqueline Olds, MD, and Richard S. Schwartz, MD, *The Lonely American: Drifting Apart in the Twenty-First Century* (Boston: Beacon, 2009), 2.
3. *Age of Aloneness*, documentary film, directed by Sue Bourne (Wellpark Productions, 2016).
4. John T. Cacioppo, "Toward a Neurology of Loneliness," *Psychological Bulletin* 140, no. 6 (2014): 1464–1504, cited in Justin Bariso, "Loneliness May (Literally) Be Killing You, According to Science," *Inc.*, September 7, 2016, https://www.inc.com/justin-bariso/new-re search-says-this-single-common-risk-factor-may-be-killing-you.html.
5. Carla M. Perissinotto, Irena Stijacic Cenzer, and Kenneth E. Covinsky, "Loneliness in Older Persons: A Predictor of Functional Decline and Death," *Archives of Internal Medicine* 172, no. 14 (July 23, 2012): 1078–83, https://doi.org/10.1001/archinternmed.2012.1993.
6. Katie Hafner, "Researchers Confront an Epidemic of Loneliness," *New York Times*, September 5, 2016, https://www.nytimes.com/2016/09/06/health/lonliness-aging-health -effects.html.
7. Joseph R. Myers, *Organic Community: Creating a Place Where People Naturally Connect* (Grand Rapids: Baker Books, 2008).
8. Marina Keegan, "The Opposite of Loneliness," *Yale Daily News*, May 27, 2012.
9. Keegan, "The Opposite of Loneliness."
10. Keegan, "The Opposite of Loneliness."

Excursus: Social Capital

1. Robert D. Putnam, *Bowling Alone: The Collapse and Revival of American Community* (New York: Simon & Schuster, 2007).

Chapter 10 The Promise of Homecoming

1. *The Book of Common Worship: Pastoral Edition* (Louisville: Westminster John Knox, 1993), 226.

2. Brueggemann introduces this idea in *The Land: Place as Gift, Promise, and Challenge in Biblical Faith* (Philadelphia: Fortress, 1977), 5; John Inge takes Brueggemann's concept and paraphrases it as "storied place" in *A Christian Theology of Place* (Burlington, VA: Ashgate, 2003), 36.

Excursus: Place Attachment

1. For the purposes of this book, we are not considering virtual places as legitimate places.

Chapter 11 The Promise of a Good Story

1. Lenore Skenazy, *Free-Range Kids: How to Raise Safe, Self-Reliant Children (without Going Nuts with Worry)* (San Francisco: Jossey-Bass, 2010).

2. Lenore Skenazy, "Why I Let My 9-Year-Old Ride the Subway Alone," *New York Sun*, April 1, 2008, https://www.nysun.com/opinion/why-i-let-my-9-year-old-ride-subway-alone /73976/.

3. Skenazy, "Why I Let."

4. Brené Brown, *Rising Strong* (New York: Spiegel & Grau, 2015), 80.

5. Robert A. Burton, *On Being Certain: Believing You Are Right Even When You're Not* (New York: St. Martin's Press, 2008), quoted in Brown, *Rising Strong*, 79.

6. "Culture and Values," Starbucks, accessed July 10, 2019, https://www.starbucks.com /careers/working-at-starbucks/culture-and-values.

7. CJ Casciotta, *Branding Is for Cows. Belonging Is for People. Break Free from the Herd and Make Stuff That Matters* (ebook).

8. Casciotta, *Branding Is for Cows*.

Excursus: Thick and Thin Language

1. Michael Walzer, *Thick and Thin: Moral Argument at Home and Abroad* (Notre Dame, IN: University of Notre Dame Press, 2002).

Chapter 12 Three Pieces of Glass: The Crisis of Belonging in Relationships

1. "Household Travel in America," chap. 1 of "2010 Status of the Nation's Highways, Bridges, and Transit: Conditions & Performance," US Department of Transportation, Federal Highway Administration, last modified April 1, 2019, https://www.fhwa.dot.gov/policy /2010cpr/chap1.cfm.

2. John Ortberg, *Everybody's Normal till You Get to Know Them* (Grand Rapids: Zondervan, 2014).

Chapter 13 The Declining Civic Realm: The Crisis of Belonging in Places

1. Mark C. Childs, *Squares: A Public Place Design Guide for Urbanists* (Albuquerque: University of New Mexico Press, 2006), 27.

2. Law of the Indies no. 112, in Dora P. Crouch, Daniel J. Garr, and Axel I. Mundigo, *Spanish Planning in North America* (Cambridge, MA: MIT Press, 1982), 13–15, quoted in Childs, *Squares*, 28.

3. Childs, *Squares*, 32–33.

4. Robert Fishman, *Bourgeois Utopias: The Rise and Fall of Suburbia* (New York: Basic Books, 2008).

5. Fishman, *Bourgeois Utopias*, 53.

6. William Cowper, *The Task*, book 3, "The Garden" (London: Kessinger Publishing, 2004), 49.

7. Cowper, *The Task*, book 1, "The Sofa," 23.

8. Fishman, *Bourgeois Utopias*, 56.

Chapter 14 Busy: The Crisis of Belonging in Story

1. See Ernest Becker, *The Denial of Death* (New York: Free Press, 1973).

2. "Residential Buildings Factsheet," Center for Sustainable Systems, University of Michigan, 2018, http://css.umich.edu/factsheets/residential-buildings-factsheet.

3. Kathleen Norris, *Acedia & Me: A Marriage, Monks, and a Writer's Life* (New York: Riverhead Books, 2010), xv.

4. Lynell George, "Kathleen Norris Battles 'the Demon of Acedia,'" *Los Angeles Times*, September 21, 2008, https://www.latimes.com/entertainment/la-ca-kathleen-norris21-2008 sep21-story.html.

5. George, "Kathleen Norris."

6. Eugene Peterson, *The Contemplative Pastor: Returning to the Art of Spiritual Direction* (Grand Rapids: Eerdmans, 1993), 18.

Chapter 15 Communally Shaped Choices

1. Abraham H. Maslow, *The Psychology of Science: A Reconnaissance* (New York: Harper & Row, 1966), 15.

2. Actually, it's not impossible to conceive of something like this. One could offer "walkability credits" for purchase. The way it would work is when someone buys a home in an automobile-oriented neighborhood, they could dedicate an additional 5 percent of the purchase price toward "walkability credits" that would be used to subsidize someone else purchasing a home in a walkable neighborhood.

3. The Walk Score tool can be found at https://www.walkscore.com/. For further discussion, see "Walkability" in chap. 18.

4. Although as we'll see in chap. 17, more and more young home buyers are considering such things.

5. N. McGuckin and A. Fucci, "Summary of Travel Trends: 2017 National Household Travel Survey," Federal Highway Administration, Office of Policy and Governmental Affairs, report no. FHWA-PL-18-019, July 2018, https://nhts.ornl.gov/assets/2017_nhts_sum mary_travel_trends.pdf.

Chapter 16 Policy-Shaped Choices

1. Village of Euclid, Ohio, et al. v. Ambler Realty Co., 272 U.S. 365 (1926).
2. Euclid v. Ambler.
3. Michael Kwartler, "Legislating Aesthetics: The Role of Zoning in Designing Cities," in *Zoning and the American Dream: Promises Still to Keep*, ed. Charles M. Haar and Jerold S. Kayden (Chicago: Planners Press, 1989), 205.
4. Kenneth T. Jackson, *Crabgrass Frontier: The Suburbanization of the United States* (Oxford: Oxford University Press, 1985), 170.
5. Charles L. Marohn Jr., *Thoughts on Building Strong Towns* (Lexington: CreateSpace Independent Publishing Platform, 2016).
6. See Marohn, *Thoughts on Building Strong Towns*; see also the website for Strong Towns, https://www.strongtowns.org.

Chapter 17 Liturgically Shaped Choices

1. James K. A. Smith, *Desiring the Kingdom: Worship, Worldview, and Cultural Formation* (Grand Rapids: Baker Academic, 2011).
2. Smith, *Desiring the Kingdom*, 22.
3. N. McGuckin and A. Fucci, "Summary of Travel Trends: 2017 National Household Travel Survey," Federal Highway Administration, Office of Policy and Governmental Affairs, report no. FHWA-PL-18-019, July 2018, https://nhts.ornl.gov/assets/2017_nhts_sum mary_travel_trends.pdf
4. See *Godspeed: The Pace of Being Known*, documentary film, created by Matt Canlis (The Ranch Studios, 2018), https://www.livegodspeed.org/home.
5. Of course there are a number of people for whom walking as a form of transportation is physically impossible. For this and other reasons, it is important to note that walking is not the only liturgy of belonging that can help one make meaningful connections within one's neighborhood.
6. Score was obtained using Walk Score, accessed July 11, 2019, https://www.walkscore .com/WA/Tacoma/98403.

Chapter 18 Belonging by Design

1. Walk Score is a pretty good measure of walkability, but in some ways is very inaccurate. Walk Score's algorythm is weighted heavily toward density of activity. It underweights design elements like road widths and curb cuts, both of which affect walkability. Some sprawling suburban shopping environments get higher Walk Scores than they should because of the quantity and diversity of commercial establishments. See Robert Steuteville, "The Value of Walkabilty and Walk Score Inaccuracies," *Public Square: A CNU Journal*, September 19, 2016, https://www.cnu.org/publicsquare/2016/09/19/value-walkability -and-walk-score-inaccuracies.
2. Joe Cortright, "Walking the Walk: How Walkability Raises Home Values in U.S. Cities" (Cleveland: CEOs for Cities, 2009), 2, https://community-wealth.org/content/walking -walk-how-walkability-raises-home-values-us-cities.
3. Jeff Speck, *Walkable City: How Downtown Can Save America, One Step at a Time* (New York: North Point, 2013).
4. James Rojas, "The Enacted Environment: The Creation of 'Place' by Mexicans and Mexican Americans in East Los Angeles" (master's thesis, Massachusetts Institute of Technology, 1991).

5. Cited in Charles Montgomery, *Happy City: Transforming Our Lives through Urban Design* (New York: Farrar, Straus & Giroux, 2014), 128–29.

6. Montgomery, *Happy City*, 132–33.

7. Hazel Boyers, personal correspondence, July 6, 2018.

8. Ray Oldenburg, *The Great Good Place: Cafés, Coffee Shops, Community Centers, Beauty Parlors, General Stores, Bars, Hangouts, and How They Get You through the Day* (New York: Paragon House, 1989).

9. Jan Gehl, *Life between Buildings: Using Public Space* (New York: Van Nostrand Reinhold, 1987).

10. Mark C. Childs, *Squares: A Public Place Design Guide for Urbanists* (Albuquerque: University of New Mexico Press, 2006), 23–24.

Chapter 19 Belonging through Proximity

1. These definitions of "parish" come from Eric O. Jacobsen, *The Space Between: A Christian Engagement with the Built Environment* (Grand Rapids: Baker Academic, 2012), 194.

2. Paul Sparks, Tim Sorens, and Dwight J. Friesen, *The New Parish: How Neighborhood Churches Are Transforming Mission, Discipleship and Community* (Downers Grove, IL: InterVarsity, 2014).

3. Jay Pathak and Dave Runyon, *The Art of Neighboring: Building Genuine Relationships Right outside Your Door* (Grand Rapids: Baker Books, 2012).

4. We borrowed this name from the For Gannet campaign in Atlanta, but we're going about our campaign a little bit differently.

Chapter 20 Belonging by Placemaking

1. "What Makes a Successful Place?," Project for Public Spaces, accessed July 11, 2019, https://www.pps.org/article/grplacefeat.

2. Thomas Lueck, "Up, but Not Running, on the West Side," *New York Times*, July 25, 1999.

3. Metro Parks Tacoma with SiteWorkshop, "Master Plan for Wright Park," January 2005, https://www.metroparkstacoma.org/wp-content/uploads/2019/05/WrightPark_Master-Plan-Report.pdf

Chapter 21 Belonging and Local Culture

1. Wendell Berry, "The Work of Local Culture," in *What Are People For? Essays* (New York: North Point, 1990), 153.

2. Berry, "The Work of Local Culture," 155.

3. "Olmstead Anthony," poster by Beautiful Angle, Tacoma, WA, May 2006.

4. Berry, "The Work of Local Culture," 155.

5. C. S. Lewis, *The Last Battle*, Chronicles of Narnia (New York: Collier Books, 1956), 183–84.

INDEX